THE INTERPRETATION OF ENGLISH NOUN SEQUENCES ON THE COMPUTER

NORTH-HOLLAND 51
LINGUISTIC STUDIES

THE INTERPRETATION OF ENGLISH NOUN SEQUENCES ON THE COMPUTER

ROSEMARY LEONARD

Stockport
Cheshire
England

1984

NORTH-HOLLAND
AMSTERDAM • NEW YORK • OXFORD

ISBN: 0 444 87658 8

Published by:
ELSEVIER SCIENCE PUBLISHERS B.V.
P.O. Box 1991
1000 BZ Amsterdam
The Netherlands

Sole distributors for the U.S.A. and Canada:
ELSEVIER SCIENCE PUBLISHING COMPANY, INC.
52 Vanderbilt Avenue
New York, N.Y. 10017
U.S.A.

Library of Congress Cataloging in Publication Data

Leonard, Rosemary, 1938-
The interpretation of English noun sequences on the computer.

(North-Holland linguistic series ; 51)
Bibliography: p.
Includes index.
1. English language--Noun phrase--Data processing.
2. English language--Compound words--Data processing.
3. English language--Semantics--Data processing.
I. Title. II. Series.
PE1205.L46 1985 425 84-21183
ISBN 0-444-87658-8 (Elsevier Sci.)

PRINTED IN THE NETHERLANDS

ABSTRACT

This book postulates rules by which noun sequences may be interpreted. The term 'noun sequence' includes compound nouns and nominal compounds. The book reports and evaluates the results of an investigation in which the output of these rules was tested on the computer. About 2,000 noun sequences are used, e.g. sponge-bag, armchair, alder cone, nightgown, fruit-preserving season. The examples come from approximately 300,000 words of English fiction written between 1700 and the present day. A computer simulation is attempted of a native speaker's interpretation of each noun sequence. The nouns are marked with semantic features and collected into a dictionary; and the interpretation program reads the data, consults the dictionary, and applies a grammar. It outputs, e.g. sponge-bag: Locative type 3030: A bag for or containing a sponge or sponges. At a generous count, 76% of the interpretations are possible ones in English. An appendix contains samples of the computer output.

In memory of my mother,
my father, and my aunt
Anne Leonard

with thanks to St. Martin de Porres.

ACKNOWLEDGEMENTS

I am especially grateful to these people:

The library staff at Lancaster University, in particular those in the Inter-Library Loans department;

Mr. Graham Greene and Mr. John Braine, for their elucidatory advice;

Elizabeth van Heister, who helped me with some German;

Dr. Dion Bell and Mr. A. McCracken, for their expert information;

David Hainsworth, Laurie Hirsch, John Gardner, Paul Nixon, Bobbie Rees and particularly Chris Cartledge, who have all helped with the implementation of the program on the computer at various stages;

Professor Bryan Higman and John Hampton for teaching me Algol and for enlightening discussions;

Eileen Grimes, who has been a wonderful help in typing this book and putting up with my revisions;

Jamie McCarrick, who drew the diagrams and inserted the odd symbols;

Brian Noble and Dr. S. Smith, who gave me constant encouragement and enabled me to keep on with the work;

Professor Geoffrey Leech, whom I cannot thank enough for all his generous advice and help over the years that this book was in preparation.

Longman Group Limited for giving copyright permission to reproduce a figure from, Towards a Semantic Description of English, G.N. Leech (Longmans, Green and Co. Ltd., London, 1969). (See p. 155, this volume).

CONTENTS

TABLES AND CHARTS

THE INTERPRETATION OF ENGLISH NOUN SEQUENCES ON THE COMPUTER

CHAPTER 1

INTRODUCTION

This book postulates rules by which noun sequences may be interpreted, and reports and evaluates the results of an investigation in which the output of these rules was tested on the computer. About 2000 noun sequences are used, e.g. sponge-bag, armchair, alder cone, nightgown, fruit-preserving season. The examples come from approximately 300,000 words of English fiction written between 1700 and the present day. A computer simulation is attempted of a native speaker's interpretation of each noun sequence. The method is as follows:

1. The nouns constituting the sequences are listed and then marked with semantic features. Some also take verbs: gown : wears.

2. The dictionary program converts the feature-list into a dictionary.

3. The interpretation program reads the data, consults the dictionary, and applies a grammar. It yields semantic identifiers for each example, e.g.

sponge-bag : Locative.

It then offers one or more interpretations, e.g.

A bag for or containing a sponge or sponges.

At a generous count, about 76% of the interpretations are possible ones in English.

The use of the computer enables one easily to alter the grammar and test it on a large set of data.

Chapter 1 describes the corpus and my typology. It also mentions some precursors.

Chapter 2 describes the dictionary and the semantic features.

Chapter 3 describes the interpretation program, and traces sample analyses.

Chapter 4 evaluates the same program and describes heuristic changes in rule ordering.

Chapter 5 discusses semantic features.

Chapter 6 summarizes what has been done.

The appendices consist of a sample of the data, the whole feature-list, an index of procedures, and a sample of the output interpretations.

This book is offered as a contribution to the study of English word-formation and extra-syntactic attachment; and also as a contribution to the technology of using computers as a means of testing and evaluating linguistic hypotheses.

The Corpus

A sample of the data is given in Appendix I. The sixteen books from which the data are taken are listed here. The first 20,000 words of each book are used, except for Braine, Deighton and Marsh. The high frequency of noun sequences in these three authors threatened to swamp the data, so from these three authors the extracts are of 15,000 words only.

For ease of reference if desired by the reader, the page numbers given are those of recent editions. The first edition was consulted in every case, and where a first edition contained a passage excised from the later edition (as with Thackeray), the noun sequences were collected from the original passage (e.g. pewter room) and the extract from the later edition was correspondingly curtailed.

Full details of these first and later editions are in a Bibliography at the end of this book.

The Life and Adventures of Robinson Crusoe, Daniel Defoe, 1719 and 1965, 20,000 words, pp. 27-70 Penguin.

Pamela, Samuel Richardson, 1740 and 1966, 20,000 words, pp. 1-43 Everyman.

The History of Tom Jones, Henry Fielding, 1749 and 1966, 20,000 words, pp. 51-98 Penguin.

The Castle of Otranto, Horace Walpole, 1764 and 1967,[1] 20,000 words, pp. 109-155 Everyman. (The high page numbers are due to the fact that Shorter Novels: Eighteenth Century contains Rasselas, The Castle of Otranto and the next novel in this list, Vathek.)

The History of the Caliph Vathek, William Beckford, translated by Henley, 1786 and 1967, 20,000 words, pp. 195-241 Everyman.

The Mysteries of Udolpho, Ann Radcliffe, 1794 and 1965, 20,000 words, pp. 1-50 Everyman.

Headlong Hall, Thomas Love Peacock, 1816 and 1965, 20,000 words, pp. 7-98 Everyman.

The Heart of Midlothian, Walter Scott, 1818 and 1952, 20,000 words, pp. 17-59 Collins.

Vanity Fair, W.M. Thackeray, 1847 and 1954, 20,000 words, pp. 21-61 Collins.

Wuthering Heights, Emily Brontë, 1847 and 1965, 20,000 words, pp. 45-101 Penguin.

The Old Wives' Tale, Arnold Bennett, 1908 and 1966, 20,000 words, pp. 3-49 Everyman.

Sons and Lovers, D.H. Lawrence, 1913 and 1948, 20,000 words, pp. 7-68 Penguin.

Spinsters in Jeopardy, Ngaio Marsh, 1954 and 1960, 15,000 words, pp. 9-51 Fontana (Collins).

Room at the Top, John Braine, 1957 and 1959, 15,000 words, pp. 7-47 Penguin.

A Burnt-Out Case, Graham Greene, 1961 and 1963, 20,000 words, pp. 9-65 Penguin.

Only When I Larf, Len Deighton, 1968 (the first edition), 15,000 words, pp. 9-51 Sphere Books Limited.

All these extracts total 305,000 words.

The present approach to noun sequences

Noun sequences consist of two or more nouns in sequence, e.g. sponge-bag, armchair, alder cone, night-gown, fruit-preserving season. These can be described as noun + noun sequences, noun-noun sequences and noun sequences. For euphony I prefer the last of these three terms.

In Leonard (1968) I showed that there is a great increase in the occurrences of noun sequences in prose fiction from 1750 to the present day. This alone is a justification for the further investigation of noun sequences. Other writers (the most pertinent of whom will be mentioned in this chapter) have made classifications of noun sequences (or nearly related structures, e.g. Levi (1978)). There are two main differences between their work and mine. One is that I am taking the point of view of the reader: my rules are interpretive rather than productive (such as those of Lees (1960), for example). The other is that I am implementing these rules on the computer, so that with the program they can be tested objectively on a large set of data. The program is so designed that the main ordering of the rules can be changed and the rules can be tested in various orders.

After mentioning linguistic precursors, I also mention precursors in the field of computing.

First Encounter

For the purpose of this book, the interpretation of a noun sequence is what takes place when the human being first reads (or hears) the sequence. Many examples, e.g. armchair, waistcoat are so familiar that they may be learned as whole words. But what I am seeking is the meaning which the noun sequence had when it was coined.

The process leading to interpretation is as follows:

1. I collected the noun sequences from the novels.

2. I added from the first editions any omitted noun sequences (curtailing the extract accordingly).

3. The noun sequences were sorted into alphabetical order.[2]

4. I bracketed the nested sequences.

5. Where the relationship between the nouns was unclear, I consulted dictionaries and expert informants.

6. I extracted all the nouns from the data.[3]

7. I sorted them into alphabetical order.[4]

8. I marked the nouns with semantic features, to give the Features list.

9. I operated a program[5] on the list of Features, to give a dictionary inside the computer, and a brief printout of comments.

10. I operated on the data the program with which this book is chiefly concerned, using the dictionary.

11. This program yielded

    (a) the type and type-number,

    (b) the underlying sentences where necessary, and

    (c) one or more paraphrases of each noun sequence.

12. Professor G.N. Leech and I independently marked the output, so as to evaluate the interpretation program. The occasional differences were discussed, and a consensus arrived at.

My Typology of Noun Sequences

My typology is based on that of Leonard (1968). This is a rough outline of my present typology:

A. Sentence, e.g. hire car.

B. Locative Sentence, e.g. birthday.

C. Locative, e.g. Lincolnshire estate.

D. Annex, e.g. hillside.

E. Equative, e.g. baby crocodile.

F. Material, e.g. stone lion.

G. Additive, e.g. Lampton-Lufford report.

H. Reduplicative, e.g. plop-plop.

I shall now give a more detailed account of my typology. All the examples are from the data, except weather theme and divorce case, which are of a type not represented in the data. Type identifiers consist of letters and numbers. Thus the type encompassing Lincolnshire estate, pocket-handkerchief and holiday afternoon is referred to as Type C1S1. Its paraphrase in the program is in or on:

An estate in or on Lincolnshire;

A handkerchief in or on a pocket;

An afternoon in or on a holiday.

This is a locative type, as the C shows. It is the first of three locative types; hence it has the label C1. The S stands for subtype: C1 subtype 1: something that is in or on something else.

The types A1 and B1 (hire-car, birthday) are output not with type numbers but with numbers that refer to the underlying sentences printed before the paraphrases. (B1 is not distinguished from A1 as the presence of a locative in the sentence is easily seen):

hire-car

Sentence 5

Underlying Sentence(s):

A car or cars travels something or someone

A car or cars travels

Someone travels something or someone in a car or cars

Someone travels in a car or cars

Someone hires a car or cars

Interpretation(s):

A car that someone hires.

birth+day

Sentence 1

Underlying Sentence(s):

Someone is born in a day or days.

Interpretation(s):

A day that someone is born in.

In the output, the program gives the contents of the input card first, including the author, the page number, and the noun sequence (which may be, for example, hire-car). The program recognizes that car has a related verb, travels, and that hire has a related verb, hires. It sets up five sentences built around the verbs. The program then chooses among the sentences, according to semantic rules, and decides on Sentence No. 5:

Someone hires a car or cars.

It then forms the corresponding noun-phrase form, and outputs the interpretation

A car that someone hires.

Birthday is easier to analyze because of the limitations on birth, so the program sets up only one sentence and outputs its corresponding interpretation.

Hire-car is an example of the A type and birthday, having the locative day, is an example of the B type. The interpretations, however, are simply stated as 'Sentence 5' and 'Sentence 1', as the type can easily be seen from the underlying sentence.

Hire in *hire-car* is an overt verb; *travels* in *hire-car* is a covert verb: a verb unrelated lexically to the noun, but semantically related. In this case the overt verb is given priority in the interpretation over the covert verb. However, some interpretations use covert verbs, e.g. *aerobatics team*:

The team *performs* aerobatics;

and *Mongo language*:

The Mongo *speaks* a language.

Performs and *speaks* are yielded for the interpretation by the definitions of *aerobatics* and *language* in the computer dictionary (to be described in the next chapter).

It has not been practicable to include a full set of rules for the agreement of prepositions, so that *in* represents a base form which may be realized as *on* or *at* as well as *in*:

A day that someone is born in.

We now move to a list of examples of all the types.

Types A and B of Leonard (1968) are now subsumed under the Sentence label, the syntactic relationship being evident from the underlying sentences.

Examples of types

(Some are rare and so will yield few examples)

Sentence type (A).

A1 hire-car (overt verb in modifier, i.e. first noun);
bank manager (overt verb in head, i.e. second noun);
aerobatics team (covert verb *performs* in modifier);
Mongo language (covert verb *speaks* in head).
body-guard; family disagreement; bone-setter; bookmaker.

We have now seen several examples of Sentence type A1. The following A types cover several areas where the interpretation is based on a sentence and where many different nouns have features implying one sentence interpretation, e.g. a material noun modifying a mechanism: Type A2 *oil stove*, *airgun*, paraffin cooker. Types A2-A5 are all of this kind.

A2 Fuel

powered by

paraffin cooker.

A3 Disease

causing or caused by

sleeping sickness; homesickness; train-fever.

A4 Ownership (of place, mechanism or furniture)

made by or belonging to

Hamilton watch; Knoll desk; company jet[1];[6] council house; family domain; family estate; school magazine; Lincoln hire-car.

A5 Ownership

belonging to

Corporation money; City Guard; household matter; town property; Security Guard coat.

Locative Sentence type (B1) (subsumed under Sentence type)

birthday (overt verb in modifier);
cave-dweller (overt verb in head);
tea-table (covert verbs drinks or eats in modifier);
nightgown (covert verb wears in head);
fruit-preserving season; towel disposal bin; home letter; breakfast-room.

Locative type (C)

C1S1 in or on

Lincolnshire estate; bay[1] window; pocket-handkerchief; carpet-rod; country[1] free-school; evening hour; holiday afternoon.

C1S2 that lives in or comes from[7]

Newark man; Bay Street friend; Amalgamin Ltd. Bahamas company; Arniston chield [Scots]; Edinburgh gentleman;

Flanders mear [Scots]; Gimmerton band; H.Q. Squadron.

C1S3 that lives in or works in

millgirl; housewife; bosom friend; cabin-passenger; chambermaid; dairy woman; heath-lark; liftman.

C1S4 The kind of ... used in or on

deckchair; cloakroom-knob.

C1S5 The kind of ... found in or on

water jacinth; marsh-mallow; mountain-ash[1]; cayenne pepper; corn-poppy.

C1S6 ... to ...

parlour stair; chamber door; city gate; dispensary door; foot[1]-mantle; house-stair; safe door; street door.

C2 ... at ... (Words such as top and side which are annex when head but locative when modifier)

front door; side garden; bottom block; front seat; back garden; top block; top button.

C3 ... for or containing ...

sponge-bag; sick chamber; bathroom; beehive; bone-house; bonnet-box; bookcase; brook valley.

Annex type (D)

D1 ... of ... (The head is an annex, i.e. it denotes a part of something.)

bed-string; clay colour; hillside; battle-pitch[2]; bell-rope; blood pressure; bone structure; mountain top.

D2 ... of ... (Both nouns belong to the same semantic field.)

fir-bough; goose skin; beech leaf; boot button; car horn; coat-tail; cellar step; chapel window.

D3 ... in ...

Army captain; choir-boy; clergyman.

D4 ... with ...

armchair; brandysnap; cherry-tree; chestnut avenue; cheval glass; cream-tart; currant bush; egg-nog.

Equative type (E)

Most of the Equative examples belong to the same type: E1: *baby crocodile*: *a crocodile that is a baby*. The subtype letters merely show from what source in the program the Equative type was reached: e.g. a verb procedure yields *actor-manager* while a procedure dealing with semantic fields yields *oak-tree*.[8]

E1(a) ... *that is* ...

baby crocodile; birdman; bitch pointer; boy apprentice; fisherman; boy friend; girl-widow; cousin Garbel.

E1(b) ... *that is* ...

oak-tree; claw-hand; cocoa stew; court-yard; divan bed; dormer window; fir-tree; hospital block.

E1(c) ... *that is* ...

actor-manager; computer brain; picture puzzle; token gesture.

E1(d) ... *that is* ...

rain-water; fly-leaf; signboard; washer-woman.

E1(e) ... *that is* ...

clearance sale; clucking sound; fainting fit; jog-trot; marriage ceremony; trick question; rumbling sound; tinkling sound.

E1(f) ... *that is* ...

branch line; bumper-dram; cherry cheek; vinegar face<d>.[9]

E2 ... *that is* ...

This abstract type is not represented in the data. Examples are: weather theme, divorce case.

Material type (F)

F1 ... *of* ...

stone[1] lion; clay hut; brass plate; brick cottage; red- brick university; calico snap-bag; cambric apron; gold chain.

F2 AND 3 ... *for or in the form of* ...

The program cannot distinguish between *leather for shoes* and *leather in the form of a shoe*. So F2 implies F3. shoe-leather; hearthstone; plate glass; cardboard.

F4 ... *of* ...

⟨brown⟩ paper bundle; haystack.

F5 ... *of* ...

thorn hedge; tree-clump; booby form; burgher family; leper village; pine forest; pine plantation; privet hedge; pro class.

Additive type (G)[10]

G1 ... *and* ...

Lampton-Lufford report.

Reduplicative type (H)[11]

H1 ... *a repeated sound of* ...

plop-plop.

In the sample of output at the end of this book, the types are named and, in certain cases, given as numbers. A conversion table is to be found at footnote 12 if desired.

Selected work by others in the field

Although the two subjects overlap, I shall deal first with linguistic work, and then with computational work. Each set will be dealt with in order of publication.

Otto Jespersen (1942)[13] treats noun sequences (as well as other features of language) in a valuable way because he takes into account the hearer as well as the speaker. I have therefore been led to consider what is going on in the brain, and this has caused me to attempt a working method of interpreting noun sequences.

To use this method in a dynamic way is different from treating the patterning of noun sequences as a set of interrelationships between types, independent of the action of the mind. It is the latter view which is implicit in many classifications, as if the linguist says: Example (i) belongs to Type A, example (ii) belongs to Type C, and so on. None of the linguists about to be discussed makes suggestions as to how the hearer might perform the analysis which leads to classification.

It is, of course, true that in _la langue_ there are patterns by which meanings are arranged according to interrelationships and contrasts. Thus the eight main types of noun sequences can be differentiated from and contrasted with one another, as if on a flat map. A particular example can be placed in one or other region, or in several regions (or types).[14] I am not rejecting Saussure's picture of _la langue_:[15] rather I am trying to focus on the manner in which, at a given moment, a hearer (or reader) understands a noun sequence, so that he can recognize that it 'belongs to' a particular type or types. The process of understanding or recognition is probably a dynamic one.

Jespersen says that the merit of compounds lies in their conciseness. He continues:

> Compounds[16] express a relation between two objects or notions, but say nothing of the way in which the relation is to be understood. That must be inferred from the context or otherwise. Theoretically, this leaves room for a large number of different interpretations of one and the same compound, but in practice ambiguity is as a rule avoided. Many compounds have become traditional names for one definite thing, thus giving up their other potential meanings ... a _goldfish_ looks like gold, a _gold-digger_ digs for gold, while a _gold-smith_

> works in gold ... goldsmith could not possibly be used of a smith with a gold-like appearance....[17]

Here it is clear that Jespersen distinguishes several different semantic types. It is helpful that he also quotes examples formed for temporary use and not intended to name something, so that a study of noun sequences is not entirely concerned with word-formation: '"I'm only a beer teetotaller, not a champagne teetotaller"'.[18]

Robert Lees (1960) attempts to explain all noun sequences as transformations from sentences, e.g.

'Subject-Object': steamboat, car thief:
    Steam powers the boat;
    The thief steals cars, etc.
'Object-Prepositional Object': bull ring, apple sauce.

Lees's approach is most helpful when one part of the noun sequence is a lexical verb or is related to one; but in cases like bull-ring and iron gate the syntactic method is less useful than Jespersen's semantic approach. Lees's approach also differs from Jespersen's in general by disregarding the process of understanding. He gives in detail the processes of transformation by which the main types are formed from kernel sentences. However, he does not consider the motivation for forming noun sequences instead of using the corresponding kernel sentences or phrases. He also treats many examples as transforms of sentences which might alternatively be derived from phrases or adjective + noun constructions. The semantic homogeneity of many of the examples in each of his lists enables us to see that the categorization is done with valid intuition; but in many cases it is not clear why an example should be derived in one way rather than another, when the same lexical items could be fitted into acceptable kernel sentences of quite different patterns.[19] Lees's type 'Subject-Prepositional Object' includes four kinds of relationship: locative, purposive, metaphorical and constitutive (material).

> His prepositions comprise not only "from","on", "at", "in" in its usual sense, and so on, but also "for", "like", and "in" in the sense of "in the form of". The preposition "for" enables purposive compounds such as "hairbrush" to be included, with underlying sentences such as "the brush is for the hair". The preposition "like" enables metaphorical compounds such as "dragonfly" to be included. The preposition "in" meaning "in the form of" enables compounds such as "snowball" to be included....[20]

Lees's analysis does not show how an interpreter would operate the transformations backwards in order to arrive at a set of kernel sentences and a sequence of transformations.

The typologies of Jespersen and Lees have each given something to the typology developed in Leonard (1968), and used as the basis of the typology for the computer program. Unlike Lees's model, my model does not assume that all noun sequences are ultimately derived from sentences, but offers phrasal interpretations in many cases without reference to sentences.

Hans Marchand (1960), like Jespersen, touches on the problem of selecting a significant aspect of the meaning of each word according to its mate in the sequence:

> Words are different in different situations: a <u>finger bowl</u> is "a bowl for the fingers", a <u>fingernail</u> is "a nail of the finger", a <u>finger post</u> "a guide post bearing a finger

> index", a <u>fingerprint</u> "a print, an impression made by the fingers", <u>finger waves</u> are "waves produced by the help of the fingers".[21]

In Leonard (1968) I classify the noun sequences that occur in a corpus of nearly 100,000 words of English prose fiction written from 1750 to the present day. (The five books from which the 1968 corpus is taken are different from the sixteen books used for the present work.) The corpus yields 514 noun sequences, 427 of them being lexically distinct examples ('types', not 'tokens').[22] It is demonstrated that noun sequences are much more frequent in present-day prose fiction than they were two centuries ago:[23]

	Total	Lexically distinct examples
Johnson (1759)	10	8
Jane Austen (c. 1813)	39	34
Dickens (1840)	89	75
Meredith (1875)	147	112
Isherwood (1962)	229	198

The increase shows signs of affecting the style of English. This is one reason why noun sequences deserve to be examined thoroughly.

The question must be faced: whether semantic features are a working reality. For example, I wrote:

> <u>inkstand</u>, <u>love-passages</u>, <u>music books</u>, <u>newspaper</u>, <u>suitcase</u>:
>
> The second part has a locative semantic element and the first denotes an entity that is capable of being located by the second.[24]

Here, a Locative semantic element is being postulated. One may compare the pure locative type in this book, which also depends on a locative semantic element (or, as I now express it, semantic feature). (The first two head-nouns, <u>stand</u> and <u>passage</u>, have become locatives of overt verbs in this book.)

In the next example, it is not a Locative feature (which is general) that is being postulated, but a feature of belonging to a particular class of things.

I wrote about an annex type:

> <u>apron-strings</u>, <u>backbone</u>, <u>bacon fat</u>, <u>coat-collar</u>, <u>finger nails</u>, <u>lock-gates</u>:
>
> The first and second parts of this type [i.e. modifier and head] each denote independent entities, and the link of dependence is made by the fact that the referents of the two parts are related in the real world situation: for example, an "apron" generally has "strings" and a "finger" generally has a "nail". In terms of semantic elements this can be restated: the second part has a semantic element of membership of a larger entity, and the first part is a suitable larger entity. ... A "bone" is a feature of the body; the name of any part of the body or the name of a suitable species of animal would be a suitable first part to a sequence containing "bone" as its second. "Fat", in its noun function, will associate with the name of any type of meat. A "collar" can be part of a garment and will associate with the name of any garment reaching to the neck. Thus each of the referents of these words is potentially a member of a larger entity, while

> having also potential independence, as in "a ball of string", "a coffin-nail" and a "dog-collar" ... here [where no one element distinguishes the type], what is operating is an element that is present in almost any example of any type; but here the two parts match: the "nail" matches the "finger" and the "collar" matches the "coat".[25]

One may compare with the above the Semantic Fields matches which take place in the annex part of the program and occur in the second, third and fourth Annex types. The features of semantic fields belong to the tertiary group of features in this book.

The ramifications of a hypothesis about the objective use of semantic features are partly recognized in Leonard (1968). I write of <u>dinner-jacket</u>, <u>fishing-rod</u>, <u>travelling-cap</u> etc.:

> The link is in the first part but in several examples the second part has a semantic element of activity or use that helps the interpreter. For instance, in "dinner jacket" the first part has an element of activity that implies an animate, and generally a human subject ... the object of "eating" is a "meal" of some kind, and this is given by "dinner". Thus the second part "jacket", is not the object of "to eat". It cannot be a locative like the second part of "dinner table" because it has no locative semantic element. Its main semantic element is one of activity: "to wear". But this element does form a link with the implied human subject of "to dine". This gives the complete relationship: "John wears the jacket while dining". Thus a "dinner

> jacket" is "a jacket one wears while dining".[26]

Leonard (1968) also suggests that features might be so distributed as to interfere with one another. It is a major function of the program described in this book to find the best order for the interpretation rules, and to display how the rules postulated sometimes act to give a wrong interpretation first.

A. Schwartz (1970) opens the topic of transforming nouns and other parts of speech into sentences, the reverse of Lees's derivational process:

> ... it is possible to express the sense of "derivation" behind a form like <u>muddying</u> by allowing secondary rules like V $\longrightarrow$ A and A $\longrightarrow$ V to interact with a primary rule like VP $\longrightarrow$ V AP.[27]

He concludes that

> ... the monstrous involutions [of the transforming process] that quickly emerge suggest that severe constraints operate somewhere and somehow to keep the process in check ... what is a problem is the refinement of notions like "verbal force" and "implied subject".[28]

It is particularly the notion of 'verbal force' that is a relevant problem.

H. E. Brekle (1970) uses a 'sentence-semantic' (<u>Satzsemantik</u>) approach which assumes the presence of underlying sentences for noun sequences, but which represents their derivations by formulae like those of formal logic, rather than by transformations. For example, in his system

mousehole

begins with

living in a hole

and then has the subject mouse added. The following formula[29] describes mousehole:

AFF[LOC(R,y), w]

where R represents living, y represents hole, and w represents mouse. LOC and AFF represent the relations of 'location' and 'thing being affected' (a kind of passive Subject-Verb relationship).

Brekle does not deal with all the types I have found, nor with nested examples, nor with examples of which the meaning is indicated in the preceding context. Unlike me, he treats causality as a relational element on the same level as location and attribution. Like most other precursors, he does not show how one can work back from a given noun sequence to the sentence from which he postulates that it is derived.

The work of Jerrold J. Katz and Jerry A. Fodor (1963) provides some useful notions about semantic features in general. Katz's book (1972) proves more relevant, by discussing theoretically many of the processes that have been attempted in my computer dictionary and my program. However, the input to Katz's set of projection rules is a sentence, whereas mine is a noun sequence. My lexicon is much more limited than the one he conceives: for instance, my program says that a dog-kennel is a kennel for or containing a dog, but it does not say that it is a small, usually wooden house ... for a canine quadruped....

Katz uses redundancy rules on the lexicon, 'to eliminate any semantic markers from a lexical reading whose occurrence is predictable on the basis of the occurrence of another semantic marker in the same reading'.[30] When a sentence is interpreted, the compressed readings are filled out again. The experience of using my program suggests that it may be better for the computer to store all the features in the definition, rather than operate such rules compulsorily for every word that is encountered.

A problem found in using my program is that of two locatives of place. For instance, how does the human being know that a park lake usually means a lake in a park and not a lake with a park in it? Compare also garden path, staircase door and bedroom corridor. These seem to demand a knowledge of the configuration of a house and garden which would be difficult to store as features on the single words.[31] Such examples seem to require an internal 'picture of the world' which Katz's postulated lexicon is not designed to deal with (and which I deal with in only a rudimentary way).

Julius Laffal (1973) assigns about 23,500 words of English to 118 categories. My markers of semantic fields, though there are only nine of them, resemble some of his category headings. He says:

> I began to group words into categories, using at first the criterion of synonymity, and subsequently the additional criteria of similarity and relatedness. Auto and car are synonyms, auto and truck are similar, and auto and train are related.[32]

He has used his concept dictionary in 'comparing the speech content of separate speakers as topic changed'[33] and 'comparing the language content of psycho-therapists with that of their patients'.[34]

His study shows that semantic fields are practicable concepts, and it supports my use of them.

Some light is also thrown on the problem of the two locatives. Laffal has a feature PLAC (locative of place) and a feature HOLW (roughly equivalent to 'hollow'). Relevant sequences are box room, country case (a case used for country holidays), and White House cup. For all these, my program would yield two interpretatives, as for bookcase. In order to get the correct interpretation, box, case and cup could be marked HOLW so that they would fit inside room, country and White House. But in bookcase, case is the outer container, so case would fail in one or other of the interpretations (of bookcase and country case) whether it had PLAC (locative of place) or HOLW.

Cistern seems an ideal word for the feature HOLW (Laffal has it); and with the HOLW item inside the PLAC item it would yield a single correct interpretation for cistern cupboard:

a cupboard for or containing a cistern or cisterns.

However, in the field of archaeology one may meet with cisterns large enough for boating on the water.[35] One is still left with the problem of the two locatives and the need for knowledge of the world.[36]

Valerie Adams (1973) devotes one of her fourteen chapters to 'noun compounds', compounds, for her, as for Jespersen and Lees, including two-word sequences such as door knob. She includes several examples which would baffle my program and present problems to other methods of deriving interpretations from noun sequences by means of semantic features. These act as spurs to a further development of my program, e.g.:

honey bee (cf.: the bee produces honey)
silk worm (cf.: the worm produces silk)[37]

concert pitch	milk tooth
credibility gap	nose dive
fire sale	sex appeal
gallows bird	shotgun marriage
kitchen garden	toothmug[38]
light year	

Her comment on these difficult examples is that

> Our understanding of compounds depends on our knowing what it is in the outside world that they denote, and it seems that, in many cases, the first element functions chiefly as a sort of mnemonic device, a reminder of the nature and associations of the object or notion that the whole refers to. For example, we may understand banana republic to mean "a small country dominated by a more powerful one", without knowing that such countries are so called because they are economically dependent on the export of fruit, and on foreign capital.[39]

Speaking of the difficult shotgun marriage, Adams says that perhaps we can interpret it as an '"instrumental"' example, like insulin shock:

> "The shotgun - or a method which calls such an object to mind - is instrumental in bringing about the marriage"; though this interpretation still leaves out a piece of "knowledge of the world" ... as Sweet ... remarked....

> This very vagueness is the chief reason why composition is resorted to ....[40,41]

These passages show the limitations of my program. However, I do not agree that vagueness is deliberately sought, and therefore I believe that it is always relevant to seek a precise relationship between the constituent nouns. Secondly, I feel that the idiomatized meanings acquired by sequences such as <u>banana republic</u> had an original formation open to analysis by methods such as that of my program.

Pamela Downing (1977) criticizes Lees[42] on the arbitrariness of underlying structures and the irrecoverable deletion of meaningful material. The original aspect of Downing's work is her testing of the formation and acceptability of English 'compounds'.[43] She finds that

> ... subjects asked to propose interpretations for novel compounds ... came up with responses no less complex than those given for lexicalized forms.[44]

It is important to recognize, as she does, that noun sequences can be formed for a temporary purpose only, both (a) because one may wrongly include them in discussing word-formation, and (b) because they often occur in novels or in real life accompanied by explanatory context. Downing has a very good example of this:

> Thus a friend of mine was once instructed to sit in the <u>apple-juice seat,</u> i.e. the seat in front of which a glass of apple-juice had been placed.[45]

Downing's corpus of noun sequences consisted of a written account of a film sequence by 150 subjects, and several passages of published prose. Her classes agree roughly with mine. She also experimented with the composition and interpretation of noun sequences in isolation. With respect to the context-free interpretation, she says:

> The fact that comparison was a favoured relationship on the CFI task (e.g. <u>autumn-pebble</u> 'many-colored pebble') ... appears to be at odds with the absence of attested compounds based on the same relationship. This suggests that comparison may be a last-resort or default relationship, considered by the addressee when no other useful underlying relationship seems plausible.[46]

This conclusion is in accord with my own analysis. I have in my corpus examples such as <u>branch line</u>, yielded by default, belonging to the Equative type.

Among the factors that Downing says the speaker must consider are that

> ... the semantic weight of these forms is not merely the sum of the meanings of the two elements concatenated in surface structure; it is up to the hearer to discover the missing link ... If ... the compound is based on a temporary or fortuitous relationship, it is unlikely that the hearer will be able correctly to deduce the nature of the class denoted by the compound, unless he was actually present at the moment the relationship occurred, or was specifically told of it ... the interpretation

> of novel compounds is often (perhaps usually) facilitated by contextual cues ....[47]

Downing does not say whether 'temporary' compounds are formed (however obscurely) according to the same types as institutionalized compounds. 'The apple-juice seat' might be treated by the program as

> A seat that someone sits on when someone drinks apple-juice,

but I would not expect all 'temporary' compounds to fit into my classes.

Beatrice Warren (1978) categorizes 4566 noun sequences from 360,000 words of American prose.[48] Her corpus is somewhat larger than mine and she has a great many more examples (mainly because my data go back to the eighteenth century when noun sequences in novels were few). Her main purpose is to achieve a typology, and my typology is not very far from hers.

Warren excludes overt verbs. I feel little need to defend my hire car, fruit-preserving season as noun sequences with overt verb-morphemes. What is in need of some support is my use of covert verbs. Warren uses covert verbs, though usually more general ones than mine. Discussing the 'Location' type (sand fleas, sea horse) she says:

> The covert semantic relation is specialized in roommates, teammates, campmate, classmate, schoolmate (because of the meaning of mate (= companion)?) being something like be in the same.[49]

Writing of the subgroup including afternoon clerk and weekend guests, she says:

> In compounds where B [the head] is animate, the covert semantic relation can be represented either by "work", "operate", "be in action in, at or on".[50]

With respect to her next type, she writes:

> ... the most frequent semantic relation is the one represented by "appear in, at, on": wartime circular, ... day school.[51]

For the latter I have the covert verb studies, which would yield:

> Someone studies in a school in a day.

Again, in defining another subgroup, Warren says:

> All compounds in this subgroup have in common that they may be paraphrased according to the pattern "B is for verb-ing A with".[52]

Her examples include ball bat, tapestry needle and teaspoon. This leads easily into my definition of e.g. spoon to include eats or stirs, though I have no Purposive category.

Thus the assumption that underlying sentences play a part in the analysis of some examples is clearly present in Warren's very objective corpus-based study, though she does not, as I do, attach to a noun a verb or verbs that will come into play on all occasions when that noun is the head.

Warren does not experiment, as I have done, with the ordering of interpretation rules.

Judith Levi (1978) classifies quite a large number of noun sequences (not from a corpus). She says:

> The principal purpose of this book is the exploration of the syntactic and semantic properties of complex nominals (CNs) in English, and the elaboration of detailed derivations for these forms within a theory of generative semantics. The book also represents an attempt to incorporate into a grammar of English a model of the productive aspects of complex nominal formation.[53]

Her two demonstrations of the formation of examples involving the underlying verbs cause and be run well to the output form (e.g. heat stress, marginal note), but one cannot trace them backwards, as so much is deleted.

Altogether, there is only a certain amount of correspondence between Levi's types and mine. My Locative type finds no corresponding type. Many of Levi's types and subtypes contain examples which would be in different categories of mine. For instance, one of her types contains picture album (my Locative) as well as pet spray and plant food (my Sentence types).

Parts of my categorization are supported by Levi. Also, Levi's category containing grain alcohol, rye whiskey is attractive: these examples would fall into my Annex type but could bear a closer analysis. Levi does not depend on covert verbs as much as I do, though she uses general verbs such as be and have as covert verbs. She allows for underlying sentences with overt verbs.

It would be interesting to experiment with her three causal types (e.g. sob story); my program would treat such examples as having underlying sentences like this, without a marker of causality:

> Someone sobs when someone narrates a story or stories.

The general causal relationship does not fall within the scope of my program.

Finally, Levi does not experiment, as I have done, with the ordering of rules.

Now I shall briefly describe some computer work relevant to this book.

Van Overbeke (1971) splits compound words on the computer, something I have had to do by hand before feeding them into the computer. There is, besides the lexicon, a list of morphemes possible within the compound. Such morphemes would scarcely be found in English. Van Overbeke finds, as I do, that the problems posed by automatic bracketing cannot be settled without reference to syntactic and/or semantic links between the members of compounds.

Joyce Friedman (1971) presents a model originally intended to help linguists write and test transformational grammars describing the syntax of natural language (e.g. French or English). It resulted in a formal model of transformational grammar. She points out that a rule of grammar may behave as intended in isolation, but that in the grammar it must interact properly with all the other rules. In the writing of my program I have repeatedly found examples of this. Friedman's lexicon is composed, somewhat like mine, of feature definitions and lexical entries. Complex symbols are described, e.g.[54]

```
[ + N       ]
[ + ANIMATE ]
[ - HUMAN   ]
[ + SG      ]
[   dog     ]
```

Friedman's lexicon does not allow for homography, though it gives two separate lists of features for each of the verbs eat, grow and wear, which is similar to my treatment of them during the analysis of nouns related to verbs. Friedman's system must be told what type of input trees to expect; and whether to generate a tree around a skeletal input or whether it is necessary only to insert lexical items. (My program does not use a tree for sentence-structure, but its use of rows of slots is somewhat in the scale-and-category manner.)

In testing the input grammar, Friedman's program is not unlike mine, which works backwards from the noun sequence to a basic sentence or phrase.

Woods, Kaplan and Nash-Webber (1972) enable an inquirer, such as a lunar geologist, to ask in a normal English sentence for information of various kinds respecting different kinds of chemicals found on the moon. The program answers usually with a list of the names of relevant samples. The parsing system is a general one, able to provide a logical and semantic internal structure for several kinds of questions and commands. There is a dictionary, and as data a list of chemical details.

The file contains (or did in 1972) 18,000 chemical analyses of the lunar samples, and references to documents 'currently some 10,000 postings. ... The language processor has a vocabulary of some 3,500 words'.[55]

The program resembles mine in trying to transform input backwards: its work with sentences is interpretive.

My program also resembles this program in various ways common to the other programs hitherto described, but there is a particular similarity in the giving of precedence to parts of interpretations according to semantic criteria.

Terry Winograd (1972) wrote a remarkable system which, to quote his own abstract,

> ... answers questions, executes commands, and accepts information in an interactive English dialog. ... The system contains a parser, a recognition grammar of English, programs for semantic analysis, and a general problem solving system. ... The program is given a detailed model of a particular domain. In addition, the system has a simple model of its own mentality. It can remember and discuss its plans and actions as well as carrying them out. It enters into a dialog with a person, responding to English sentences with actions and English replies, asking for clarification when its heuristic programs cannot understand a sentence through the use of syntactic, semantic, contextual, and physical knowledge. Knowledge in the system is represented in the form of procedures, rather than tables of rules or lists of patterns.[56]

Winograd continues:

> By developing special procedural representations for syntax, semantics, and inference, we gain flexibility and power....[57]
>
> For our experiment, we pretend we are talking to a simple robot, with a hand and and eye and the ability to manipulate toy blocks on a table. The robot responds by carrying out commands (in a simulated scene on a display screen attached to the computer), typing out answers to questions, and accepting

> information to use in reasoning later on.[58]

Examples of semantic features used by Winograd are: #HUMAN, #GREEK, # FALLIBLE. Winograd's concept of such markers also includes the names of objects: mine includes features only.

Winograd poses the problem which I try to meet with my fourth set of features: the relative size of the referent. He says,

> The order of analysis simplifies handling of "relative" modifiers. There is no absolute definition for "big" or "little"; a "big flea" is still not much competition for a "little elephant". ... each definition ... can ... produce an appropriate meaning relative to the object being described. This may be an absolute measurement (e.g., a "big elephant" is more than 12 feet tall) or a relative ... description of the form "the number of objects fitting the description and smaller than the one being described is more than the number of suitable objects bigger than it is".[59]

Winograd does not deal with the relationships within uninflected noun sequences. He says:

> There are some places in English where the relation between a set of words is not indicated by syntactic clues, but is largely based on semantics. One example is [sic] chain of classifiers before a noun. In "strict gun law", the law is strict, but in

> "stolen gun law", the gun is stolen. It is possible to combine long strings like "an aluminum soup pot cover clearance sale", in which a large amount of semantic information must be combined with the ordering to find the correct interpretation. The current system handles classifiers by assuming that they all separately modify the head. This needs to be changed, to use both the semantic markers and complex deductions to find the real relationships.[60]

This is precisely what my program is designed to do.

Donald E. Walker (1973) describes an attempt to understand spoken English.

Accepting spoken input, the computer tries to predict what the next word will be, in order to avoid long tests on the input words.

Walker's analysis is like that described by Winograd, but differs from Winograd in some ways, e.g. (in a parsing tree):

> Winograd tested to eliminate the least likely alternatives first, checking the longest possible constituent and cutting back when that failed ... With voice input, it is necessary both to test for most likely alternatives first and to have a more general mechanism for following alternative paths through the grammar in case of failure.[61]

In its chief instructions, my program begins by testing for three relationships not the most likely to occur, but very likely to be correctly analyzed. Next come two relationships highly likely to occur: the Locative and Verb relationships, which are deliberately ordered with respect to one another according to the most likely to succeed. The unlikelihood of the modifier-material sequence is the reason why it is placed near the end of the test. Walker's and my program are similar in this.

However, the procedure of mine dealing with verbs related to the nouns looks for several unusual conditions, some even leading to an equative type, before it reaches the tests for normal verb structures. In this, my program resembles Winograd's.

Yorick Wilks (July 1973) has a concept of 'elements' which supports my concepts of certain semantic features and the semantic fields:

> ELEMENTS are sixty primitive semantic units used to express the semantic entities, states, qualities and actions about which humans speak and write. The elements fall into five classes, which can be illustrated as follows (elements in upper case):
>
> (a) entities: MAN (human being), STUFF (substances), THING (physical object), PART (parts of things), FOLK (human groups), ACT (acts), STATE (states of existence), BEAST (animals), etc., (b) actions: FORCE (compels), CAUSE (causes to happen), FLOW (moving as liquids do), PICK (choosing), BE (exists) etc., (c) type indicators: KIND (being a quality), HOW (being a type of action) etc., (d) sorts: CONT (being a container), GOOD (being morally acceptable), THRU (being an aperture) etc., (e) cases: TO (direction), SOUR (source), GOAL (goal or end), LOCA (location), SUBJ

(actor or agent), OBJE (patient of action), IN (containment), POSS (possessed by) etc.[62]

A number of these features can be matched exactly, and others near-matched, by some of my features: eleven of them are reasonable matches.

Footnotes to Chapter 1

1 'First included in Everyman's Library 1930''reprinted 1967.' I am not sure whether the format has been changed between 1930 and 1967, so I am giving the date of reprinting. The date 1930 is also given in the Bibliography. The same sort of thing is true of the other books in Everyman's Library.

2 This was done kindly by Mr. Paul Nixon, with a program in Cobol.

3 This was done by a program of mine in Algol 60.

4 This was done by a program of mine in Algol 60.

5 I wrote both of these programs in Algol 60.

6 The numbers in square brackets indicate homographs of other nouns, e.g. jet[1], the plane; jet[2], the spouting; and jet[3], the black material.

7 That lives in or comes from causes a clause to be output, but this type is not a sentence type: it is merely that the clause is the best way in which to paraphrase this example, which is actually a purely Locative type in its base form. The same applies to Types C1S3, C1S4, C1S5 and C3.

8 These are the subtypes of E1:

E1(a) baby crocodile: from Findfields, if head and modifier are each either human or animal, and both are not agents: i.e. human, animal; human, human; animal, human; animal, animal.

(b) oak-tree: from Findfields, if there is a Fields match and head and modifier are of equal size.

(c) actor-manager: from Verbinterp, where the head has a verb, the modifier is a subject and has an overt verb, or both head and modifier are subjects and the head has an overt verb.

(d) rain-water: from Verbinterp, where the modifier has an overt verb and is a subject.

(e) clearance sale: from Verbinterp, where both head and modifier are 'activities', i.e. constitute the verb of the underlying sentence.

(f) branch line: from Equifind, which acts by default, i.e. when no other type has been yielded.

9 In context this refers to 'vinegar-faced Joseph', i.e. 'Joseph with a face like vinegar'. Apart from the modifying morpheme -d (for -ed), vinegar-face is a noun sequence of the equative kind, with in this case an overriding metaphorical relationship.

10 By additive I mean something different from the dvandva relationship which Marchand (1969), p.41, calls additive.

11 Some examples of reduplication do not just represent sounds, but have a syntactic relationship. Compiler-compiler (not in the data) a compiler which compiles compilers (in computers), would be picked up by Verbinterp long before reaching Addifind.

12 In the sample of output at the end of this book, the types are named and, in certain cases, given as numbers. Here are the equivalents:

A2	1020	C2	3020	E1(e)	5014
A3	1030	C3	3030	E1(f)	5015
A4	1040	D1	4010	E2	5020
A5	1050	D2	4020	F1	6010
C1S1	3011	D3	4030	F2 AND 3	6020
C1S2	3012	D4	4040	F4	6040
C1S3	3013	E1(a)	5010	F5	6050
C1S4	3014	E1(b)	5011	G1	7010
C1S5	3015	E1(c)	5012	H1	8010
C1S6	3016	E1(d)	5013		

13 Jespersen (1909-49); especially Part VI (1942).

14 Thus one can conceive not only of relationships between the two nouns in a noun sequence, but also of relationships and contrasts between the whole classes of noun sequences, of which eight are distinguished in this book (Types A and B with underlying sentences, and types C-H with phrasal interpretations).

15 Saussure (1916), passim.

16 Jespersen includes two-word sequences in his term 'compounds', e.g. life member, Part VI, op.cit., p.144.

17 Op.cit., Part VI, p.137.

18 Op.cit., Part VI, p.139. (Jespersen quotes from G.B. Shaw.)

19 Cf. Leonard (1968), p.49.

20 Op.cit., pp.49-50.

21 Marchand (1960), p.22. I have found this first edition more helpful than that of 1969.

22 The total is 458 when examples occurring only in first editions are included.

23 Leonard (1968), p.264: The first 17,500 words of: Samuel Johnson, Rasselas; Jane Austen, Pride and Prejudice; Charles Dickens, The Old Curiosity Shop; George Meredith, The Ordeal of Richard Feverel; Christopher Isherwood, Down There on a Visit.

24 Op.cit., p.183.

25 Op.cit., pp.199-200.

26 Op.cit., p.123.

27 Schwartz (1970), p.302.

28 Op.cit., p.304.

29 Brekle (1970), p.149.

30 Katz (1972), p.44.

31 Katz and Fodor (1963) acknowledge a similar (though much more restricted) problem with regard to horse shoes and alligator shoes.

32 Laffal (1973), p.vii.

33 Op.cit., p.x.

34 *Op.cit.*, p.xi.

35 E.g. in Istanbul.

36 *Cf.* *water tank*, *water-hen*.

37 Adams (1973), p.66. I have not reproduced her stress-marks.

38 *Op.cit.*, p.88.

39 *Op.cit.*, p.88

40 Sweet (1891), p.449, section 1560. (The British Museum catalogue dates it 1892.)

41 Adams, *op.cit.*, pp.88-89.

42 Lees (1960), (1966), (1970).

43 Like Jespersen (1942), Downing includes two-word sequences among 'compounds'.

44 Downing (1977), p.820.

45 *Op.cit.*, p.818.

46 *Op.cit.*, p.830.

47 *Op.cit.*, p.837.

48 The Brown Corpus, from which she took her samples, is described in Kučera and Francis (1967).

49 Warren (1978), pp.171, 172.

50 _Op.cit_., pp.178, 179.

51 _Op.cit_., p.179.

52 _Op.cit_., p.205.

53 Levi (1978), pp. 5, 121 ff., 126 ff.

54 Friedman (1971), p.53.

55 Woods, Kaplan and Nash-Webber (1972), in the Abstract on the last page.

56 Winograd (1972), p.1.

57 _Op.cit_., p.1.

58 _Op.cit_., p.2.

59 _Op.cit_., p.129.

60 _Op.cit_., p.157.

61 Walker (1973), p.5.

62 Wilks (July 1973), p.3.

CHAPTER 2

THE DICTIONARY

In order to analyze a noun sequence, the program has to look up each noun in a 'dictionary' to see what semantic features it has. The program then finds connexions between the nouns according to their semantic features. For instance, the noun _side_ has the semantic feature of being an 'annex': a part of something. Thus the noun sequence _mountainside_ is interpreted as _the side of a mountain_. The noun _field_ has a locative feature, and so a _daisy field_ is _a field with daisies in_. The noun _maker_ has a feature that relates it to a verb, _to make_. It also has the feature of denoting an agent. Thus the program interprets _music-maker_ as _someone that makes music_. In the noun sequence _travelling-cap_ both nouns have features that relate them to verbs, and, because _cap_ is the object of the related verb _to wear_, the action of _travelling_ is assumed to be simultaneous. The program therefore outputs the interpretation _a cap that someone wears while someone travels_. We can see that in some cases the interpretation results from the features of one of the nouns, and in others it results from the features of both nouns. But it can be seen that we require a list of the features of every noun that we are likely to encounter during the analysis. This list, although it includes only nouns and verbs, is loosely called the 'dictionary'.

The dictionary program has been run on a machine with a 24-bit machine word, but none of the program is dependent on 24 as an upper limit, and with very slight alterations it could be run on a machine with fewer bits than 24.

The initial capital has been found useful. As a likely marker of place-names among locative nouns, it enables the interpretation program to output

a man that lives in or comes from Newark

as the likeliest meaning of Newark man, whereas it outputs

a man that lives in or works in a lift

as a likely meaning of liftman.

With regard to the two courts, the Court with an initial capital is marked with the human feature, and is treated not only as a locative but also as a likely subject of a sentence; whereas the court in lower-case letters is merely the locative.

Unfortunately the distinctness of the form with the initial capital results in some wasteful duplication in the dictionary, but it has been retained for its usefulness in the analysis of noun sequences.

Definitions limited to those features required for the analysis of noun sequences.

Features such as 'annex', 'location', 'agent' and 'relationship to a verb' are relevant to the analysis of noun sequences. There are many other semantic features belonging to nouns that are probably not relevant to the behaviour of the nouns in sequence. Therefore, such features as 'soft' and 'hard', 'cold' and 'hot', 'dark' and 'light', have been ignored for the purposes of this program. The matter of setting up relationships of dependency and implication between the senses of nouns has also been ignored. Thus there are no structures inside the dictionary that resemble Katz's semantic tree for bachelor.[1] Some of the features used in this dictionary imply dependency or class-inclusion, such as the feature 'human' and the nine features that denote membership of certain semantic fields. But it is not intended to include all possible semantic relationships.

Nevertheless, the structure of the dictionary is such that if it were desired to add many more semantic features, it would be quite possible to do so. The structure adopted here is capable of extension to function as a dictionary for a more general purpose than the analysis of noun sequence. The great problem for the lexicographer would be to identify those semantic features and relationships that would provide a manageable set of definitions and reasonably short searches. A number of these relationships are likely to be things that the dictionary for human use can take for granted as common knowledge, but that the computer dictionary must include in an explicit way. Because they are implicit in human use of language, some of the features may prove hard to identify.

Parts of speech

The dictionary for use in this program has deliberately not included a marker of 'part of speech'.[2] However, in general, experience with this dictionary suggests that if it were to be extended to include words other than nouns and verbs, it would need markers of the 'part of speech', or of several possible parts of speech, for each lexical item. In particular, the inclusion of adjectives, which has been avoided but which would be the next step in extending the dictionary for noun sequences, would probably require a special marker. Furthermore, while the definitions in this dictionary have very much the same structure for verbs as for nouns, the structure of the cross-references (e.g. between painter, painting and paints) varies according to whether the word is a noun or a verb, and so it might be said that the part of speech is identified by the structure of the entry.

Pragmatism in the construction of the entries

Pragmatism has been an important principle in the construction of the dictionary. As few semantic features as possible were used in the first version, and features were added only as they were thought necessary. The nine semantic fields that are used are simply those into which all those noun sequences fell that had an 'annex' or 'equative' relationship, and that could not be analyzed by using the 'pure annex' feature that belongs to such words as front, side and top. Thus, boot button, thighbone and so on call for the establishment of semantic fields such as 'clothing' and 'part of the body'. Among those features that do not denote class-inclusion, there are some such as 'location' and 'pure annex' that quickly help us to analyze examples such as Lincolnshire estate and table top. There are also some syntactic features such as 'plural' and 'non-count' that are included merely to enable us to use the right article during the output of a sentence containing the word trousers or gravel. But features such as 'speed' or 'direction', which might appear in an implementation of the definition of to play by Katz and Fodor,[3] are not relevant to this program and are not included. Especially it has been found necessary to beware of distinctions made by the physical scientists which are not found to operate in natural language. For instance, air operates more frequently in connexion with flight than as a kind of substance. It carries the connotation 'flies or lands' more often than it acts as a material noun: contrast airfield with air-pump. The term horse is quite different from the terms for most of the other quadrupeds, in implying several functions such as to carry and to pull. The dictionary program contains the facility to give horse several verbs, though here we have given it only two. In this program its connexions with notions denoted by verbs are explored before the marker 'animal' is taken into consideration. This is in contrast to many definitions in normal dictionaries; the definition in the Concise Oxford Dictionary, for instance, begins with 'Solid-hoofed quadruped with flowing mane and tail'. Admittedly, in a dictionary not concerned primarily with noun sequences the verb functions might be less important; but this is a small illustration of the way in which it seems that the names of certain animals and objects may denote their uses rather than their physical properties, and that biological classification seems to be comparatively unimportant.

How a Dictionary entry is input and stored

An entry in the dictionary is composed of four parts: the word, its semantic features, its alphabetical position, and in some cases the pointers to other words with which it is connected.

Each word is entered with its semantic features. The dictionary program carries out the alphabetical ordering and sets up any pointers that are required.

How the semantic features are input and stored

A full list of the semantic and other features is given in the next chapter.

Four self-evident primary features are Verbness, Location, Material and Annex (a part of anything). Two self-evident secondary features are the features of Transitivity and Object of an Overt Verb. The tertiary features denote membership of a class such as clothing or part of the body. The fourth kind of feature denotes proportionate size: e.g. a hand, #3, is larger than a finger, #2.

In fact, there are several features used besides the ones that have already been described, but at present we are concerned with the way in which the features are input and stored. The significance of each of the other features will become clear in later chapters. Suffice it to say that in practice they are all accommodated in the four groups of features. A few semi-syntactic features, such as non-count, are included in practice among the primary features, and theoretically a case could be made for non-count to have semantic significance.

Let us suppose we are dealing with the word gold. It has three primary features and no other features. The three primary features are that gold is a material, that it has a physical existence (as opposed to, e.g., humour or pleasure), and that the noun is a non-count noun.

The features are each represented by a number. In the list of primary features, these particular features are numbered:

material	3
physical existence	6
non-count	10

The entry that is input by the linguist will therefore look like this:

GOLD 3 6 10

If a word has secondary features, they are distinguished by the sign $<$ before the number. The noun charge is associated with the verb to charge, the verb is transitive, and the noun denotes the object of the verb:

Someone charges a pound (for the ride).

This sentence might underlie a sequence such as

pound charge.

The features are numbered as follows:

The noun is associated with a verb	1 (a primary feature)
The verb is overt (as opposed to, e.g. pound <u>fare</u>)	<1
The verb is transitive	<5
The noun denotes the object of the verb	<8

When we input the noun, we also input the third person singular form of the verb with which it is associated. The entry for <u>charge</u>, therefore, looks like this:

CHARGE 1 CHARGES <1 <5 <8

The tertiary features denote membership of a class, and are always associated with a feature of the fourth kind, denoting the comparative size of the referent within its class. The tertiary features are marked with the % sign, and the features of size are marked with the # sign.[4]

A <u>cuff</u> is a <u>small</u> part of an item of <u>clothing</u>, and so it is marked as follows:

Has a physical existence	6 (a primary feature)
Is or belongs to an article of clothing	%8
Is almost the smallest item in its semantic field	#2

The entry for <u>cuff</u> looks like this:

CUFF 6 %8 #2

Occasionally a referent belongs to more than one semantic field. For instance, a <u>door</u> can belong to a <u>cupboard</u> (an item of furniture) or to a <u>house</u> (a building). A <u>lift</u> is both a mechanism and a part of a building. In these cases there are two markers of semantic fields.

Linguistic weaknesses of the system of markers used in the programs

It must be admitted that there are three weaknesses of the system of markers used in the programs. They could all be solved, but the solutions would involve alterations which would detract from the main purpose of the interpretation program, especially by adding appreciably to the time taken to perform the analysis and therefore making the program too cumbersome to perform many experiments in the more important areas of analysis.

The first, and probably the most serious weakness, is that when more than one verb is associated with a noun, it is not possible to specify the noun as having different functions for each of the verbs. For instance, the entry for master gives the following semantic features:

Is associated with a verb or verbs	1
Human	4
Has a physical existence	6
The verbs are not overt but covert	<2
The noun denotes the subject of the verbs	<11

MASTER 1 CONTROLS OR TEACHES 4 6 <2 <11

However, in dealing with a noun such as message it might be desirable to mark it as the object of the covert verb to send as well as the subject of the covert verb to convey:

telephone message
(Someone sends the message by telephone)

condolence message
(The message conveys condolence.)

If this weakness were to be overcome, the storage allowed for references to verbs would have to be augmented by storage for separate function-markers for all the verbs, whereas at present the functions are stored very economically as 'bits', the smallest available units of storage, and can be inspected as boolean variables belonging to the noun, once only for each noun. It has been decided not to increase the storage or the inspection time by allowing for this variety of functions. The variety of verbs with their functions does not occur with overt verbs, and, while the absence of a provision for it may weaken the case for the use of covert verbs, it is probably safer to exclude such a provision while trying to demonstrate that covert verbs can, in fact, validly be used at all. There are only one or two cases in the corpus where a clear improvement might be made by including such a provision. The weakness is a syntactic and a semantic problem, involving not only problems of storage.

The second and third weaknesses are concerned with the sizes within semantic fields. The second weakness is that it is not possible to mark a referent as being, for instance, of small size within the field of buildings but of large size within the field of furniture. Thus a door has the size-marker #2 whether it belongs to a piece of furniture or to a building. To overcome this weakness would involve much more time in inspecting the features of size. Very few examples in the corpus would be better defined in this way.

The third weakness is encountered when a single word can denote 'annex' items of more than one size within the same semantic field. A word such as floor cannot be marked with two sizes within the field of the building. In one sense it denotes the lower horizontal plane of a room; in its larger sense it denotes a horizontal plane extending throughout a building: *first floor*, *second floor*, and so on. An example used by Deighton, *office floor*, is ambiguous in this way, although the context shows that it means *that level of the building on which the office or offices are located*. In fact, *floor* is the only case in the corpus that shows this duality of sizes, and it could be dealt with (albeit brutally) by entering two different definitions for *floor*. This third weakness is easier to overcome than the other two, as the structure of the dictionary within the machine could easily accommodate several sizes for one word. The complication would be in the interpretation program, which would have to inspect the sizes one by one, as bits, instead of once only, as one integer.

Variations permissible to the linguist writing the input

The input can be used by a linguist who is not a programmer. An example is given in the List of Features, an appendix. The noun is written first. Then the features are written, immediately preceded by their special markers if they are features of verbness, semantic fields, or sizes. If one or more verbs are to be related to the noun, they are input anywhere in the line after the noun. If there is more than one verb, the linguist can write, for example:

MASTER 1 CONTROLS OR TEACHES 4 6 <2 <11

or he can write

MASTER 1 CONTROLS TEACHES 4 6 <2 <11

The dictionary will accommodate up to five verbs for one noun. The word OR can be used instead of a space to separate all or any of them. The program that makes the dictionary will print a warning if more than five verbs are input, or if it is puzzled by any of the feature-markers, and then it will carry on entering the next noun.

The verbs and the features need not be entered in any special order. Thus the above entry could be written in any of the following ways:

```
MASTER CONTROLS TEACHES <2   6   4   <11   1
MASTER   <11   4   <2   1   CONTROLS   6   TEACHES
MASTER   4   6   CONTROLS   <11   1   TEACHES   <2
```

This means that the linguist can keep a set of words with their definitions on cards or file, and can add new features or new associated verbs without having to rewrite the cards. If he is using a file-editing system, it is a great relief not to be bound by numerical ordering, although of course a well-ordered list of features is easier to read.

If the linguist omits from the definition of any particular noun the first primary feature, 1, which means that the noun has one or more associated verbs, the dictionary program will still read the verbs into the dictionary, but the interpretation program when it is carrying out the analysis will fail to notice them. If such an omission is later discovered, the addition of the feature-marker 1 will cause the interpretation program to find the verbs satisfactorily.

There is no marker for the end of an entry; the end of the line or the end of the card is the end of the entry. Up to 99 characters are permitted on a line.

Theoretically, any number of spaces may be used to separate words and features from one another.

If the dictionary program is puzzled by certain kinds of small error in input, it will bypass one or more verbs or features but it may well input the noun and the rest of the features. In that case it will print a warning, giving the location on the line of the assumed error. If it skips a whole entry because of an error, it will print a warning and print the line that it has not entered.

A word is limited to 30 letters, which seems a reasonable limit for unhyphened nouns in English. If a longer word is input, it is curtailed and a warning is printed.

The linguist using this program to compose a dictionary is free to define the meanings of any of the features except those which are marked with the sign <. (Several of these secondary features are used within the dictionary program to establish syntactic links between nouns and verbs.) Thus, if the marker < were not used, the dictionary program could be used to set up any kind of dictionary at all, allowing for up to 69 features. But such a dictionary would be only an alphabetical storage system; its value would depend on the way in which the features were defined, and on the kind of program that would make use of it. Grammatically, the most valuable part of the dictionary program is the fact that it sets up cross-references between nouns and verbs.

Covert Verbs

The impression may be gained that the covert verbs have been chosen in view of the examples which they are then used to interpret. However, in general I have postulated normal uses for the nouns, which may not fall within the data.

Cheque : pays for would be all right for e.g. *gravestone cheque*

> a cheque that someone pays for a gravestone with.

The program gives a wrong interpretation: *Amalgamated Minerals cheque*

> a cheque that someone pays for Amalgamated Minerals with.

Scarf : wears would be all right for e.g. winter scarf:

a scarf that someone wears in the winter.

The program gives a wrong interpretation: artificial silk scarf:

a scarf that artificial silk wears.

Piano : plays would be all right for e.g. piano time:

a time that someone plays a piano in.

The program gives a wrong interpretation: piano top:

a top that plays a piano or pianos.

Thus the verbs are not just chosen ad hoc, but do reflect the more normal usage of the language.

Metaphor

Metaphor usually occurs in the Equative type, with no reason to make an alteration in the dictionary. However, in Thackeray (1847), Mr. Sedley makes fun of his son (the Collector of Boggley Wallah) by saying that a 'buggy' is 'a one-horse palanquin'. A 'mechanism' feature has had to be added to palanquin (a sort of litter) to enable the horse to pull it.

Other alterations

A few other special features have had to be added to definitions: e.g. the same feature, 'mechanism', has had to be added to cab[1] to enable it to be seen as a part of e.g. a lorry.

Homographs

Provision is made for homographs, but they are not a primary concern of this book. Only approximately 65% of them are correctly analyzed by the program.

Homographs may be distinguished in the dictionary by the addition (immediately following each word) of numbers in square brackets. For instance, the two kinds of <u>tank</u>, the one a receptacle and the other a tracked armoured vehicle, may be entered as follows:

TANK [1] 2 6 %1 #3
TANK [2] 1 TRAVELS <2 6 <11 %1 #4

Up to 9 homographs of any noun can be accommodated in the dictionary.

The linguist may find that he has input a noun early in his list without realizing that it has a homograph. In that case, he can input the second occurrence of the item with the marker [2] even though the first occurrence was not marked with [1]. All subsequent entries of that item, however, must be marked with numbers, so he must always know how many homographs of any particular item there are in the dictionary. If he marks an entry with a number that has already been used, or with a number higher than is suitable, the entry will be rejected as a duplicate, and a warning will be printed.

If a noun is entered twice without being marked as a homograph, a warning will be printed.

For the present purpose, the existence of homographs has not been diligently explored, as the main purpose was to get the program working for the corpus under consideration. Quite a large number of homographs are included. The facility is available for the user interested in a more general application.[5]

There is one minor linguistic disadvantage in the arrangement of homographs in the dictionary. The homographs are ordered in the way in which they are input. Thus the primary use of a lexical item may happen to occur second or third in the store. Interpretations printed by the program may include a lexicographically secondary meaning first. If the dictionary is printed out, it may list the tank that is a vehicle before the other tank because the 'vehicle' happens to have been input first.

It would be easy to re-order the numbers in the list before use; but it could be very complicated to set them in order after new words had been added to the dictionary. The facility has not been felt necessary for the present purpose.

How the linguist makes and adds to a dictionary

In order to make the dictionary, the linguist needs a list of entries such as have just been described. In the case of the present work, the semantic features have been chosen for each noun in a mainly intuitive manner. Features have been added to or deleted from each noun in the light of the interpretations output by the program during its development. New features have been defined, too, in the light of experience. Dictionaries, and in particular the Concise Oxford Dictionary, have been consulted in some cases, but most of the features marked in the computer dictionary are regarded as too obvious to mark in a dictionary for human use. The kind of thing on which it has been useful to have the opinion of the Concise Oxford Dictionary is how far a court is felt to be human, and whether a palanquin is a mechanism. Informants (other than the writer's own intuition) have scarcely been used at all. I have, however, consulted others over difficult cases. The decisions about which features to mark on each word are assessable according to the quality of the interpretations that are output by the program.

Having written the entries for each noun, consisting of the features and any associated verbs, the linguist puts them into a list, in the present case Features, which need not be in alphabetical order. He feeds this list into the computer, and operates the dictionary program on it. The result is a dictionary.

How the dictionary is composed

In the composition of the dictionary, first, the noun sequences are collected from the novels, and listed on cards or file, one sequence to a line. If it is desired to precede each sequence with bibliographical or other information, such as the author and page number of the book, or information about stress-patterns, then this information can be inserted before the noun sequence. The noun sequences must always begin on the same location on the line: in practice, they are preceded by author and page number, and begin in location 25.

Samples of input can be seen in the appendix Data.

The noun sequences can include adjectives and conjunctions, which must be placed in brackets like <THIS>. They can also include (NEST-MARKER) BRACKETS like these. Non-nouns and round brackets are ignored by the noun selection program.

The boundary between nouns in an unhyphened sequence such as *housemaid* must be marked by a + sign. An equals sign[6] is also treated as a boundary. A slash between words is treated as a unifier, e.g. *grade/one mistress*, where *grade one* acts as a noun though *one* is not a noun.

A program picks out the nouns, another program sorts them,[7] and the linguist must edit in the features and related verbs.

The dictionary program is then run on the feature list, producing a dictionary which can be output to file or tape.

When more noun sequences are collected, the same process is performed, but the linguist checks with the feature list and crosses out those nouns that are already in the dictionary. (This can be done by the computer.) The linguist then adds the features to the new nouns.

He inputs the existing dictionary, and then the new nouns with their features. The dictionary program inserts the new words in the dictionary, printing a warning (but not stopping) if it meets a noun that is already in. If a verb is re-encountered, but this time with a newly marked feature, the new feature is added to the old entry for the verb.[8]

The composition of the dictionary

(Please see following page.)

The composition of the dictionary

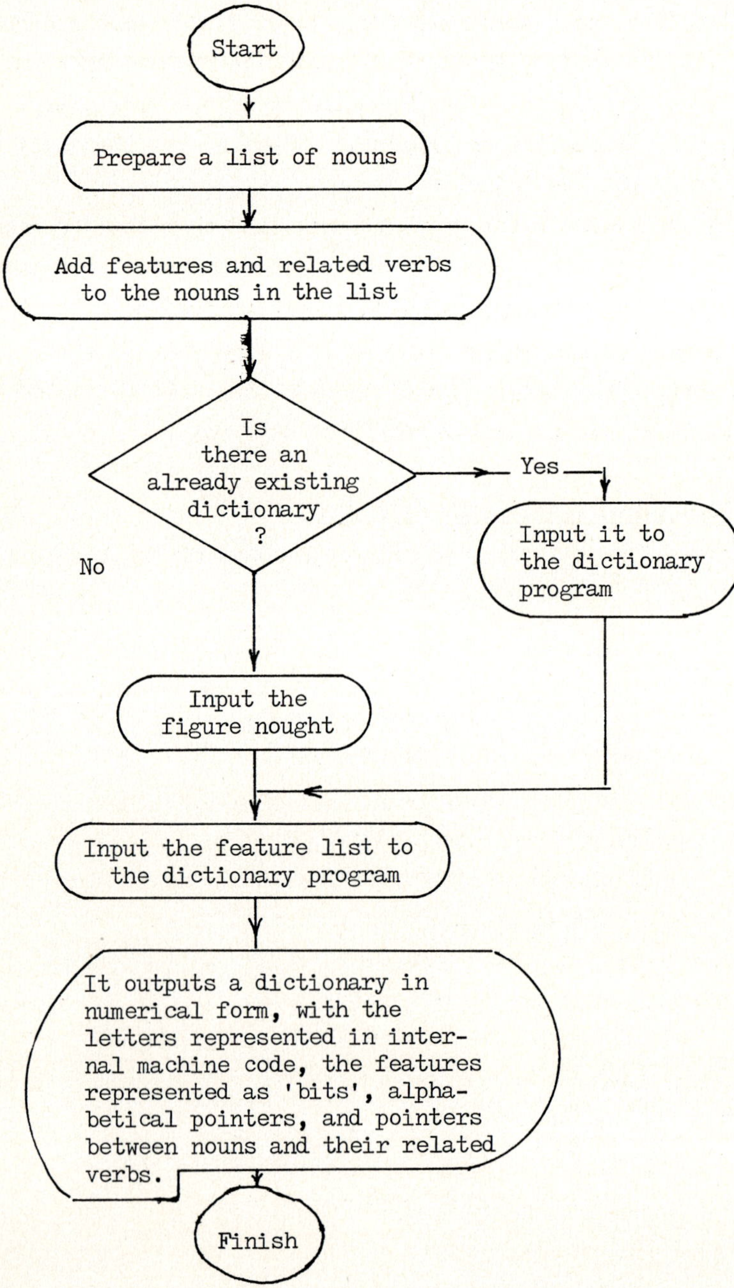

Footnotes to Chapter 2

1 Katz and Fodor (1963), p.186.

2 Compare Chomsky (1970).

3 Katz and Fodor (1963), p.184.

4 # is known as 'hash'.

5 Kelly and Stone (1975) have an extremely high rate of success with homographs. However, (a) most of their disambiguation is between parts of speech, and (b) they are able to use several words of context.

6 An equals sign indicates a hyphen occurring at the end of a line in the text, which may mean a hyphen but may also be used in a one-word sequence.

7 On the first making of the dictionary there is some redundancy in that the alphabetical sorting is done twice. But there is an advantage to the linguist in having the first, very long word-list in alphabetical order. Once inside the dictionary, it has to have pointers added. The earliest version of the dictionary-making program operated on an already sorted list, but if the verbs are to be mixed with the nouns, the dictionary-making program must repeat the sorting process.

8 This facility could be used for nouns too, but it is safer not to use it for nouns as it could result in the insertion, unawares, of incompatible features, or the ascription to the same lexical item of features belonging to two quite separate homographs.

CHAPTER 3

THE NOUN SEQUENCE INTERPRETATION PROGRAM

The program for interpreting noun sequences has three components. These are the analysis (or interpretation), the input process and the output process. Of these, the analysis is by far the most important, but the input and output are necessarily quite complex.

The Analysis

The analysis inspects the example for nine different patterns. If it finds one of the patterns, it makes a further inspection, e.g. to see whether the nouns belong to the same semantic field (fir-bough), whether they have a related verb (birthday), or whether they contain locatives (Lincolnshire estate). Further checks are then made and, if appropriate, an interpretation is stored in the Nest. (By far the most complex of these analyses occurs when there is a related verb.)

The interpretations yield the eight main types of noun sequence. There are nine kinds of search, not eight, because some of the noun sequences have to be sought in two different ways for the same type, and one pattern merges two types. One of the types with two searches is the Annex type, which can have the pattern of two members of the same semantic field (fir-bough) or one noun with an Annex feature (hillside). The other is the Material type, where a material feature in the modifier is sought early (stone lion) whereas the test for the material head comes much later (*tree-clump*, *shoe-leather*). The search that inspects for two types is the verb search, which may yield a purely verbal example (*headache*) but may, on the other hand, yield a verbal locative (*birthday*). These are merged because it may be at quite a late stage that the locative noun is fitted into the sentence-slots set up by the verb.

The nine searches will now be described.

1. *The search for a match in semantic fields*.

The tertiary features (mechanism, human organization etc.) are inspected and a match is found between *fir* and *bough* in the feature 'plant or tree'. The quaternary features (relative size) are then inspected. *Bough* is smaller than *fir*. Hence the Annex relationship is yielded: one entity is a part of the other:

The bough of a fir.

The type number is put into the 'left-hand side' of the Nest.[1] The paraphrase will be output later.

2. *The search for a material modifier*.

An inspection is made to see whether the modifier denotes a material. It does so in an example such as *stone lion*. The example is then inspected to see whether the head can be composed of a material, and does not consist of only the verb item in a sentence, e.g. *stone speech*. However, such a metaphorical construction is allowed, provided that the feature <5 (transitive) is not present. Thus *silver laughter* can mean

laughter made of (sounding like) silver,

but a *stone-breaker* is unlikely to be *a breaker made of stone*.[2]

The type number is then placed in the Nest.

3. The search for a pure annex.

This search is to find whether one noun is a pure annex to the other. A 'pure annex' is, for example, side in hillside, because a side (or a top or even the noun colour) denotes purely a part or an attribute of something. In this way it is different from, e.g. fir-bough, where a bough has an existence independently from a fir.

When a pure annex is found, the number denoting the type is placed in the Nest.

If one of the nouns is nested, e.g. (table-top) polish, a rule comes into force. An inspection is made to see whether the modifier is a material noun, e.g. (soap+stone) ornament. If so, the normal rules apply. But in the case of (table-top) polish, the features of the nested modifier (table) are attached to its head (top), for the sake of the highest-level interpretation: e.g. (table-top) polish must be analyzed as

the polish for the top of a table,

not

top polish for a table.

4. The search for a related verb.

This search is to find whether there is a relationship involving a verb, e.g. birth + day. Verb relationships are discovered by inspecting the storage of verbs taken from the dictionary entries of each noun.

A digression is made to check whether the head-noun is horse or man, as in barm-man.[3] This is because the nouns horse and man can each carry several different verb relationships, one of which is selected according to the semantic content of the other noun.

The appropriate verb is sought on <u>horse</u> or <u>man</u>, and a sentence is yielded:

A horse pulls a tram or trams;
A man sells barm.

Next, we want to know which are the sentence-functions of the noun that is related to the verb. It may be the subject, verb, object, instrument or locative of place. In <u>birth + day</u>, <u>birth</u> is simply the verbal noun. (In the other cases, various types are yielded, including an Equative type for 'subject + subject': <u>producer-director</u>.) The functions are looked up in the material taken from the dictionary.

When the possible functions of the noun have been found, a verb structure is set up based on the noun. For <u>birth + day</u> a new, empty row of sentence-slots is found, and a sentence is set up in that row:

S	V	O	Instrument	Locatives: Place	Locatives: Time	Manner
Someone	is born	Ø	0	0	0	0

The Object slot is blocked, as <u>is born</u> has no Object.

After the row has been set up, we try to fit the other noun[4] into the sentence. We first inspect it to see whether it is related to a verb. In the case of <u>birth + day</u> it is not. An ordered cycle of operations comes into force to try the other noun in each of the sentence-slots. It fits into the slot of Locative of Time:

S	V	O	Instrument	Locatives: Place	Locatives: Time	Manner
Someone	is born	Ø	0	0	a day or days	0

The position of the word in the array of slots is linked with its record in the Nest, by putting -1 into the Nest, a reference to the row in which the sentence is stored. (A second sentence, e.g. one with the intransitive sense of hurt, would have the number -2.)

In the part of the Nest where type numbers are stored (the 'left-hand side' of the Nest), a positive number denotes a phrasal type, e.g. Material (a house of stone), and a negative number denotes a sentence type. Thus the storage is distinct when output is required.

If the other noun is related to a verb, e.g. riding in riding breeches, we seek its function and find that riding, like birth, denotes the activity of the verb. We move down to the next empty row of slots, and set up a sentence in that row:

	S	V	O	I	Loc_{pl}	Loc_{tm}	M
-1	Someone	wears	breeches;				
-2	Someone	rides.					

Finally, by inspecting the possible functions of the second sentence, a link is made to the sentence above, and a more complex sentence is created:

	S	V	O	I	Loc_{pl}	Loc_{tm}	M
-1	Someone	wears	breeches;				
-2	Someone	rides;					
-3	Someone	wears	breeches	0	0	someone rides	0

The slot of Locative of Time implies the conjunction when.

The second row is copied in case another interpretation is found. A reference to the fully-formed sentence in the third row, -3, is placed in the 'left-hand side' of the Nest. (Because the number is negative, the output process will find the expression in the Slots.)

5. The search for a locative relationship (excluding one with a verb).

We test each noun to see if either or both the nouns are locative. If there is a locative in the head only, e.g. sponge-bag, the type number is put into the Nest.

If the modifier denotes a time and the head denotes a place, e.g. summer mist, a sentence is set up in a slot which will be output as

The mist as it is in the summer.

A reference is placed in the Nest to the row of Slots.

If the noun sequence consists of two similar locatives, we test for various possible relationships. There may be two locatives of place, or two of time. A gallery chamber may be

a chamber with a gallery in it

or

a chamber in a gallery.

One or more phrasal type numbers are yielded, which are placed in the Nest.

If the sequence has a locative only in the modifier, e.g. pocket-handkerchief, the fact is ascertained and the appropriate type number is put into the Nest.

6. The search for a material head.

An inspection is made to see whether the head denotes a material. In the head, the material element need not be like that in stone or glass, for example. It can denote a collection of things, e.g. clump, herd, tribe, so that the meaning is 'head composed of modifiers'. We detect by its collective feature, e.g. clump as being a collective word, and find that tree-clump can be

a clump of trees.

The type number is then put into the Nest.

7. The search for an additive relationship.

Here we seek two hyphened proper nouns, e.g. May-June, (Lampton-Lufford) Report, and treat them as 'modifier added to head':

May and June.

The number denoting the additive relationship is placed in the Nest.

8. The search for a reduplicative relationship.

Here we are dealing with sequences of identical words, e.g. plop-plop. They are treated as reduplicative sounds:

a repeated sound of 'plop'.

The number denoting this relationship is put into the Nest.[5]

9. The search for an equative relationship.

The search for an equative relationship is made at the end of the analysis, and any noun sequence not analyzed comes by default to this category: e.g. branch line where, through the action of metaphor, the appropriate interpretation is

a line that is a branch.

Equative examples are yielded at other places in the program, especially in the search for verbs (e.g. fighter-bomber, of a

Verb type), but the equative search is the one which saves other Equative examples from slipping through the net.

An Equative type number is placed in the Nest.

The nine main searches deal with the eight types as follows:

1. Semantic fields match.	D: Annex types. Also one Equative type.
2. Material modifier.	F: Material type (modifier).
3. Pure annex.	D: Further Annex types.
4. Verb.	A and B: Sentence and Locative-Sentence types. (Also a few Equative types.)
5. Locative.	C: Locative type.
6. Material head.	F: Material type (head).
7. Additive members.	G: Additive type.
8. Reduplication.	H: Reduplicative type.
9. Equative members.	E: Equative type (by default).

The order in which the nine searches are made will be discussed later.

The input process

Now that a description of the process of analysis has been given, the process of input will be described. It is treated second, not first, because experimentation has found that there is only one good way of ordering the analysis, but there are several possible ways of performing the input. The method here described is therefore less important than the analysis.

A card containing the noun sequence to be analyzed is read into a storage array. The input process then sets out to extract the nouns and place them in the Nest.

There are six steps in the input process. They ultimately relate the contents of the card to the dictionary entries.

1. Finding an opening bracket.

The input process usually starts to operate by transferring a noun into storage, but it first checks whether there is an opening (round) bracket before a noun, as in (horse + hair) sofa. In such cases the process moves down one level in the Nest. If there are two brackets, as in school ((foot + ball) game),[6] it moves down a further level. (Horse + hair) sofa is of this structure:

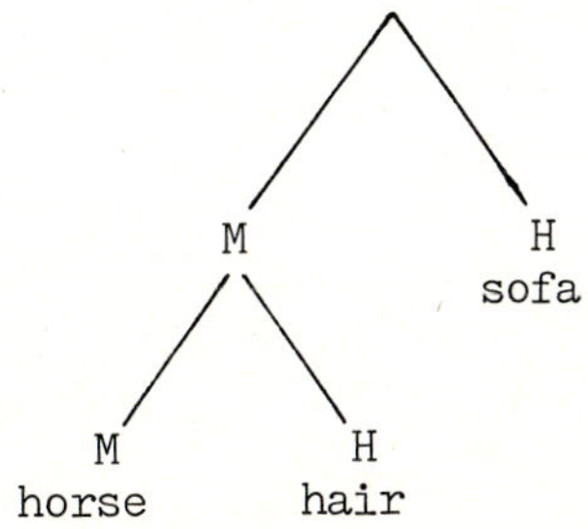

It appears thus in the Nest (where 1 on the x-axis denotes the head and 2 the modifier):

1	2	
sofa	-2	-1
hair	horse	-2

School ((foot + ball) game) is of this structure:

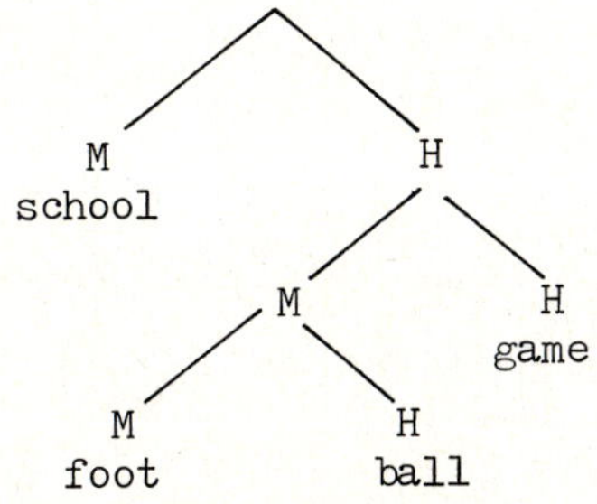

It appears thus in the Nest:

1	2	
-2	school	-1
game	-3	-2
ball	foot	-3

Thus we check for an opening bracket to see whether there is such nesting, and if there is we cause the correct placing of the noun in the Nest. Noun sequences without brackets are simply placed at the top of the Nest: head + ache:

1	2	
ache	head	-1

2. Transferring a noun.

We transfer the nouns found on the card into a storage array, from which each will be sought in the dictionary, and will eventually be copied when the interpretations are output.

Angle brackets usually indicate premodifiers.

If an opening angle bracket is found on the card we give the example special treatment, e.g.

⟨little-⟩ boy class.

We place in storage a pair of pointers to the beginning and end of the adjective. Thus it does not interfere with the analysis of the nouns but it can be recalled if required (e.g. in an annex search) and it will be recalled during the output of the interpretation.

If the word between the angle brackets is and or or, the program bypasses the card as containing a coordinator.

3. Looking up the nouns.

At this stage we look up each noun in the dictionary. When the letters match, a note is made of the position of the noun in the dictionary.

Next we collect from the dictionary the definition of the noun. The feature-markers forming the dictionary have been packed closely into computer 'words' in the dictionary, and we now expand them into boolean arrays, i.e. storage spaces where each item is not a number but is either 'true' or 'false'. Each feature is thus 'present' or 'absent': e.g. director has feature 1 (is related to a verb) but not feature 2 (locative). The features of the noun go into one boolean array and the features of any related verbs into one or more different boolean arrays.

We give special treatment to the features of nouns that have one or more homographs. We place the letters of the nouns, together with their suffixes (e.g. plane[2]), into the noun array. The separate definitions are collected from the dictionary and stored in separate locations in the boolean arrays.

If a noun is not found in the dictionary, a warning is printed and the card bearing that noun is skipped.

We move up the Nest as closing brackets are encountered. Items left over on the card after all the nouns have been matched are mentioned in the printout. The juncture between each pair of nouns may be +, *, - or a space. Information about this is stored at each level of the Nest.

The output process.

When the analysis has been made, the output process is used. Some of the interpretations are in the form of phrases, e.g. sponge-bag:

A bag for or containing a sponge or sponges.

On the other hand, some contain or consist of clauses, e.g. hire-car:

A car that someone hires.

The former kind of interpretation is output when the type number in the 'left-hand side' of the Nest is positive. When the number is negative, the clausal form is output, accessing the material from the sentence-slots.

When giving a phrasal output, we pick up the reference to the articles, and accordingly print a definite or an indefinite article, or no article at all, before each noun. We also print a preposition or other linking word, which is determined by the stored meaning: e.g. Type D2 adds two articles and the preposition of to bough, fir:

The bough of a fir.

A plural can also be added: sponge-bag:

A bag for or containing a sponge or sponges.

When nesting occurs, the output is performed at each level of the Nest, e.g. (horse-hair) sofa:

Hair of a horse;
A sofa made of hair of a horse.

When accessing material from the sentence-slots, we print the head of an of-phrase or a relative clause linked by that. Thus book-keeping has the sentence

Someone keeps a book or books;

and the interpretation

The keeping of a book or bocks.

The relative clause occurs in e.g. hire-car:

A car that someone hires.

Locative heads are picked out thus from the sentence (dining-room):

Someone dines in the room;
A room that someone dines in.

A locative realized as a sentence is treated thus with the interpolation of when or where (riding-breeches):

Someone wears breeches;
Someone rides;
Breeches that someone wears when someone rides.

An Instrument is output thus (breakfast apparatus):

Apparatus that someone breakfasts with.

Farthing (rush-light), with its nesting, is output:

Light of rushes that costs or is worth a farthing.

The verb to shine is not required in the output.

Key to the Semantic Features marked on the Nouns in Features[7]

The list Features, containing all the nouns and their dictionary definitions, is to be found in an Appendix. Almost all these features are used in the program, and some occur in the accounts of procedures after this list.

Primary Features

1. The noun is related to a verb, e.g. attack, director, aerobatics, master, book.
2. Locative, e.g. Lincolnshire, bag, case, house, gallery, chamber, water, book, town, Sunday, day, season, summer. (Also see 12 below.)
3. Material, e.g. iron, lace, stone[1], glass, paraffin.
4. Human, e.g. Hamilton, Lampton, conjuror, boy, company. (Does not include arm, leg etc.)
5. Pure Annex, e.g. edge, part, number, pattern, colour. (Cf. no. 20.)
6. The referent exists physically, e.g. tree, radio (but not love).
7. Animal but not human, e.g. pig, goose, pigeon, lion, horse.
8. A species of anything, e.g. canary, laurel. (Not used in the program.)
9. Plural, e.g. minerals, breeches.
10. Does not normally take the indefinite article, and does not normally become plural, e.g. Lampton, Roqueville, gold, coal, heat.
11. Go to a special procedure of the same name as the noun, e.g. procedure Man, procedure Horse. This procedure selects the verb to go with the other noun in the sequence. (The working of this feature depends on the verbs being input in Features in a definite order.)
12. Locative of time, e.g. Sunday, day, season, summer. (Feature 2 must also be marked.)
13. Normally unique, e.g. Bahamas, sun, sky, country[1] (paysage), sea, grass. Takes the definite article.
14. Manner, e.g. style, manner, scheme, rate[1], tenor, security.
15. Related to an adjective or adverb that takes a sentence as object, e.g. It is probable that he will come →

probability, likelihood. (Not used in the program.)

16. A 'reading' locative, e.g. book, letter, note, message. (Cf. Warren (1978), pp. 172-3.) (Not used in the program.)
17. Collective, e.g. bunch, bundle, herd[2], set[2], hedge, clump, class, stack, family, kind.
18. Marked on fellow etc. for use when it is a modifier, to convert it to a head: fellow-citizen: someone that is also a citizen. E.g. also deputy, fake, dummy.
19. Takes to, e.g. door, trader, stair, letter, thrust (a stair to a parlour).
20 Annex that is locative as a modifier, e.g. top, side, back, front, corner, section.
21. Puts to on the related verb, e.g. waist, knee (breeches that someone wears to a knee or knees).

Secondary (Verb) Features

<0. Pure verb (with suffix e.g. ø, -ion, -ance, -ence), e.g. (overt) attack, breakfast, hire, ache, birth, tip[1], fright, clearance, sale, entertainment; (covert) light (shines), account[1] (describes), concourse (meets), course[1] (runs).

<1. Related to an overt verb, e.g. reception, fright, servant, maker, leading, nominee, dweller.

<2. Related to a covert verb, e.g. accident (happens), account[1] (describes), concourse (meets), gown (wears), tea (drinks), bride (marries), broker (deals in).

<3. Agent of overt verb, e.g. servant, maker, teacher, producer, director, actor, guard, lift, help.

<4. Verb + ing, e.g. leading, adding, advertising, bathing, sleeping, keeping, riding.

<5. Transitive verb, e.g. account[1] (describes), reception (receives), maker (makes).

<6. 'Impo' verb, i.e. the verb implies its own object, e.g. adding, fisher, entertainment, examination, sees, eats.

<7. Takes a Human object usually, e.g. call (stewardess call-button), dressing (dressing-room), education (house-education).[8] The program cannot implement the 'usually': its rule is 'must be human'.[9]

<8. Object of an overt verb, e.g. building, cutting, snap[1], organization. (It nearly always denotes the result.)

<9. Causative verbs, e.g. slide, shut, work, break. (These can also be called ergative.)

<10. Instrument of an overt verb, e.g. saw, pick, covering, cooker, zipper.

<11. Subject of a covert verb, e.g. Court (judges), fellow (is also), ferry (travels).

<12. Object of a covert verb, e.g. food (eats), passenger (carries), farthing (costs or is worth).

<13. Locative of a covert verb, e.g. bed (lies), barge (travels), bench (sits).

<14. Instrument of a covert verb, e.g. blade (cuts), ear (hears). Apparatus, instrument and tackle are marked <14 with no covert verb: the noun is connected with the main verb during analysis, e.g. fishing-tackle:

Someone fishes with the tackle.

<15. Transmissive, e.g. poisons:

Someone poisons the food;
The food poisons someone.

<16. Can take a sentence as object, e.g. guard, key, inclination, teacher, order, lesson. Dancing lesson:

Someone teaches that someone dances:
(Someone teaches someone to dance.)

<17. Dangerous action, e.g. it burns. (Not used in the program.)

<18. Can take an abstract object. (Not used in the program.)

<19. Cannot take a concrete thing as object, e.g. decision, habit[1] (tends to), letter (writes).

<20. Takes an object that can be read, and is therefore not subject to the 'concrete' feature <19, e.g. writes: letter, story, journey. (Not used in the program.)

<21. Underlying verb takes the head as object, e.g. fellow, test. (Overlaps with Feature 18 and is not used in the program.)

<22. Locative of an overt verb,[10] e.g. manufactory, mine, residence.

Tertiary Features (Semantic Fields)[11]

%1. Mechanism, e.g. phone, car, tram.

%2. Human organization, e.g. clergy, police, class, company, council, town, Corporation.

%3. Part of the body (human or animal), e.g. head, leg, tail, skin, hair.

%4. Plant or tree, or part of one, e.g. fruit, olive, apple, fir, bough, branch, laurel, plane[2], tree, hedge, clump.

%5. Food or drink, e.g. ham, beer, apple, fruit, barm, dinner, food.

%6. Furniture, e.g. table, leg, chair[1], sofa, furniture.

%7. Building, or part of one, e.g. parlour, stair, house.

%8. Clothing, e.g. button, collar, coat, breeches, cloak.

%9. Disease, e.g. fever, leprosy, sickness.

Quaternary Features (Relative Size)

#1. e.g. nail, knob.

#2. e.g. toe, stair.

#3. e.g. leg, parlour.

#4. e.g. body, house.

#5. collective nouns, e.g. clump in tree-clump.

It will be seen by reading them vertically that these nouns illustrate semantic sets.

Having given the key to the semantic features, I can now go on to give an account of one of the procedures of the program. This account illustrates the amount of detail in the program. I have chosen for this purpose the procedure which looks for a match in semantic fields. Although it is an important procedure, it is comparatively straightforward: it does not have involuted working nor frequent calls of other procedures.

A Detailed Account of the Procedure 'Findfields', for Matching Semantic Fields.

This procedure yields interpretations when the two nouns belong to related semantic fields. The head and modifier may belong to the same semantic field, e.g. fir-bough (%4), parlour stair (%7). In this case several things may happen. Where the head belongs to the field of 'parts of a building' and also takes 'to', the procedure yields type C1 subtype 6, i.e. with to:

a stair to a parlour.

Where the head has the feature of 'a collection of things' (17), type F5 is yielded: tree-clump:

a clump of trees.

Where the modifier denotes something larger than the head, type D2 is yielded: fir-bough:

the bough of a fir.

Where the reverse is true, type D4 is yielded: cherry tree, armchair:

a tree with a cherry or cherries;
a chair[1] with an arm[1] or arm[1]s.

Where the head and the modifier are of the same size, an equative type is yielded: E1: fir-tree:

a tree that is a fir.

We have now dealt with the features of the tertiary type. There are also some primary features which imply membership of certain semantic fields.

Where the head has the primary feature 4, thus denoting a human being, and the modifier denotes a human organization (%2), the former is a member of the latter: type D3, clergyman:

a man in the clergy.

Where the head denotes a part of the body (human or animal) and the modifier denotes a human being or an animal, type D2 is yielded: horsehair, Alan Ladd deadpan:

hair of a horse;
the deadpan of Alan Ladd.[12]

Where the modifier denotes a part of the body (%3, e.g. kidney, horn) the case is somewhat different from the above. If the modifier is not at its deepest position in the nest (e.g. tail in fantail pigeon),[13] and the head denotes a human being or animal, type D4 is yielded:

a pigeon with a tail that is a fan.

Type D4 is also yielded when the modifier is itself modified: one-kidney patient; short-horn cattle:

a patient with one kidney;

cattle with short horns.

Where the head and modifier each denote a human being or an animal (4, 7), the equative type E1 is yielded: catfish, bird-man, queen bee:[14]

a fish that is a cat;
a man that is a bird (an aviator);
a bee that is a queen.

(The equative relationship is metaphorical in all these three examples.)

There is an exception to this rule. If the head and modifier both denote subjects of a verb (represented by the feature <3) then the procedure Findfields bypasses the example (e.g. actor-manager) as it is dealt with under the procedure Verbalfind.

Thus the procedure Findfields concludes.

An Illustration of the Operation of the Mainprogram.

There now follows a section of the program seen from a different viewpoint. Having seen the action of one procedure on several examples, we will now follow the action of the whole program on one example. We see, among other things, how the program tests for all eight types. I have chosen an example for this illustration that has two acceptable interpretations.

The example is council house (with or without initial capitals).

First we enter the Mainprogram. A card is read in bearing council house.[15] It just may be the terminator of the data, but in this case it is not, so we proceed in the normal way to print the contents of the card. The two nouns are transferred into a storage array. A number denoting each noun is put into the Nest where the interpretation rules are applied. It is this number that identifies each noun throughout the analysis. The Nest holds the head number in location 1 and the modifier number in location 2. The modifier may be bracketed, e.g. (horse + hair) sofa. If so, it will be stored at a low level in the Nest; but it is not so in this case. The nouns council and house are looked up in the dictionary and their features are placed into another storage array whose locations correspond to the numbers in the Nest. When the head is dealt with, a test for a bracket in front of it is also made, in case the example is of this structure: cambric (head-clothes).

When there is only one noun so far in the Nest, we inspect the nexus. Council house has a space between the words (rather than being hyphened or spelt as one word), and this information is put into the Nest.

When both nouns are in the Nest, we return to the Main-program. Since neither the head nor the modifier is further nested, the analysis begins here. The numbers denoting the head and the modifier are picked out. We inspect the storage for homography, but it does not occur in this example. Using the procedure Findfields (described above) to test for a D type, we ask whether the two nouns belong to the same semantic field, or have permutations of the human and animal markers. In this case, though council has a human marker, house has not. So we return to the analysis procedure. We next seek a material interpretation (an F type). The head (house) has no feature of collectivity (e.g. tree-clump), and the modifier (council) does not denote a material (e.g. clay hut), so we return to the analysis procedure. We next test for another D type by asking whether one of the nouns denotes a part of anything (e.g. side garden, desk top). Council house does not have such a noun, so we return to the analysis procedure.

We now set out to look for a locative feature. Where the head is related to a verb, e.g. attack (attacks), aerobatics (performs), a diversion is made to deal with the example as a verbal one. Otherwise a locative feature is sought in the head, e.g. Lincolnshire, house. If the modifier has an overt verb, e.g. attacks but not performs, another diversion is made to the verb procedure. If the modifier is locative as well as the head, e.g. Lincolnshire estate, there is some doubt as to which contains the other, and a procedure is called to deal with this. In all other cases where the head is locative, type C3 is yielded: one meaning of council house:

a house for or containing the council.

We then return to the analysis procedure.

One interpretation having been made, we offer a priority number to be placed in the Nest, in case of homography.

The next inquiry is to seek a verb relationship. If neither noun is related to a verb, the modifier is inspected. First we see whether it begins with a capital letter. Inspection is also made for the 'human' feature and the feature 'human organization'. These patterns allow for Council and council. If the head has the locative feature, type A4 is yielded:

a house made by or belonging to a council.

We return to the analysis procedure.

Two possible interpretations for council house have been found, but an analysis has to be attempted for every possible type. We see whether the modifier denotes a material, e.g. cambric apron. It does not, so we next see whether both nouns have initial capitals and the nexus is a hyphen. In such a case an additive type is sought, e.g. Lampton-Lufford in Lampton-Lufford report. Council house does not belong to this type. Returning to the analysis procedure, we see whether the nouns are identical (e.g. chug-chug). This not being the case, we return to the analysis procedure. If no interpretation had been made, an equative one would be made here, e.g. archetype orphan, but we have made an interpretation, so this equative type is not yielded.

We return to the analysis procedure for the last time. We are next passed on to the procedure which brings the interpretations out of the Nest and prints them. The example we are using now is a simple one, but various measures have to be taken in case we are dealing with a nested example.

First we check whether the modifier and head are at their deepest positions in the Nest. Council house is. Then we ask whether there are examples of homography not yet analyzed. There are not. Next we ask whether there are any underlying sentences recorded in connexion with this example, e.g. The moon shines for moonshine. We have none.

We write Interpretation(s), and, checking at each stage to see whether we have exhausted the contents of the Nest, we begin to output the interpretation. First we give the C3 output. We construct a phrase with for or containing, the indefinite article with each noun, and a singular and a plural object.

A procedure checks whether the head noun, house, begins with a vowel. If it were, an would be written; in fact, a is written. Then the noun is inspected to see whether house is modified by an adjective. It is not. House is written, followed by for or containing. The modifier is duly inspected for a vowel and none is found, so a is written. The adjective check is made. We then write council. A plural is possible, so we also write or councils, giving the C3 interpretation

A house for or containing a council or councils.

We deal with the second interpretation in the same way. House and council are similarly inspected. The A4 interpretation does not admit of a plural, and so we get

A house made by or belonging to a council.

Thus we come to the end of the procedure which brings the interpretations out of the nest and prints them. We return to the Mainprogram. As all the interpretations of council house have been printed, we conclude the operations on this example. When all the examples have been dealt with, we come to the end of the Mainprogram.

The example of council house in the data has the A4 interpretation:

'"I wasn't a builder of council houses or factories."'
Greene (1963), p.45.

The C3 interpretation is found in the NED:

'A house in which a council meets for deliberation.'

It is still current, with reference to Bristol Town Hall:

'I spend a lot of time at the archives down at the Council House.'[16]

Thus the A4 and C3 interpretations are both correct.

The Treatment of Homography and Polysemy in the Program

In the dictionary for the program, I shall follow normal dictionary senses of homography and polysemy.

A homograph is defined by the NED as 'A word of the same spelling as another, but of different origin and meaning'.[17] It is defined by the COD as a 'word spelt like another, but of different meaning or origin'.[18]

Homography does not appear in the NED in a relevant sense, and is not included in the COD, but the Shorter Oxford[19] gives as its most relevant meaning '2. Homographic spelling'.

Polysemy is not in the main NED but appears in the NED Supplement as 'the fact of having several meanings'.[20]

It will be seen that, strictly speaking, the COD permits polysemous words to be included among homographs: 'of different meaning *or* origin'. Of seven dictionaries consulted,[21] three (including the COD), among the most modern, permit this.[22] I shall adopt this same position. In fact, I shall apply the term *homography* to all cases of duplicated nouns analyzed in the program.

The recognition of homographs in the program is determined partly by practical considerations, i.e. whether it is necessary for the interpretation of noun sequences. It is determined also by whether there is a homograph in the language, even if the homograph is not in the data. I claim some validity for the program outside the present data, so it is fairer to include a large number of these, though they sometimes yield poor interpretations.

Some of the duplicated nouns in the dictionary are simply spelt alike, with no semantic relation between them, e.g. *lime*[1] (oxide of calcium), from Anglo-Saxon, and *lime*[2] (the fruit), from French. Others are historically related, but do not retain much semantic similarity, e.g. *chest*[1] (part of the body) and *chest*[2] (the container). There is a third group in which the nouns are historically related and still retain a noticeable semantic similarity, e.g. *stone*[1] (rock or a fragment of rock) and *stone*[2] (the kernel of a pulpy fruit). *Chest* and *stone* can be called polysemous. They can also be called homographic, and are so called in the context of this book. I have suffixed them in Features in the same way as unrelated homographs, and they come under the term *homography* in the text.

It is not my practice to subsume *all* polysemous words under homographs. Sometimes the likeness of meaning is very close, and no separate definition is needed. <*middle-*>*class home* and

⟨little-⟩ boy class find the same definition of class in my dictionary. Thus the dictionary does not make such fine distinctions as the entry in the COD (1976), which takes them to be cases of polysemy: 'class ... 1. Rank or order of society ... 2. Set of students taught together.'

Polysemy is sometimes represented by the giving of different verbs to one noun:

master: controls or teaches.

In addition, a few polysemous homographs such as building are under one entry in Features but are marked with such features as 'gerund' (the act of building) and 'object' (the result), yielding two verb-related meanings before its simply locative meaning:

⟨Pan⟩ Am building: (Pan Am = the Pan-American Airways company)

The building of Pan Am (cf. body-building[23]);
Something that Pan Am builds;
a building made by or belonging to Pan Am.

Footnotes to Chapter 3

1 I.e. Nest [-x, y, z]. Some other types are also yielded which I shall not discuss here.

2 These two examples do not occur in the present corpus.

3 It is not implied that the only possible relationship between man and a food is one of selling. It can be one of enjoying: the milk lady : the lady who takes a lot of milk (used by a friend of mine). But the 'selling' relationship is the one more frequently encountered.

4 I.e. not the noun which was used to set up the sentence. The 'other noun' is day in this case. The 'other noun' may have a verb also.

5 A syntactic relationship such as that found in e.g. killer-killer would be picked up by the Verb search and so would not be treated as a sound.

6 Not in the present data, which has no examples of this structure, except one involving co-ordination:

(Continuum Building)((Coffee and (Do-nut)) shop)

The program does not analyze co-ordinated examples. The example in the text is from Leonard (1968), pp.373, 384. The nearest in the present data is (front (drawing-room)) twilight, which does not demonstrate the pattern so well.

7 Some features are given a greater number of illustrative examples than others because in some cases there is variety within the semantic area covered by the feature, and in other

cases certain examples are mentioned for various purposes elsewhere in the book and this key may be consulted for them.

8 Some of these examples have Locative relationships which without <7 would be wrongly yielded as Object-Verb.

9 Therefore it was necessary to mark *love* as always taking a 'human' object. *Dream lover* is correctly analyzed:

Someone that someone loves when someone dreams.

But the following interpretation is blocked:

Someone that loves dreams.

10 Different from *building*, which is marked as a Pure Locative or the object of *builds*.

11 These features of semantic fields are mainly used in the interpretation program where a match between semantic fields is sought, but are also used elsewhere occasionally, e.g. for *Lincoln (hire-car)*.

12 This is the only human example of this type in the data. It refers to the expressionless face of a film star. A simpler example would be *baby face*.

13 These examples are taken from outside the data as the data do not contain a good example of the pattern.

14 These examples are from outside the data.

15 Or *Council House*.

16 A Bristol man on Channel 4 television, 5.15 p.m., 18th January 1983.

17 NED (1888-1933).

18 COD (1976).

19 Shorter Oxford (1964).

20 NED (1888-1933): Supplement (1933).

21 NED (1888-1933), Nuttall's (1929), Penguin (1965), Webster (1971), Chambers (1972), COD (1976), Shorter Oxford (1964).

22 Homograph: Penguin: 'one of two or more words having the same spelling but different meanings'. Webster: 'one of two or more words spelled alike but differing in derivation or meaning or pronunciation'.

23 Body-building is not in the data.

CHAPTER 4

EVALUATION OF THE PROGRAM AND ORDER OF ANALYSIS

Introduction to the Interpretations

1. Samples of interpretations are given in an appendix.[1]

2. Strictly speaking, my categories represent underlying logical and/or semantic relationships rather than superficial syntactic relationships. For example, there is an underlying locative relationship which may be realized syntactically by in, on or at, and the actual choice of preposition is irrelevant to the underlying classification: seaman:

A man that lives in or works in the sea.

Another example implying an underlying structure is the use of the that-clause[2] for dancing-master:

A master that controls or teaches that someone dances.

The program sets up sentences for the verbs teach and dance. Teaches in the dictionary expects an object. Therefore the sentence

Someone dances

is placed in the Object slot. The pronoun that makes it a subordinate clause. The program is not equipped to develop it further into teaches someone to dance.

So the _that_-clause can be considered as a slightly underlying form of the _to_-clause, and I accept the sentence containing it as a correct interpretation. Therefore it could be argued that the whole idea of representing the interpretation as a phrase or sentence 'in English' is misconceived. When native speakers interpret noun sequences, presumably they do not decode them into English paraphrases, but decode them into some logical or semantic relationship (or set of relationships).

However, I make an attempt at a surface or near-surface paraphrase, rather than leaving the reader with only type names to puzzle through. At the same time, I have to admit that to get a perfect English paraphrase of every example would have meant building in much more syntactic and semantic information than I could reasonably manage, given that the attainment of categories and sentence-structures, rather than correctness of the less important parts of the paraphrases, was the main aim of the program.

Occasionally, reticence is preserved; e.g. _harem_ is assigned the meliorative verb _enjoys_.

3. The dictionary and the interpretation program are equipped to deal with only some instances of the matching of prepositions to nouns and verbs. In certain paraphrases _at_, _on_ and _to_ are used, but they occur only in strictly limited circumstances. Where a paraphrase calls for a preposition but none is specially indicated, _in_ has been used. I crave the indulgence of the reader to allow a wide area of meaning for _in_ in cases such as the following:

(a) _birthday_: a day that someone is born _in_ (on, time);

(b) _head-clothes_: clothes...that someone wears _in_ a head (on, place);

(c) breakfast-table: a table that someone breakfasts in (at);

(d) casino turn (in the Monte Carlo rally): the turn in a casino or casinos (by).

4. As seen in

a sweater or sweaters
middle classs
a company or companys

the plural is formed simply by the addition of s. To store the rules for the plural would have taken a long time, detracting from the main purpose of the program.

5. In the text of this book, the data and interpretations are generally given as they are written in the computer data-lists and interpretations.

There are exceptions to this rule:

(a) I alter faulty plurals: childs becomes children;

(b) A letter preceded by an asterisk in the printout is written in capitals in the text:

*BOLOGNA SAUSAGE   Bologna sausage.

6. Round brackets enclosing words mean something different from round brackets enclosing ticks, crosses or question marks. Brackets are put round words to signify nesting, e.g. (bed+room) window. The evaluations of the interpretations are marked with ticks, crosses or question marks. In the interpretations, round brackets are used on the ticks when the sequence concerned appears elsewhere in the Interpretations, e.g. (birth+day) gift:

Something that someone gives ✓✓ in a day that
someone is born in. (✓✓)

Thus each interpretation is reckoned only once. (In this case the correct interpretation of *birthday* is noted, but is not scored for evaluation purposes.)

7. Premodifiers in angle brackets are attached to their nouns when the interpretation is output. < *stationary->train noise* is output as follows:

Noise that someone hears in a stationary-
train or stationary-trains.

(The context mentions wheel-tapping.)

8. Angle brackets can also enclose quotation marks:

<"> * conversation <"> chair.

9. The definite article is used in the paraphrase to precede an activity noun (i.e. a noun in the verb function), e.g. *child-murder*, *daybreak*:

The murder of a child or childs;
The break of a day or days.

However, some interpretations will seem odd because of this operation: *coal shortage*:

The shortage of coal

(where *a* shortage is more usual).

10. A door to *a* King Street

(for *⟨King⟩ Street door*) seems odd, but ⟨King⟩ has been stored only as a premodifier, so it is output with the general *a*.

11. In the interpretations, a noun is often given in the plural as well as in the singular. This is good in the case of *bedroom*:

> A room for or containing a bed or beds;

but it is not always felicitous:

> a room for or containing a bath
> or baths.

12. Luckily, in English we have the relative pronoun *that*. It can represent the subject and object of a sentence (unlike *who* and *whom*) and does not vary according to whether the referent is human or not (unlike *who* and *which*). *That* has been used for all the relative-pronominal functions. Without it, much work would have had to be added to several procedures, especially the one that outputs the sentences and clauses:

book-seller: Someone *that* sells a book or books;

boxing glove: A glove *that* someone wears when someone boxes;

childhood sweetheart: A sweetheart *that* someone courts in childhood.

13. *Someone or something* often has to be used in a subject or object position in the paraphrase because although a verb can have a feature 'takes human object usually', many verbs can take both human and non-human subjects and objects: e.g.

charcoal-burner: Someone or something that burns charcoal;

food poisoning: The poisoning of something or someone by a food or foods.

Thus daydream has the underlying sentence

Someone dreams in a day or days;

but also daylight has:

Someone shines in a day or days.[3]

The latter interpretation is output as

The light in a day or days,

so someone does not spoil the final interpretation.

14. The Material type 6010 is interpreted with of: clay hut:

A hut of clay.

However, when nesting occurs, the reference of of is easily lost, so the interpretation gives made of: tapestry (bell-rope):

The rope of a bell made of tapestry.

15. Sometimes nesting causes a paraphrase to be output which is correct but looks odd. The procedure for outputting sentence-based interpretations, when printing a paraphrase involving an Instrument, outputs an expression beginning with the instrument, goes to the end of the sentence and then returns to the beginning to print the subject, verb and object. (This process is described under Sentout in the Index of Procedures.) The paraphrase is then (e.g. for bread-knife):

A knife that someone cuts bread with.

The *with* at the end causes no trouble in this paraphrase, but when nesting occurs, the relation of the final *with* to the *something* can be puzzling: *(soda-water) siphon*:

> Something that someone siphons water with soda or water for or containing soda *with*.

16. A puzzling result can also occur where the main clause is interrupted in the middle. The following interpretation occurs. It is correct in the context of the novel. *Reception* denotes a room where people are received, not the receiving of radio signals. The difficulty is due to the presence of three interpretations of *radio station[2]*:[4] *(radio station) reception*:

> *Something that* a station[2] for or containing a radio or radios or a station[2] that someone transmits with a radio or radios in or a station[2] that someone transmits with a radio or radios *receives someone in*.

17. Identity of reference has to be judged by the reader, with the help of the underlying sentences. For example, in *death-bed* both *someones* refer to the same person:

> A bed that *someone* lies in when *someone* dies;

but in *confidence trick*, the first *someone* is the deceiver and the second is the person deceived:

> A trick that *someone* deceives with when *someone* trusts.

Both at once are indicated by *wedding-coat*:

> A coat that *someone* wears when *someone* weds.

18. The type name and number, and also the underlying sentences, often help the reader to understand the paraphrase. An extreme example of this is found in the interpretation of suntan:

The tan of the sun.
The tan of the sun.
The tan of the sun.

The first example is shown as a member of the Annex type 4010, meaning tan belonging to the sun. The other two are shown as sentence types, the underlying sentences being

Someone tans the sun

and

The sun tans.

So we can see that it is the last paraphrase that should be marked as correct.

19. The transformation
(a) John teaches Mary [noun phrase]. Mary dances
(b) John teaches that Mary dances
(c) John teaches Mary to dance
is carried out by the program only to (b), so that dancing-master yields

A master that controls or teaches that someone dances,

and operation money yields

Money that someone buys that someone operates with.

Also compare ignition key and rambling design (= the intention to ramble):

A key that someone locks that someone ignites with;
The design of that someone rambles.

These paraphrases are not to be confused with the structure

Someone says that someone dances.

They are examples of a near-surface paraphrase being offered rather than the dry bones of the type name and number.[5]

20. It should be pointed out that the underlying that-clause in, e.g., dancing-master, is not always yielded correctly. Machine is related to makes for cases such as cigarette machine, which is correctly interpreted:

A machine that someone makes a cigarette or cigarettes with.

Makes is allowed a sentence as Object for cases such as match[2]-maker:

Someone that makes that someone matches,

correctly constituting an underlying form of

Someone who makes someone match (i.e. marry).

In this latter example the verbs of both the head and the modifier are correctly activated. However, in some similar cases an incorrect interpretation is made, with a redundant verb, e.g. sewing-machine:

A machine that someone makes that someone sews with.

21. Apart from the New English Dictionary and other dictionaries, there are several outside sources for interpretations of individual examples, such as:

(a) Hammersmith Semiramis:

'Semiramis, a mythical queen of Assyria ... She married Onnes, an Assyrian general, and accompanied him to the siege of Bactra, where her prudent advice hastened the fall of the city....' - The Oxford Companion to English Literature, ed. P. Harvey, Oxford, at the Clarendon Press, 1st pub. 1932, this ed. 1967. The Hammersmith Semiramis is the headmistress of a girls' school, in Thackeray. She strikes poses with a Roman look.

(b) Lincoln (hire-car):

'The man who founded the Lincoln Company was Henry Martyn Leland ... Lincoln was his boyhood hero, and the man for whom he had cast his first vote. The Lincoln Motor Company was based in Lincoln, Illinois ... In 1911 the Lincoln Motor Car Works in Chicago appeared ....' - A. McCracken, letter of 13th February, 1979. Since the firm is named Lincoln, 'made by or belonging to' will be acceptable as a paraphrase.

(c) Mongo Language:

I asked Mr. Graham Greene whether Mongo was the name of a tribe or the name of a language. His secretary replied 'He is afraid he cant [sic] remember' - letter of 14th November, 1977. Thus there is a genuine ambiguity, and my interpretation

A language that the Mongo speaks

is acceptable.

(d) Nash Airflyte Eight :

'A Nash Airflyte Eight [cylinders] is a car ...

Nash = manufacturer, Airflyte - model.' - John Braine, letter of 21st December, 1978.

22. My policy about homographs has been to mark them in the dictionary

(a) when the sense in the data is an unusual sense, e.g. chair-man, a man who carries a chair (in Fielding);
chair[1] sits in
chair[2] travels in or carries;

(b) when there are two or more conflicting senses in the data, e.g.
mountain ash[1] (the tree) and
ash[2]-pit (the residue of combustion);

(c) when there is a homograph in the language which is fairly common and would probably be recalled by the reader when encountering the noun in the data, e.g.
bat[1] in bat-ear (the animal); and
bat[2] not in the data (the thing with which one hits a ball).

However, four meanings of plane were put into the dictionary to see what would happen when they were encountered during interpretation. For jet plane, where jet also has three meanings, a a correct interpretation was given second out of twenty-five interpretations.

The Evaluation of the Interpretations

The interpretations of the 1,944 examples have been evaluated and marked by Professor G. N. Leech and myself. It will be seen that in most cases the program offers more than one interpretation for the same noun sequence. In the samples at the end of this book, two ticks indicate an interpretation correct at the first attempt. One tick indicates correctness at a second or subsequent attempt. A cross indicates that all the interpretations offered are wrong. A question-mark indicates hesitation in awarding the mark, for semantic reasons or for serious ill-formedness of the interpretation. E.g.:

<u>bath+room</u>

a room for or containing a bath or baths. ✓✓

<u>border pattern</u>

the pattern of a border. ✓✓ ?

<u>breakfast-room</u>

a room for or containing a breakfast or breakfasts.

a room that someone breakfasts in. ✓

<u>block+head</u>

the head of a block. ✗

With nested sequences, two or more sets of marks are given, and these are counted as if they represented two (or more) independent sequences:

<u>(carnation-colour) silk</u>

silk with ✓✓ the colour of a carnation. ✓✓

If the left-nested sequence occurs independently elsewhere in the data, it is not counted. (All right-nested sequences are included also in their proper place in the lists, and are not reckoned twice.)

Brackets round the ticks or crosses are used to signify that a noun sequence occurs elsewhere in the Interpretation files. Among the left-nested sequences <u>birth+day</u> is represented:

<u>(birth+day) gift</u>

something that someone gives ✓✓ in a day that someone is born in. (✓✓)

However, it appears independently in its proper place later on:

<u>birth+day</u>

a day that someone is born in. ✓✓

The bracketed ticks are not included in the reckoning of the marks.

As I have said, two ticks mark a first interpretation correct; one, a later interpretation. However, in a nested sequence, if part of the later interpretation occurs in the first interpretation, it can receive two ticks:

<u>(cloak+room) knob</u>

the knob of a room for or containing a cloak or cloaks.
the kind of knob used in or on ✓ a room for or containing a cloak or cloaks. ✓✓

In reckoning the percentage of noun sequences correctly analyzed, the two ticks are counted as one mark, and the one tick as half a mark. A cross means no mark. Each of these three evaluations can be qualified with a query. In the count, ✓✓? and ✓? are reduced: two ticks with a query count as one tick, and one tick with a query counts as nothing.[6]

The totals for the Interpretation Files are as follows (see overleaf):

Interpretation File	✓✓	✓✓?	✓	✓?	✗	✗?	Total
A	276	19	142	7	55	6	505
B	228	10	85	2	39	1	365
C	292	7	78	2	39	3	421
D	268	4	71	0	32	3	378
E	157	29	53	8	25	3	275
Total	1221	69	429	19	190	16	1944

<u>The Final Count</u>

The final count is reached as follows:

✓✓	✓✓? ✓	✓?	✗	✗?
1221	69 + 429	19	190	16
	= 498	not included		
	498 ÷ 2 = 249			

The total of examples with two ticks stands alone, representing the only interpretations fully correct. The totals of examples doubtfully correct is added to the total of examples correct only at the second or a subsequent attempt. The result is divided by two, as each such example scores half a mark. The total of examples doubtfully correct at a second or subsequent attempt is rejected altogether, and reckoned with the totals of wrongly-analyzed examples merely as part of the grand total of 1,944 examples.

Each correct total is divided by 1,944 to give a percentage:

$$\frac{1221 \times 100}{1944} = 62.8\% \qquad \frac{249 \times 100}{1944} = 12.8\%$$

Thus 62.8% of the 1,944 examples are correct at the first attempt, and 12.8% represents the near-correct and partially-correct examples.[7]

$$62.8 + 12.8 = 75.6\%$$

Finally the sum of these two totals is given, being the percentage of correct analyses among the 1,944 examples, according to a last count. (This figure may be rendered as 76%.) I claim that the program is correct in a significantly high number of examples to show that it has considerable validity in analyzing the noun sequences in the data.

This percentage is even more convincing when one remembers that most of the homographs included in Features, and therefore in the dictionary, are taken from outside the data. This means that to a certain extent the program is working in a part of the language not restricted to the data.

The Evaluation of Homographic Noun Sequences

In the general count, homographic noun sequences are treated exactly like the ordinary noun sequences. However, in a special count of homographic sequences to see whether the machinery for homographs is working successfully, a distinction is made between the single tick on a sequence in which the correct homographic noun is the one first offered, and the single tick on a sequence in which the correct homographic noun is the one offered later (e.g. third or fourth). In the former case, the homograph is marked 'correct'; in the latter, 'wrong', just in this special count. E.g.:

With correct homograph ranking first:

(a) coffee-set

a set[2] of coffee.

a set[2] that someone drinks coffee with. ✓

the set[1] of coffee.

With correct homograph ranking later than first:

(b) bull pen

a pen[1] that a bull or bulls writes something with.

a pen[1] that a bull or bulls writes with.

a pen[2] for or containing a bull or bulls. ✓

It can be seen that in (a) the homograph procedures are working well, even though the correct interpretation is not given first, whereas in (b) the homograph procedures are wrong in offering the (fountain) pen together with the bull. So in evaluating the success of the homograph procedures, the tick on (a) is reckoned as a tick, but the tick on (b) is reckoned as a bad mark, to be counted against the tick on (a).

Some special cases which occur in the marking of the homographs are:

1. The pattern just described cannot be applied where there are two homographs in a sequence, one ranking first but the other ranking later:

cab fare

a fare[1] that someone pays for a cab[1] or cab[1]s with.

a fare[1] that someone pays for a cab[2] or cab[2]s with. ✓

Here [1] is correct and ranks first, and it would be pleasant to reckon the tick in favour of the homographic procedures, but cab[2] ranks second, and so I am reckoning the tick as 'wrong', i.e. against the homographic procedures.

The same is true of air+line, air+port and drawing-board.

2. Veronica Lake (hair style) yields

The style of hair(✓✓) of Veronica Lake[2]. ✓✓

This is counted as only one example, because hair style occurs later in its own right, at its own alphabetical position, in the files of Interpretations.

3. In gold (watch chain), as watch is the homograph, the homographic relationship exists only between watch and chain. It is reckoned when watch chain occurs later. The relationship between gold and chain (unlike that between gold and ring in signet ring, where ring is homographic) is not a homographic relationship, and so gold (watch chain) is not counted as a homographic example.

4. (Sheraton-type) furniture yields

> furniture with ✓✓the type[2] of Sheraton ✓✓
> or a type[1] belonging to Sheraton.

This is counted as two examples, each involving the homograph.

5. (air-crew) slip yields (as the last of four interpretations:

> a slip[2] that a crew that flies ✓or lands wears ✓.

(The meaning is clearer with the context:

> a young man in R.A.F. uniform with the white
> air-crew slip in his cap.)

There are two homographs involved, as flies or lands is the realization of air[2]. Each relationship is counted as one mark, as neither of the sequences occurs elsewhere in its own right. The ticks are reckoned as 'with later homograph' like bull pen: thus they weigh against the ticks 'with homograph ranking first'.

The totals for the homographic examples are as follows:

Interpretation File	Good (i) ✓✓	Good (ii) ✓✓?	Good: Correct Homogr. Ranking First (iii) ✓	Bad: Correct Homogr. Ranking Later (iv) ✓	Good: Correct Homogr. Ranking First (v) ✓?	Bad: Correct Homogr. Ranking Later (vi) ✓?	Bad (vii) X and X ?
A	27	2	12	30	2	0	9
B	21	2	8	20	0	1	8
C	27	0	3	21	0	2	8
D	37	0	4	14	0	0	7
E	16	8	5	9	0	3	5
Total	128	12	32	94	2	6	37

Grand Total 311

The count of homography is reached as follows:

(i) + (ii)	(iii) + (v)	(iv) + (vi)	(vii)
128 + 12	32 + 2	94 + 6	37
= 140	= 34	= 100	

$34 \div 2 = 17$ $\qquad$ $100 \div 2 = 50$

Totals of examples with one tick are divided by 2, as has been done with same totals for the whole of the Interpretation Files.

The good and bad marks are amalgamated into two subtotals:

Good	Bad
140	37
+ 17	+ 50
157	87

Since we are here concerned simply with the opposition 'right-wrong' of homographic interpretations, the figure over which the results are placed will be the sum of the two totals 157 + 87, i.e. 244. This yields the following results:

$$\frac{157}{244} = 64\%$$

This is the total of homographs correctly analyzed by the program, as a proportion of those analyzed correctly and incorrectly.[8] The total of incorrectly analyzed homographs is $\frac{87}{244}$, i.e. 36%.

Several examples consist of more than two homographs, so that the random probability of correctness is less than 50%. 64% is a disappointing result but at least in the framework of the grammar of the program a method of dealing with homographs has been constructed. No doubt it could be improved in various ways.

In some cases, both of the homographic nouns occur in the data, e.g. stone[1] and stone[2]. Others have matches outside the data, e.g. flock[1] (wool refuse) is in the data but flock[2] (of sheep) is outside. Homographs from outside the data are usually included in the dictionary when they are obvious and omission might render the analysis unreal. More homographs could be included, e.g. lime[3] (the linden tree).

The evaluation of the interpretations of the homographic examples is much stricter than it would be if homographs from inside the data were the only ones represented in the dictionary.

The success of the main procedures

Part of the value of the present work, and particularly of the computational aspect of it, is that it offers an opportunity to vary the descriptive parameters of the model. For example, one can change the order of the major analysis procedures, in order to enhance the success of the program. The program has been gradually improved. Given the basic description, I have developed the list of Features and got the best ordering of the eight main procedures in the analysis procedure.

A Subset of the Corpus Used in Testing the Success of Procedures

A subset of $\frac{1}{4}$ of the corpus will be used to demonstrate the order of analysis, i.e. to measure the degree of success of the various procedures, related to the order in which they apply. Some of the interpretations are easy to process and easy for the reader to follow, but the more difficult ones also must be included. So a sample of $\frac{1}{4}$ of each difficult group is taken. These total 111 examples. To provide the normal samples, which must total 375 to make up $\frac{1}{4}$ of 1,944, a section from later in the output is used. So the sample is composed of the following noun sequences. All the lists of examples are inclusive.

1. From the beginning of the output: $\frac{1}{4}$ of the difficult examples, which can be seen in an Appendix. The samples are arrived at as follows:

	Total set of difficult examples[9]:	The subset (i.e. sample):
(a)	2	0
(b)	5	1
(c)	23	6
(d)	74	19
(e)	1	0
(f)	11	3
(g)	120	30
(h)	209	52
	445	111

$$445 \div 4 = 111$$

The corpus, excluding the above examples:

$$\begin{array}{r} 1944 \\ -\ 445 \\ \hline 1499 \end{array}$$

2. 375 examples are taken to represent the more normal examples in the corpus. (The appendix of samples ends with a very short list of these normal examples.)

The Frequencies of the Chief Procedures for Analysis

(a) Correct in first position means that the first interpretation offered is correct. There may be later interpretations also, which are usually wrong but sometimes provide alternative correct interpretations. E.g.:

mud hut

Material 6010/Locative 3030[10]

Interpretations:

a hut of mud (correct)

a hut for or containing mud (wrong).

music-room

Locative 3030/Locative 3011/Sentence 1

Interpretations:

a room for or containing music (correct)

a room in or on music (wrong)

a room that someone plays music in (also possible).

(b) Wrong in first position can be exemplified thus:

mud + guard

Material 6010/Sentence 1/Sentence 2

Interpretations:

a guard of mud (wrong)

someone that guards mud (wrong)

someone that guards with mud (wrong)

and thus:

mountain chapel

Locative 3030/Locative 3011

Interpretations:

a chapel for or containing a mountain or mountains (wrong)

a chapel in or on a mountain (correct).

(c) Correct in a later position:

Music-room and mountain chapel (above) exemplify 'Correct in a later position', where

a room that someone plays music in

is possible as well as the first interpretation, and

a chapel in or on a mountain

is the only correct interpretation of the latter example.

(d) Wrong in a later position can be exemplified by mud hut, music-room and mud + guard:

a hut for or containing mud;
a room in or on music;
someone that guards mud.

Mud hut has a correct interpretation first, music-room has

its wrong interpretation sandwiched between two correct interpretations, and the interpretations of mud + guard are all wrong.

In the main count of correctness only one mark is reckoned for each example. In this count of the results of the different analysis procedures, all the interpretations are taken into account. Homographs are included, with only one first interpretation being allowed in the first count, but all interpretations being allowed in the second count.

The Frequencies of the Chief Procedures in the Analysis (from the subset of $\frac{1}{4}$ of the corpus).

(See overleaf.)

<u>The Frequencies of the Chief Procedures in the Analysis</u> (from the subset of $\frac{1}{4}$ of the corpus)

	Totals of occurrences	(i) Correct in first position	(ii) Correct in a later position	(iii) Wrong in first position	(iv) Wrong in a later position
Semantic Fields Match (a kind of Annex)	61	42	5	7	7
Material Modifier	95	70	3	15	7
Pure Annex, e.g. <u>top</u>	68	33	5	20	10
Verb relationship	647	108	108	55	376
Locative	327	38	59	31	199
Material Head	20	0	3	1	16
Additive	1	0	1	0	0
Reduplicative	1	1	0	0	0
Equative	6	0	0	2	4

The Frequencies of the Chief Procedures in the Analysis, given as percentages

	Totals of which the other numbers are percentages	(i) Correct in first position	(ii) Correct in a later position	(iii) Wrong in first position	(iv) Wrong in a later position	Wrong (v) (iii)+(iv)	Correct (vi) (i)+(ii) The measure of success of each procedure.
Semantic Fields Match	61	69%	8%	11%	11%	22%	77%
Material Modifier	95	74%	3%	16%	7%	23%	77%
Pure Annex	68	49%	7%	29%	15%	44%	56%
Verb Relationship	647	17%	17%	8%	58%	66%	34%
Locative	327	12%	18%	9%	61%	70%	30%

The four other procedures yield results too small to give significant percentages.

With or without homographs, after columns (i) and (iii) yield the first examples, the totals of examples under (ii) and (iv) include all interpretations of each kind, e.g. school + boy, Sentence 1 and Ownership 1050, both possible:

Annex 4030	A boy that studies in the school;
Sentence 1	A boy belonging to a school.

Office door, Sentence 1 and Ownership 1040, both wrong:

Locative 3014	The kind of door used in or on an office;
Locative 3015	The kind of door found in or on an office.

The preceding charts confirm the ordering of the procedures in the program because they show that the procedures are ordered, in the program, according to their degree of success.

Interpretations Yielded Outside the Normal Areas of Application by some of the Procedures in the Analysis

The success of the procedures also involves their ability to identify additional interpretations as a by-product of their main functions.

In evaluating the interpretations, I wish to include not only the relationships identified with each of the chief procedures in the analysis, but also other relationships, which are interpreted as well as the more usual relationships. For example, the Semantic Fields Match usually yields Annex relationships such as in fir-bough (4020) and armchair (4040), but it also yields the Equative type 5011: oak-tree. Examples like these are relevant to the evaluation as they could make a great difference in the totals of correctness for certain of the procedures: e.g. the total of correct interpretations in first position by the Semantic Fields Match rises from 42 to 71. In the event, the difference is obscured by the figures for the correct interpretations in the later positions and the wrong interpretations, which are also affected by the extra examples.[11] In fact, the percentages of examples analyzed by the chief procedures are almost the same with the new inclusion as before.[12] Such a large difference in the raw figures as 42 rising to 71 ought to be taken into account, and this is why I am including such figures in the two tables shortly to follow.

The conditions under which these extra examples appear are given here. (The reader is advised to consult the Index of Procedures if puzzled by this account.)

(1) The Semantic Fields Match yields a Material type, 6050, when the fields match and the head has 17 (i.e. collective), e.g. thorn hedge. (The Material Modifier also yields 6050, when the modifier is human and the head denotes a human organization, e.g. booby form.)

(2) The Semantic Fields Match yields a Locative type, 3016, when the fields match and the head is part of a building and takes 'to' (19), e.g. door : office door. (Locative, through Locative Modifier, yields 3016 when the modifier is locative and the head has 19; and through Two Locatives, where the head and modifier are locative, providing that the modifier is not a time locative, and that there is no fields match.)

(3) The Semantic Fields Match yields, of the Equative type, the unsuffixed type and Subtype 1. The former is yielded when the head and modifier embody the following permutations of 'human' and 'animal': human-human, human-animal, animal-animal, animal-human (e.g. birdman). When the fields match, and the referents are of the same size, the latter is yielded, e.g. oak-tree. (These types are not yielded by any other procedure.)

(4) The Pure Annex yields the Locative type 3020, when the modifier has 20 (i.e. an annex word that is locative when modifier, e.g. front), is not nested nor premodified by an adjective, and does not have an overt verb: e.g. front door. (This type is not yielded by any other procedure.)

(5) The Verb Relationship yields, of the Equative subtypes, 2, 3 and 4. Subtype 2 is yielded when both nouns are subjects, the head being related to an overt verb; and when the modifier is a subject and is related to an overt verb, e.g. actor-manager, player king. Subtype 3 is yielded when the modifier is a subject and is related to an overt verb, the head not being related to a verb, e.g. fly-leaf. Subtype 4 is yielded when both nouns denote activities, e.g. clearance sale. (These types are not yielded by any other procedure.)

The other main procedures do not yield interpretations outside their normal fields of application.

Totals of Interpretations Yielded Outside the Normal Areas of Application. (From the subset of the corpus)

	Total of Occurrences	(i) Correct in First Position	(ii) Correct in a Later Position	(iii) Wrong in First Position	(iv) Wrong in a Later Position
Semantic Fields Match	40	29	1	9	1
Material Modifier	0	0	0	0	0
Pure Annex	6	4	1	1	0
Verb Relationship	29	2	4	17	6
Pure Locative	0	0	0	0	0

<u>Totals Yielded by Chief Procedures plus Totals Outside the Normal Areas of Application of the Same Procedures.</u> (From the subset of the corpus)

	Totals of Occurrences	(i)	(ii)	(iii)	(iv)
Semantic Fields Match	101	71	6	16	8
Material Modifier	95	70	3	15	7
Pure Annex	74	37	6	21	10
Verb Relationship	676	110	112	72	382
Locative	327	38	59	31	199

Percentages of the above list are given on the next page.

Totals Yielded by Chief Procedures plus Totals Outside the Normal Areas of Application of the Same Procedures, given as percentages. (From the subset of $\frac{1}{4}$ of the corpus)

	Totals of which the other numbers are percentages	(i) Correct in first position	(ii) Correct in a later position	(iii) Wrong in first position	(iv) Wrong in a later position	(v) (iii)+(iv) Wrong	(vi) (i)+(ii) Correct. The measure of success of each procedure
Semantic Fields Match	101	70%	6%	16%	8%	24%	76%
Material Modifier	95	74%	3%	16%	7%	23%	77%
Pure Annex	74	50%	8%	28%	14%	42%	58%
Verb Relationship	676	16%	17%	11%	56%	67%	33%
Locative	327	12%	18%	9%	61%	70%	30%

It must be remembered that the foregoing charts, those from a subset of the corpus, include every interpretation of every example analyzed by the procedures represented. The Locative and Verb Relationship offer a great many interpretations for certain examples. Therefore the figures concerned are different from those which take into account only the first correct interpretation and first wrong interpretation of each noun sequence.

The final totals form a measure of the overall success of a procedure. There are two such totals: those of 'The Frequencies of the Chief Procedures in the Analysis, given as percentages' and 'Totals Yielded by Chief Procedures plus Totals Outside the Normal Areas of Application of the Same Procedures, given as percentages'. The Semantic Fields Match and the Material Modifier practically tie for first place. The Semantic Fields Match is placed first here and in the Analysis because if it is successful, the Material Modifier and Pure Annex procedures can be bypassed in one jump. With the Material Modifier first, there would have to be two jumps (see the following two pages).

The Order of Analysis

I have now given charts which show how many examples in the whole corpus are analyzed correctly. The homographic noun sequences throughout the data have been evaluated. Using a subset of the corpus, I have tested the success of the analysis procedures. What is under discussion now is the order in which those procedures should be accessed. They have been tried in different orders and the best result is given below. What has to be decided is:

(i) whether the interpretation program ought to move to the end of the nine procedures when it has made one correct analysis;

or

(continued on p. 126)

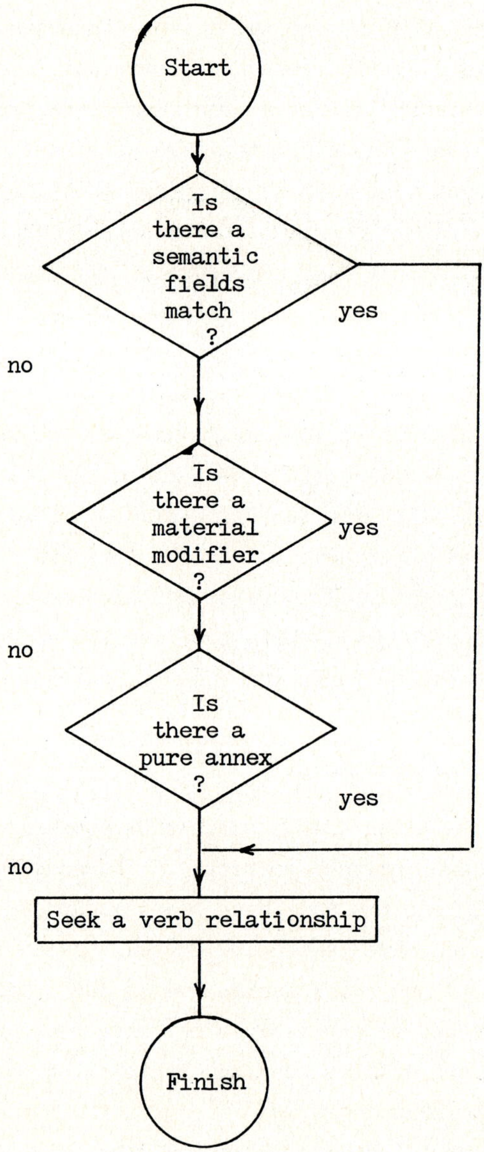
Start
Is there a semantic fields match ?
yes
no
Is there a material modifier ?
yes
no
Is there a pure annex ?
yes
no
Seek a verb relationship
Finish

[Continued]

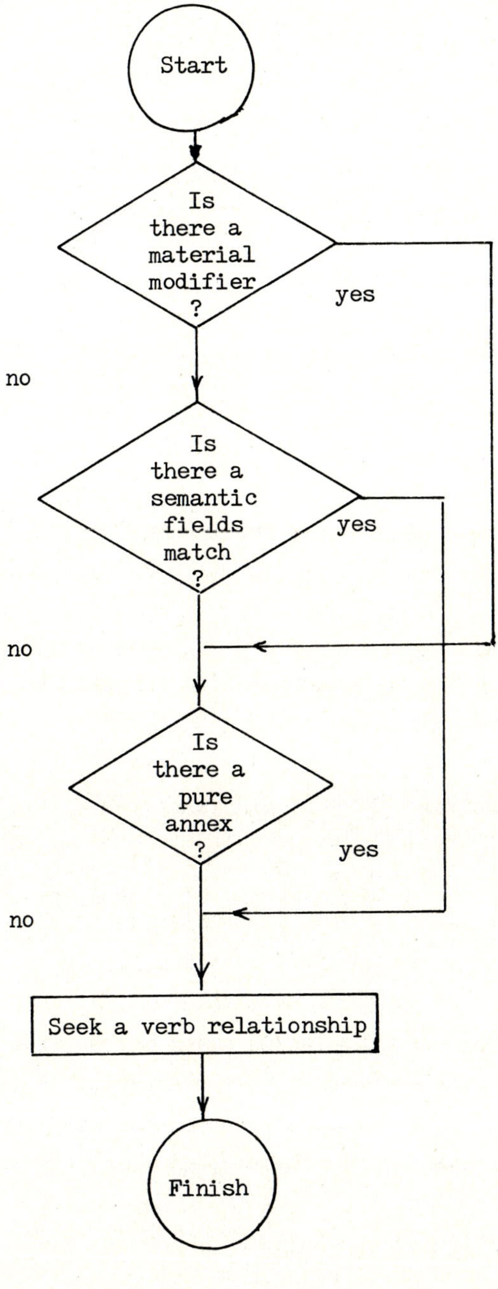
Start
Is there a material modifier ?
yes
no
Is there a semantic fields match ?
yes
no
Is there a pure annex ?
yes
no
Seek a verb relationship
Finish

(ii) whether the interpretation program should test each example with every one of the analysis procedures (Semantic Fields Match to Equative);

or (iii) whether correctness in certain analysis procedures renders certain other analysis procedures unnecessary.

A consideration of ambiguous relationships will help to determine the above questions.

Originally, I had the order:	The present order is:
Verb Relationship	Semantic Fields Match (a kind of Annex)
Locative	Material Modifier
Annex	Pure Annex
Material	Verb Relationship
Additive	Locative
Reduplicative	Material Head
Equative	Additive
	Reduplicative
	Equative

I shall ignore the Additive and Reduplicative types, e.g. (Lampton-Lufford) report, chug-chug. They are represented by only one or two examples, and in the data no ambiguous example occurs that includes them.[13]

I originally thought that after identifying the sequence as having, for example, a verb relationship, no further scanning of the types was necessary. But that was not so. We shall now look at some ambiguous examples in order to see that more than one type has to be inspected for each example. For ambiguous examples no simple linear order can be established, but in practice let us take as a framework the order given above on the right.

The ambiguity now being spoken of is not that of homography

as used in this study, (where homography identifies two different meanings of one noun, e.g. spring), but that of ambiguity in the relationship between the nouns, e.g. string bag:

A bag of string (Material)
A bag for or containing string (Locative)

and Stockholm chief:

A chief that rules Stockholm (Verb)
A chief that rules in Stockholm (Verb)
A chief that lives in or comes from Stockholm (Locative).

As shown in the last example, there can be ambiguity within the same general type, e.g. the two Verb meanings. But we are here concerned with ambiguity across types, e.g. Verb/Locative.

Several examples have apparent ambiguity but actually allow for two ways in which to say the same thing, e.g. leper village:

A village of lepers
A village for or containing lepers,

and village church:

A church in or on a village
A church made by or belonging to a village.

Other examples could be called theoretically ambiguous but in practice one interpretation is odd: mud cottage:

A cottage of mud
A cottage for or containing mud.

There is an analogue in wood shed but mud cottage is not in practice ambiguous.

In the corpus, ambiguity between types does not occur in the case of the Semantic Fields Match and the Material Modifier. In order to see whether, if there is success with the former, the program should lead into the latter, the feature-lists were searched, looking for nouns that were Material and belonged to a defined semantic field. The nouns having the material feature and also belonging to a specific semantic field were:

bone	oak
buff	paste
chocolate	plaid
cork	rush
feather	salt
fibre	skin
hair	soda
horn	teak
mutton	wood
osier	

Despite the two possible relationships of each noun (material and a match in semantic fields), a consideration of possible sequences shows that overlap is rare. Horse-hair would be part of a horse, and hair would not be likely to have the Material relationship in such a sequence. (Horse-hair) sofa, on the other hand, would have the Material relationship between sofa and hair without a match in semantic fields. The Semantic Fields Match yields an Equative type for oak tree. Oak tree can also mean a gallows-tree made of oak, but in that case we would be dealing with two meanings of tree. Cork heel and cork-tree belong to different types. So do cow's-skin trunk and pigskin. Only one of all these nouns strikes me as capable of having a match in semantic fields and also a material-modifier relationship. This is bone. Despite the relationships in such examples as fish bone and bone comb, it is to be found in the sequences *bone hand*[14] (a hand made of bone) and *bone-head⟨ed⟩*[15] (stupid: with a head made of bone from ear to ear). For these examples, the match found in the semantic fields yields a wrong interpretation, and the Material relationship is correct. However, the Semantic Fields Match would treat the match in fields (a hand with a bone) as the correct answer, and so the analysis would skip the test for the Material Modifier, thus missing the correct answer:

A hand of (made of) bone.

One solution to this would be to place the Material Modifier before the Semantic Fields Match in the Analysis. With this method, the Semantic Fields Match would yield a wrong interpretation after the correct one, but this is done by many of the other interpretations.

The other solution, which I prefer, is for the Semantic Fields Match to select all the examples of the pattern:

$$\left\{\begin{matrix}\emptyset \\ \text{premodifier[16]}\end{matrix}\right\} + \left\{\begin{matrix}\text{part of the body} \\ \text{material}\end{matrix}\right\} + \text{part of the body.}$$

The Semantic Fields Match itself would then interpret them, yielding a correct Material type and cancelling the Annex (Fields) interpretation. This involves looking ahead to give an interpretation normally yielded by the Material Modifier, but such an anticipation is already performed, for example, in the Semantic Fields Match, with regard to a Locative type (e.g. *parlour stair*).

To see whether it was safe to allow the Semantic Fields Match to bypass the Pure Annex test (which recognises, e.g. *mountain top*, *bedside*), the feature lists were searched. There are several nouns belonging to a specified semantic field and also having a Pure Annex marker.

<u>Nouns having the Annex feature and also belonging to a specific semantic field</u>:

appendix	juice
brow	knob
chestnut	mouth
crust	orange
fibre	structure
frill	stubble
head	wire

The result is that when a Fields match is found (e.g. <u>fish-head</u>), the Annex marker becomes redundant: the paraphrase would be <u>the head of a fish</u> with both the Semantic Fields Match and the Pure Annex. Where there is no Fields match, the Annex marker comes into its own: e.g. <u>straits-mouth</u>:

The mouth of a straits.

Thus the program is able to bypass the Pure Annex test where it has scored a success with the Semantic Fields Match.

At this point in the evaluation, until the end of this chapter, short names must be used to identify the procedures. This is because I am juggling with their order in the analysis and long names cannot easily be considered on the same page. They refer to their equivalents as follows:

Semantic Fields Match	Findfields
Material Modifier	Matmodfind
Pure Annex	Pannexfind
Verb Relationship	Verbalfind
Locative	Locfind
Material Head	Matheadfind
Additive	Addifind

Reduplicative	Redupfind
Equative	Equifind

The relationship between Findfields and Verbalfind will now be considered. Can the program safely bypass Verbalfind if Findfields has succeeded?

Findfields paraphrases factory chimney:

> The chimney of a factory,

whereas Verbalfind paraphrases it:

> A chimney that someone makes in a factory or factories.

Findfields paraphrases town-boy:

> A boy in the town.

Verbalfind gives it two other meanings:

> A boy that lives in or works in a town
> A boy belonging to a town.

Similarly, (radio station) reception yields, for Findfields,

> The reception of a station that someone stands
> with a radio or radios in

i.e. the room where people are received in a radio-transmitter building. For Verbalfind, (radio station) reception yields:

> The reception of someone in a station that
> someone stands with a radio or radios in

i.e. the receiving of someone's broadcast transmitted from the radio station.

Oddly enough, in context reception has the former meaning: a part of the building where incomers are received. Both meanings are acceptable.

The above three examples show that Verbalfind must be accessed as well as Findfields: the analysis done by Findfields must not allow us to skip the Verb analysis.

I had hoped to have a structure of this kind:

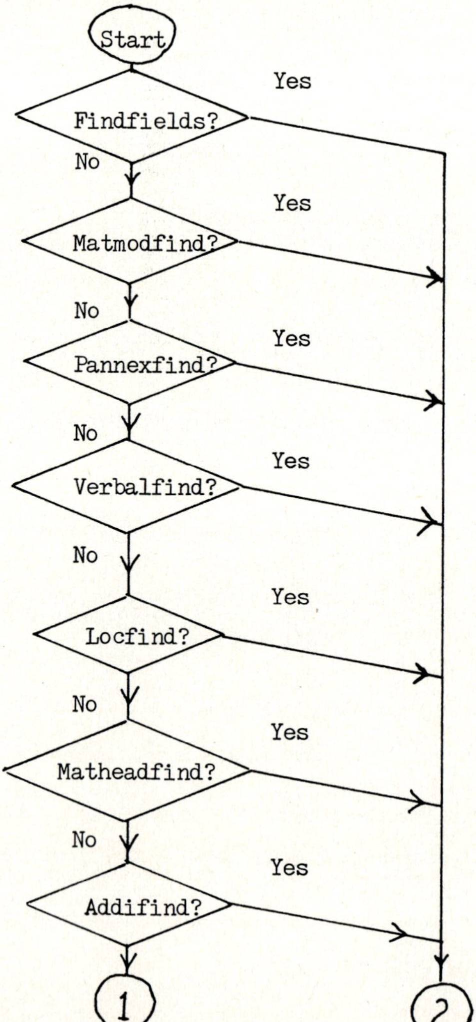

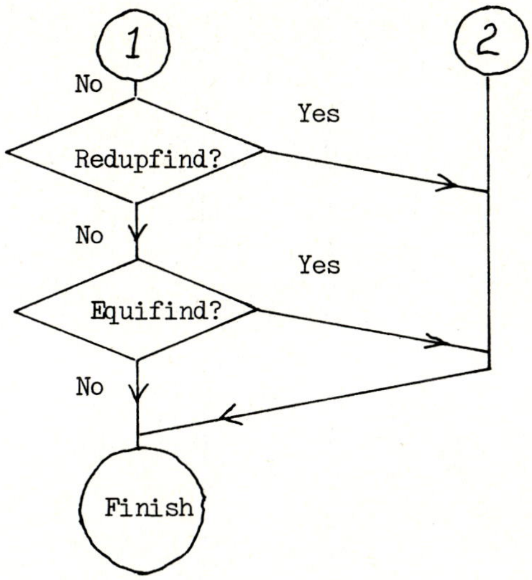

but the structure has to be more complex, because of the distribution of ambiguous examples shown overleaf:

Ambiguous Relationships

	Matmodfind	Pannexfind	Verbalfind	Locfind	Matheadfind
Findfields	-	-	factory chimney	tower wall	cake chocolate
Matmodfind		snow-flake	brick building	string bag	cardboard
Pannexfind			mine-head	town name	fence wire
Verbalfind				Stockholm chief	saddle-cloth
Locfind					cardboard

Most of the above noun sequences are from the data. In a few cases, examples had to be composed intuitively. All the nouns used are from the Feature list. Intuitively composed sequences are brick building, mine-head, cake chocolate and fence wire. Findfields yields an Equative interpretation for e.g. birdman, which is given an Equative label but which is not yielded by Equifind; the intention of Equifind is to be a fail-safe: to yield a relationship for any sequence not already assigned a relationship. By definition, Equifind does not deal with examples having ambiguous relationships.

Snowflake means (by Pannexfind),

a flake of (from) snow,

and (by Matmodfind)

a flake of (made of) snow.

Factory chimney means (by Findfields),

the chimney of a factory,

and (by Verbalfind)

a chimney that someone makes in a factory.

Brick building means (by Matmodfind)

a building made of brick,

and (by Verbalfind)

(The act of) building something in brick.

Mine-head means (by Pannexfind)

the head of a mine (machinery etc.),

and (by Verbalfind)

a head that rules a mine (the manager).

Tower wall means (by Findfields)

the wall of a tower,

and (by Locfind)

a wall in or on a tower.

String bag means (by Matmodfind)

a bag made of string,

and (by Locfind)

a bag for or containing string.

Town name means (by Pannexfind)

the name of a town

and (by Locfind)

a name in or on a town.

Stockholm chief means (by Verbalfind)

a chief that rules in Stockholm,

and (by Locfind)

a chief that lives in or comes from Stockholm.

Cake chocolate means (by Findfields)

the chocolate of a cake,

and (by Matheadfind)

chocolate for cakes or chocolate in the form of a cake.

Cardboard means (by Matmodfind)

board of (made of) card

and (by Matheadfind)

board for cards or board in the form of a card.

It is ambiguous also between the latter sense and the sense given by Locfind:

a board for or containing cards.

Fence wire means (by Pannexfind)

the wire of a fence (e.g. one strand above a wooden fence)

and (by Matheadfind)

wire for fences or wire in the form of a fence.

Saddle-cloth means (by Verbalfind)

a cloth that someone wipes or covers or lines a saddle with,

and (by Matheadfind)

cloth for saddles or cloth in the form of a saddle.

The following flowchart illustrates the relationships just described: (it omits Equifind, Addifind and Redupfind as not directly relevant here.)

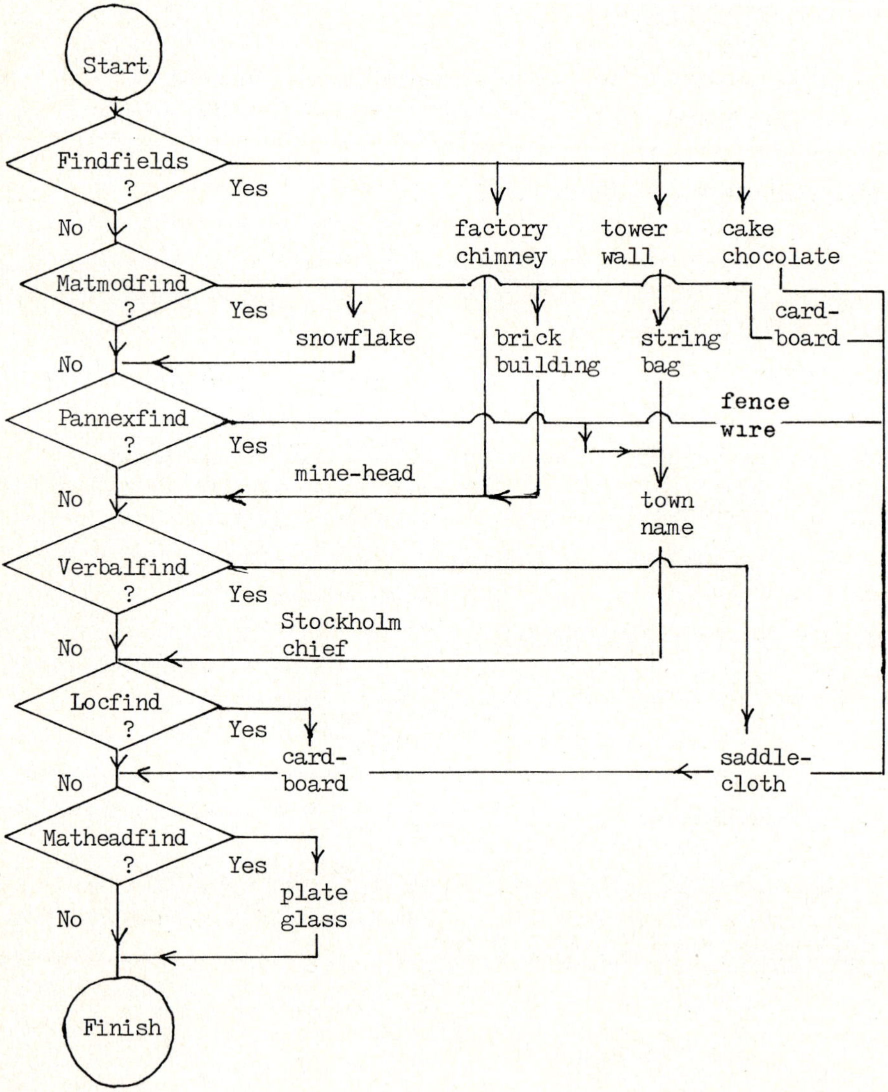

This is a flowchart showing the relationships, but it has to be rewritten to use the choices demanded by the computer language. My solution is to make almost all procedures feed into the procedure just below:

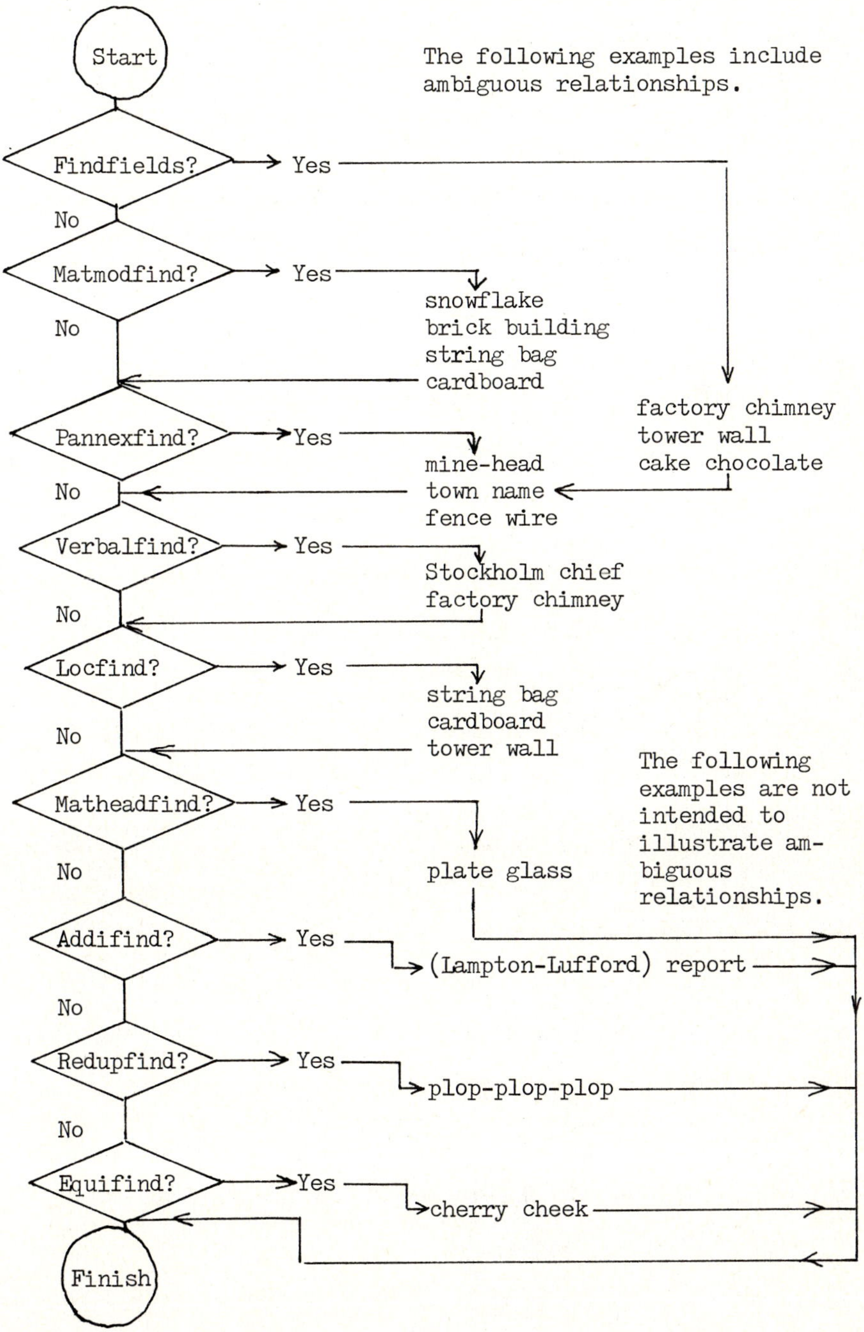
Start
The following examples include ambiguous relationships.
Findfields?
Yes
No
Matmodfind?
Yes
snowflake
brick building
string bag
cardboard
No
factory chimney
tower wall
cake chocolate
Pannexfind?
Yes
mine-head
town name
fence wire
No
Verbalfind?
Yes
Stockholm chief
factory chimney
No
Locfind?
Yes
string bag
cardboard
tower wall
No
The following examples are not intended to illustrate ambiguous relationships.
Matheadfind?
Yes
plate glass
No
Addifind?
Yes
(Lampton-Lufford) report
No
Redupfind?
Yes
plop-plop-plop
No
Equifind?
Yes
cherry cheek
Finish

During the implementation of the above flowchart, I was working with a subset of about 1/5 of the present corpus. Where there was ambiguity between Verb and Locative I found that in most examples where there was a verb in the head, Verbalfind yielded the best interpretation, followed by Locfind, as in the flowchart. However where there was a verb in the modifier (and not in the head), Locfind yielded the best interpretation, followed by Verbalfind.

I introduced this distinction into the Analysis procedure, as seen in the following flowchart, which fits in between Pannexfind and Matheadfind as on the preceding flowchart:

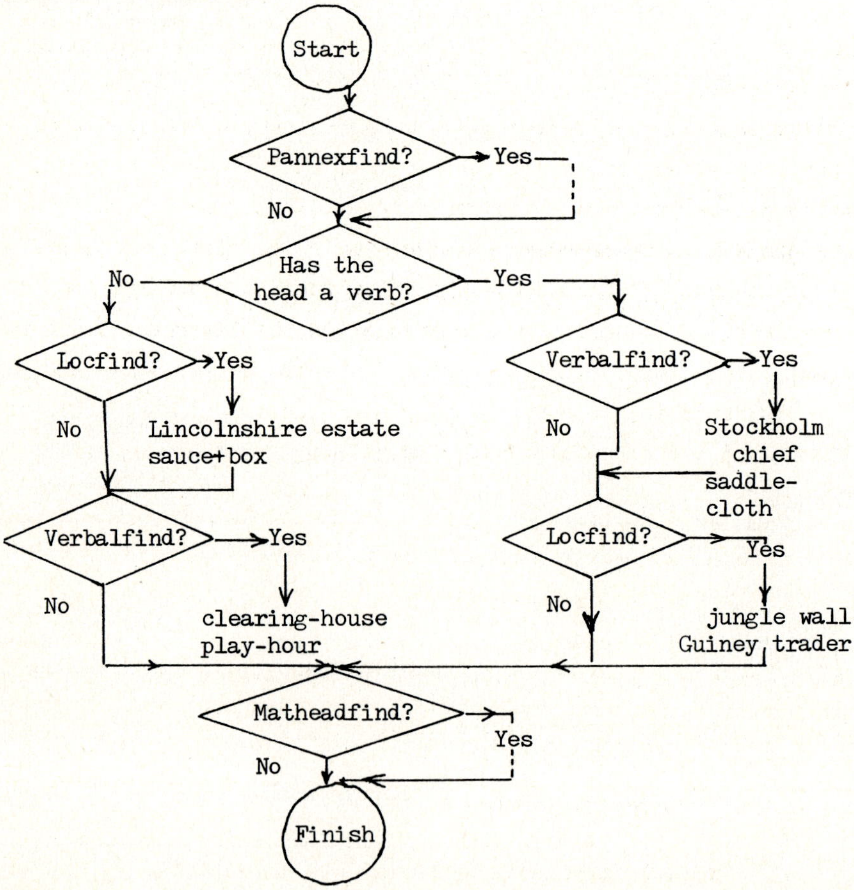

The Ordering of Relationships

The procedure following Verbalfind and Locfind is Matheadfind (e.g. plate glass), one of the two parts of the original Material procedure, which had to be split into Matmodfind and Matheadfind, as will be seen. Following Matheadfind is Addifind, for examples such as (Lampton-Lufford) report and May-June.

After Addifind comes Redupfind.

Finally comes Equifind, which must come at the end in order to pick up all unanalyzed examples and assign to them the Equative relationship.

If one interpretation (e.g. if Verbalfind) is usually better than another (e.g. Locfind), it appears sensible to make that interpretation first. Yet if we have two clearly valid interpretations (e.g. of string bag), it should not matter which of them is yielded first. For this study, the giving of interpretations in a fixed order seems to lead to satisfactory results. The program is designed to give as many interpretations as its rules produce. Ideally, all the interpretations offered should be correct. The Analysis procedure gives the interpretations in what is hoped to be the best order. A number of them are wrong, but the Analysis procedure usually succeeds in yielding these as subsequent and therefore less likely interpretations, e.g. sky scraper:

> Something or someone that scrapes the sky;
> A scraper in or on the sky.

A number are erroneously given first, e.g. note book:

> A book that a note or notes reads,

instead of the later, correct

> A book for or containing a note or notes.

But this type of shortcoming is to be expected, if one considers that the actually-occurring (and institutionalized) interpretations of noun sequences are only a subset of those which in terms of the language might theoretically occur.

What I have found is

(a) that we can give the correct meanings of noun sequences either at the first or a later try in 76% of the cases.

(b) The choice can be made in a binary way.

(c) There are ambiguities of relationship such that in most cases the analysis must proceed directly from one type to the next, and is not able to finish the course as soon as the analysis has succeeded with one type.

(d) The exceptions to this rule are:

(di) If a match is found in semantic fields, e.g. in factory chimney, then after Findfields the analysis skips the tests for the material modifier (mud hut) and the pure annex (hill top), and moves to Verbalfind.

(dii) If Matheadfind is true, the search moves to the end of the procedure Analyze: that is, none of the following types is expected to yield a second meaning to Matheadfind: Addifind, Redupfind and Equifind.

An example of these last three types may already have had a correct interpretation yielded by another procedure: e.g. for compiler-compiler Verbalfind would yield the correct

A compiler that compiles compilers,

before the action of Redupfind. For producer-director, Verbalfind would yield:

A producer that is a director,

before the action of Equifind.

One kind of ordering is that illustrated already: the ordering of groups with the Annex group resulting from *Findfields* at the beginning, and the Equative group by default (i.e. where no other test has succeeded) at the end. This means that if a *Findfields* relationship is satisfied, it is more likely to be correct than the *Verbalfind* relationship possibly yielded next: *the chimney of a factory* is more likely to be a correct paraphrase of *factory chimney* than *a chimney someone makes in a factory*.

Within groups, another kind of ordering can be seen. It is most evident in the separation of *Matmodfind* from *Matheadfind*. Originally the Material group (including the material head as well as the material modifier) was dealt with almost at the end of the list in *Analyze* (the analysis procedure). This was a relic of the earlier classification.

Activity	Verb Verb-Locative
Location	Verb-Locative Pure Locative Annex
Identity	Annex Material Equative

The material group fell neatly between the Annex (*house door*) type and the Equative (*baby crocodile*) types, and the smoothness of the transition from activity to location and then to identity was not interrupted. However, in the present work a large number of examples with material modifiers yielded unlikely paraphrases: *red-brick university*:

> A university where someone studies a red-brick or red-bricks.

Moving the Head search to the beginning yielded some absurd

paraphrases as first interpretations, so the tests for Material nouns were split into Matmodfind and Matheadfind, the former being placed near the beginning of the interpretation procedures.

The Annex group of types can be yielded by both Findfields (house door) and Pannexfind (hill-top). Both clearly have the one thing as a part of the other:

> the door of a house
> the top of a hill.

The proportion of correct analyses by Findfields (recognising the same semantic field in both nouns) is much higher than that of the analyses by Pannexfind (recognising an Annex feature in one noun), so Pannexfind was placed below Findfields and Matmodfind in the interpretation procedures.

This raises the question of whether sheer numbers ought to dictate the ordering of analyses. Surely the proportions offered above are clear of suspicion: if one interpretation is more likely to be right than another, as in factory chimney, then let the test for the one precede the test for the other. So the remaining procedures were placed in order according to frequency of correctness: Verbalfind, Locfind, Matheadfind, the oddly-composed Addifind and Redupfind, and Equifind, which comes last by definition. The way in which the major procedures in Analyze are constructed each in a self-contained way, to investigate the examples for the various relationships, is a powerful aspect of the program, as it enables these procedures to be shuffled until the best order is heuristically shown. An evaluation metric having been set up, they can be rearranged as desired.

Finally, the order of analysis for homographs, which precedes the main order, is slightly different from the main order, as it permits a jump from Findfields to Matheadfind. This may be important as it suggests that homography limits the possible relationships of a noun.

A Note on Human Analysis and the Program

For the purposes of this program, the assumption is made that each interpretation in the data is being encountered for the first time. This is a reason for supposing that the program does not exactly represent the human processes of interpretation, since it is not unlikely that well-established sequences, such as armchair, are interpreted as single unanalyzed entities. Nassau (morning(news + paper)) would be better analyzed if the dictionary had an entry for newspaper as a whole, as well as for its parts (though this would require the program to make a choice, or the linguist to edit the + sign out of news + paper when nested).

The kinds of relationships between nouns are probably changing. The present data do not go back sufficiently far to demonstrate this, except perhaps for the compounds in god+ and +groom; e.g. godfather, godparent, godson, bridegroom, which the program is unable to analyze perfectly. Changes during the last 200 years in the frequencies of the main kinds of relationships recognized by the program are demonstrated in Leonard (1968), but I am afraid I have no evidence to offer about types of relationship other than the eight kinds used in the program. So far as I can tell, only these eight kinds have been forming new noun sequences during the last 250 years.

The fact that more than one correct interpretation is offered to many of the noun sequences leads one to speculate whether the brain, when seeking the relationship between the two nouns, progresses through an ordered, even a binary choice, or makes a choice with all the possibilities simultaneously in view. A method of analysis without ordering would be to throw the features of the noun sequence at a set of resonators. Another would be to use a multi-coloured screen. Both would respond simultaneously, with just the type or types of noun sequence possible for each example.

However, the limited evidence of this research points to some ordering, if only in probabilistic terms, of the types of interpretation.

The Order in which the Slots are filled in the Sentence

So far I have written about the ordering of the procedures in Analyze. Now I should like to say a few words about the ordering of the nouns in a sentence.

I have ordered the sentence-slots as follows:

1	2	3	4	5	6	7
Subject	Verb	Object	Instr.	$Loc._{pl}$	$Loc._{tm}$	Manner

When a noun has a related verb (e.g. coat : wears), a sentence is set up around the noun:

1	2	3	4	5	6	7
Someone	wears	a coat.				

The phrase structure of the noun sequence is related as follows to a clause structure. In his Sunday coat,[17] the procedure Tryitem will place Sunday in the slot for the locative of time:

1	2	3	4	5	6	7
Someone	wears	a coat			on Sunday.	

When beginning the work described in this book, I had a hypothesis that the slots would be filled cyclically, moving from left to right (and then back again to the left if the Subject slot were free). The following four examples show the cyclic movement: e.g. towel disposal bin, fruit-preserving season, birthday, stewardess call-button:

Subject	Verb	Object	Instr.	Loc.$_{pl}$	Loc.$_{tm}$	Manner
1	2	3	4	5	6	7
Someone	disposes of	a towel		in a bin		
Someone	preserves	fruit			in a season	
Someone	is born				in a day	
Someone	calls	a stewardess	with a button			

The output corresponds to the cyclic input:

A bin that someone disposes of	a towel or towels	in.
A season that someone preserves	fruit	in.
A day that someone is born		in.
A button that someone calls	a stewardess or stewardesses	with.

<u>(Towel disposal) bin</u> demonstrates the locative of place, and <u>(fruit-preserving) season</u> the locative of time. Instrumental nouns are, for example:[18] <u>button</u>; <u>whisk</u>; <u>rake</u>; <u>knife</u>, and Manner nouns are <u>style</u>, <u>manner</u>, <u>security</u>.

A made-up example with all the slots filled will now be given.

One might postulate a sentence in the kind of setting of <u>Sons and Lovers</u>[19] where someone might rake the coal in the kitchen in the evening:

1	2	3	4	5	6	7
Someone	rakes	coal	with the rake	in the kitchen	in the evening	in miner's style.

The above structures can give rise to a number of noun sequences:

<u>kitchen coal-rake</u>:

Something that someone rakes coal with in the kitchen;

evening coal-raking:

Raking coal in the evening (with the rake);

miner's style coal-rake:

Something that someone rakes coal with like or in the style of a miner.

The sentence might be transformed into:

Kitchen evening miner's-style coal-rake.

One can pick out from this monstrosity several acceptable noun sequences. However, the fact that we seldom have nouns for all the slots is one proof that filling every available slot from left to right is highly likely to fail.[20]

Some interpretations work well on the left-to-right principle:

kitchen coal-rake:

Something that	1	2	3	4	5	6	7
	Someone	rakes	coal	with	in the kitchen.		

However, when filling the slots from left to right with no constraint on the relevant noun, it is easy to fill the Instrument slot wrongly: *Someone rakes coal with the kitchen; *Someone preserves fruit with the season.

Evening coal-raking would put evening in the $Loc._{pl}$ slot, though that might not matter: witness

Nassau morning newspaper.

Here, both paper and Nassau are place locatives, and Nassau is shifted to the $Loc._{tm}$ slot, while morning is shifted to the Manner slot.[21]

miner's style coal-raking

should be

1	2	3	4	5	6	7
Someone	rakes	coal	with a rake			like or in the style of a miner,

but 'style of a miner' would go into the $Loc._{pl}$ slot. 'In' would look right, but the Loc. meaning is wrong.

miner's style coal-raker (e.g. the small son of a miner, raking the coal) should be

1	2	3	4	5	6	7
a raker	rakes	coal	with a rake			like, or in the style of, a miner

but in practice the style would go into the $Loc._{pl}$ slot.

The result of these considerations is that I have rewritten the directly relevant procedure, so that while it must always fill a free Object slot, it must fill the other slots according to the semantic features of the nouns concerned. This works well for the Instrumental and Locative nouns; Manner nouns do worse, and the program needs improvement in that direction. Subject nouns are often correctly placed because they are human or the agents of verbs.

Naturally, every sentence has the Verb slot filled. If the head is the subject, e.g. teacher, it will fill the Subject slot. If not, the Subject slot will contain the number 4, denoting a 'human' noun. It will normally be filled after the other slots. In the case of sunrise, the non-human sun is allowed to fill the Subject slot as it has not the features to fill any of the other slots.

Notes to Chapter 4

1 All the unusual examples were chosen statistically as described later in this chapter. There occur examples with premodifying adjectives and left-nested examples. These, especially the latter, generate labyrinths of interpretation. The reader may wish to begin his inspection of the interpretations with the normal examples at the end of the sample of interpretations.

2 By a that-clause I mean a dependent declarative clause: Quirk et al. (1972), p.734.

3 One could ask: why not output for daylight:

Something or someone shines in a day or days.

After all, charcoal-burner is output as

Someone or something that burns charcoal.

The answer is that in the procedure Slotout, under certain conditions, if the head of the noun sequence is a subject, someone is written in the output sentence. If the head has a 'mechanism' feature or is not human, or something is added. Hence

Someone or something that burns charcoal.

Daydream and daylight are realized as the verbs in the underlying sentences, not the subjects, and no provision was made for the insertion of something as the subject in such cases.

4 Station has two meanings: [2] denotes the second homograph. The homography does not interfere with the point being made here.

5 One could ask: why not output the infinitive in

A master teaches that someone dances?

(cont'd.)

The procedure that yields *someone dances* is a recursive use of the procedure that yields *a master teaches S*. *That* is written to link the two sentence-structures. *To dance* is not the only possible subordinate structure: one might have

Someone watches that someone dances
someone dance
someone dancing

or Someone reads that someone dances (on Friday evenings in the square).

The program has no mechanism for (a) treating the sentence structure differently in a recursive use from its treatment for a sentence without embedding; nor for (b) distinguishing between the structure of the object with such verbs as *teach*, *watch* and *read*.

6 The only use of ×? is to indicate my doubt to the reader. ×? does not count as a positive mark of any kind.

7 The figures need not balance at 100% as the rejected half-marks merely count as nothing. An area of doubt is validly present.

8 If the 157 and 87 are placed over the grand total 311, the results are:

Correctly analyzed: 50%, as against the
wrongly analyzed: 30%.

9 Excluding noun + noun + ed, e.g. *chocolate-colour<ed>*.

10 3030 simply means 'Type 3 (Locative), Subtype 3'.

11 E.g. the interpretations made by the Semantic Fields Match which are 'wrong in first position' also rise, from 7 to 16.

12 This may possibly be a sign that the evaluation process is correct in a more general way than was expected.

13 Outside the data occurs compiler-compiler, a compiler (in computing) that compiles compilers. This would be picked up first by the Verb procedure which precedes the Reduplicative procedure. (This suggests that the Reduplicative should come after the Verb procedure, at least, in this analysis.)

14 Dickens (1904 ed.), p.20: 'He [Dick Swiveller] ...carried a yellow cane having at the top a bone hand with the semblance of a ring on its little finger and a black ball in its grasp'.

15 Mair (1973), p.100.

16 A premodifier would make the example a possible Fields example: one-bone finger, three-finger hand.

17 Cf. Sunday (tail-coat) in the data.

18 Cf. Fillmore (1968), p.22: John broke the window with a hammer. In my dictionary, rake and hammer would be marked 'Instrument'.

19 Lawrence (1913).

20 In a sentence, 5 and 6 could be reversed:

Someone shows fashions in Lancaster in the evening;

Someone shows fashions in the evening in Lancaster.

However, in some cases, the derived noun sequence seems to demand the locative of place before the locative of time:

Lancaster evening fashion show;

* Evening Lancaster fashion show.

But consider also:

country morning walk

morning country walk

where neither is totally unacceptable.

Slots 5 and 6 can be ordered only in a probabilistic way.

21 Another factor which should be mentioned is that there ought to be several slots each for Loc.$_{pl}$ and Loc.$_{tm}$: there can be more than one place and time identifier in a noun sequence. The program has not in fact been altered for this:

1	2	3	4	5	6	7
Someone	publishes	news		in the paper	in Nassau	in the morning.

This shows how, without two Loc.$_{pl}$ slots, morning is forced into the Manner slot.

CHAPTER 5

THE PERFORMANCE AND INTERACTION OF FEATURES

Chapter 5 is intended to show what happens when the features operate in an integrated model of linguistic understanding.

There have been a number of quite detailed attempts to specify sets of semantic features for the semantic description of English.

Many users of semantic features (e.g. Katz,[1] Fillmore[2]) show them in a few contexts or in comparative isolation. Leech (1969) improves on this when he outlines what he calls 'the "general taxonomy" of the language'. He identifies the system of 'concrete'/'abstract' as the most basic notion (while showing that kindness and bribery are not abstract but are derived from adjectives and verbs respectively). His diagram is as follows:[3]

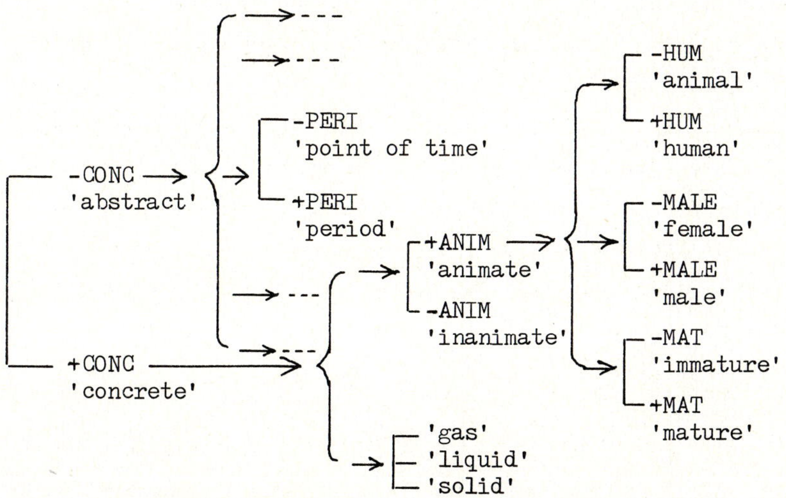

Winograd (1972) has a similar diagram. However, it is designed to work in his program's 'world' of objects of various different shapes and colours, so that the more particular features are concerned only with that 'world'.

One of the significant contributions of this book is that it shows how such features can interact in the interpretation of noun sequences.

This is why it is worthwhile to discuss what my program does with these features. (This chapter does not evaluate the features.) The fact that the program gets 76% of the examples right gives plausibility to the set of features I have chosen.

In dealing with the features, sometimes only one alteration is needed to produce correct interpretations of several examples. E.g.: the verb sells is marked on shop. But this interacts infelicitously with staff as the modifier: shop-staff:

The staff that someone sells in a shop or shops.

If I merely make one alteration, if I mark the verb works on staff, I can get a good interpretation, which will also apply in the cases of railway staff, airport staff, etc.

Such a change can make a useful generalization.

Though I am apparently relating only to my data, the changes also have predictive value.

I offer here an account of the performance and interaction of features in the world represented by my data. The functions of certain features are evaluated, and the behaviour of certain features in different contexts is displayed. The focus will sometimes be on one or two features and at other times on one or more examples exhibiting similar features. Locative features are dealt with first.

(a) Locative features, independent (Pure Locatives) and in sentences (Sentence Locatives), according to a survey of 280 interpretations.

1. Locative features

With regard to the three possibilities for a Locative word: Object, Sentence Locative and Pure Locative,[4] a survey was made of the interpretations obtained for approximately 2000 distinct examples in the corpus of data.[5] In 280 cases with a Locative noun, the program yielded more than one of these relationships. Frequently the Locative noun appeared in the Locative function in a sentence, and also as the container in a Pure Locative relationship. E.g. evening news:

> News that someone publishes in an evening or evenings;
> News in or on an evening.

Sometimes all three relationships, Object, Sentence Locative and Pure Locative, were yielded for one example. E.g. Stockholm chief:

> A chief that rules Stockholm;
> A chief that rules in Stockholm;
> A chief that lives in or comes from Stockholm;
> A chief in or on Stockholm.

The first interpretations offered were more often right than the second or subsequent interpretations, but the final version of the program attempts to give priority to some correct interpretations that were, when this check was made, offered as second alternatives.

In more cases only one relationship was correct. In some cases the correct relationship was an Annex or Equative one, e.g. jet-fighter, and the various Locatives were yielded as alternatives after the right relationship had already been given.

Nevertheless, it was worth while attempting to reduce the number of faulty interpretations.

2. *A 'human' Subject*

In the final version, Feature <7 requires the verb to take a 'human' Object, but there is no feature requiring a 'human' Subject. I investigated whether such a feature would improve the program's performance as follows:

If the Subject were required to be filled by a 'human' noun, how many wrong interpretations would be possible? Of the 280 examples, 60 yielded sentences with 'non-human' subjects. E.g. *evening breeze*, *Modley bus*:

A breeze that blows in the evening
A bus that travels to Modley.

There were also five more cases in which the interpretation was possible although wrong in context, e.g. *water-cart*:

A cart that travels in water

as well as

A cart that water travels in.

33 of these examples wrongly yielded inanimate subjects, e.g. *bedroom*:

A room that lies in a bed.

Of these, 16 were yielded by examples which have a covert verb in the modifier. I thought of excluding these by alterations to the program which would forbid a Subject slot to be filled by the head when the head is locative and the verb is covert and is in the modifier.

One of these alterations, to prevent the modifier from providing an inanimate Subject, is a simple insertion in the procedure for interpreting structures that include verbs, before the procedure to set up a sentence is entered; but the other alteration, to prevent the head from providing a Subject under these circumstances, would have had to be made in the procedure which tries to fit nouns into the sentence-slots. This meant that in a theoretically context-free procedure a distinction would have been made according to whether the verb was originally provided by the head or by the modifier. This alteration has not been made since in any case it would not lead to a significant improvement. The rules that limit the role of the verb related to a modifier, on the other hand, are helpful in cases such as *bedroom*.

I would require a 'human' marker for the Subject of *lies*; I have not got such a feature at present. (Cf. Feature <7.)

3. *An animate Object*

As we have seen, Feature <7 requires the verb to take a 'human' Object.[6] How many Objects are animate? Of the 280 examples, 12 had animate Objects, six of them correctly placed as Object and the other six incorrectly placed. There was no correspondence between correctness and whether the verb was in the head or the modifier. The six correctly analyzed examples had the locative in the modifier, but so did some of the wrongly analyzed examples. Thus one cannot demand an inanimate Object under these circumstances, nor use the presence of a verb in the modifier to exclude or include animate objects. Feature <7 stands, for such examples as *dress* and *education*.

4. *Features cannot be vague*

I wanted <7 to mean '*usually* takes a "human" Object' but I had to limit it, to mean '*must* take a "human" Object. The marking of *loves* with ⟨7 yields for *dream lover*

Someone that someone loves when someone dreams,

which is correct in context; but for *dog-lover* ⟨7 bans

Someone that loves dogs.

The main problem here is that vagueness is disallowed. Compare L.A. Zadeh in Kaufmann:

> At present, we are unable to design machines that can compete with humans in the performance of such tasks as recognition of speech, translation of languages, comprehension of meaning, abstraction and generalization, decisionmaking under uncertainty, and, above all, summarization of information.
>
> In large measure, our inability to design such machines stems from a fundamental difference between human intelligence, on the one hand, and machine intelligence, on the other. The difference in question lies in the ability of the human brain - an ability which present-day digital computers do not possess - to think and reason in imprecise, nonquantitative, fuzzy terms.[7]

This inability to be vague crops up more than once among the features, but this 'human Object' is the best example of it, and so it is mentioned here.

5. Pure Locative examples with 'animate' members

I could have postulated that all the 27 examples with an animate member and a verb should yield a Sentence interpretation and not be allowed to yield Pure Locative interpretations. However, there was no direct correspondence between the animacy of a member and whether the relationship was a Pure Locative one or a Sentence one. 12 relationships out of 32 were Pure Locative ones. *School* entered into one Sentence relationship and two Pure Locative ones, with different features active in the relationships.

There were 8 animate locatives (e.g. *bank*, *parish*), occurring 13 times, 11 of them being analyzed correctly as Sentence Locatives but also wrongly as the Container in a Pure Locative relationship. Only *town* was found as a possible Container (as in *town-crier* or *town-clerk*). (It must be remembered that we are here concerned only with cases involving verbs; *town* etc. are of course found elsewhere in purely Locative roles.)

Since *town* was an exception, no general rule could be made about animacy as a criterion in the choice between a Sentence interpretation and a Pure Locative interpretation, even though it might have seemed likely that Pure Locative interpretations would have been confined to 'inanimates' in cases where a sentence was possible.

Thus the marker 'animate' (and 'human') is of little use in choosing between the three places for Locatives: Object, Sentence Locative and Pure Locative.

6. *Transitivity and the Implicit Object*

'Transitivity' is a feature marked as <5 on very many of the verbs. The feature <6 denotes 'can imply its own Object', e.g. *makes* <5: *morning pastry-making* can be interpreted:

Someone makes pastry in the morning;

but not

*Someone makes in the morning.

On the other hand, for Stockholm chief and night attack both are acceptable:

rules <5 <6: Stockholm chief

> The chief rules Stockholm;
> The chief rules in Stockholm.

attacks <5 <6: night attack

> Someone attacks in a night or nights;
> Someone attacks a night or nights.

A point I wish to make here is that the interpretations found acceptable in this book go beyond the usual sense of 'Object understood'. It is well known that drinks is allowed in John drinks because alcohol is understood as the Object. But I have found that with many verbs, where nouns having other functions (e.g. locatives) complete the sentence, no need is felt for an Object: the verb implies its own Object. This I call an 'impo' verb, and treat specially in the procedure which constructs the sentences, e.g. not only rules, attacks, adds, advertises, but also clears (clearance), compares (comparison), bars (barrier), hits (bat[2]).

There is another point that I wish to make about 'impo' verbs: the marking of the implicit object for one example must be done carefully as it can ruin the interpretation of other examples.

With respect to dispensary door: the first interpretation is correct. However, we are also given

> A door that someone dispenses in a dispensary
> or dispensaries.

Dispenses is not usually 'impo' (having an implicit object), but one could, for example, say of a chemist

He dispenses in the afternoons.

One wishes that *dispenses* could be marked in some way to allow only pharmaceutical goods, but one also has to accommodate

He dispenses wisdom.

The verb *indicates* is used on *card* and *ticket*. *Air*[2] *ticket* is correct at the third attempt:

A ticket that admits to or indicates that
someone flies or lands.

Admits to and *indicates* have <16 ('can take a sentence as object') with <5 but no <6 (impo).

Card, *directory*, *finger* and *hand* also have *indicates*. Thus for *place card*[8] the interpretation is

A card that indicates a place.

Telephone directory (which Warren would call *telephone (number) directory*[9]) yields

A directory that someone indicates a telephone
or telephones with.

These two examples demonstrate a correct transitive interpretation. They have no 'impo' interpretations.

Fingers and *hands* of clocks *indicate* the time.

One has therefore to be careful not to mark <6 on any new noun with *indicates*. However, in a railway station the term *indicator* is used without an object (*train time indicator*); theoretically one could argue that this use is restricted to the station, where the trains are.

Another example of the 'impo' feature is *exhibition-room*, with *exhibition* marked <6, which yields

A room that someone exhibits;

A room that someone exhibits in.

The first interpretation here is wrong, but it need not be altered[10] as the pattern would be correct in the case of <u>show house</u>:[11]

A house that someone shows,

the first house completed in a row of new houses, round which prospective buyers are shown. The 'impo' feature allows

A room that someone exhibits in

and must therefore be kept.

7. <u>Locatives and the Implicit Object</u>

There is a strong correspondence between the presence of a Locative and the suppression (or implicitness) of an Object: for instance, a <u>clearing-house</u> is

A house that someone clears in,

not

A house that someone clears.

The question that led to the observation of this correspondence was: Do I want to forbid the program not only to place the head in the Subject position, but also forbid it to form <u>any</u> sentence where the covert verb is in the modifier and a noun has the Locative feature?

From the list of 280 examples, those examples were chosen which derived their verb from the modifier (excluding those with an inanimate Subject, which had already been considered). 46 examples were correctly analyzed (even if at the second or third attempt) and 29 were wrongly given a Sentence interpretation (though perhaps also analyzed correctly as Pure Locatives). The 46 examples show that it is necessary to allow a covert verb in the modifier to form a sentence, e.g. music room:

A room that someone plays music in.

Inspection of the 46 examples showed that in none of these instances did the Locative word act as the Object in the correct interpretation. Where the verb was intransitive, the correct interpretation was given immediately, e.g. bowling-green:

A green that someone bowls in.

Where the non-locative noun was marked as the Object, it fell naturally into place: supper-room:

A room that someone eats supper in.

However, where the verb was transitive and the non-locative was not the Object, the interpretation offered first was wrong in all 23 cases:

dipping-hole:

*A hole that someone dips;
A hole that someone dips (something) in.

clearing-house:

*A house that someone clears;
A house that someone clears in.

This led to the idea of a rule that in cases where the head is locative and a covert or overt verb which can imply its object is provided by the modifier, the head should fill the Locative slot. The program was amended accordingly.

8. The Sentence Locative versus the Pure Locative

The presence of a Locative feature is very significant for the choice of a slot in the sentence, and is more significant than the presence of a 'human' feature for the form of the sentence. But there do not seem to be easy correspondences to determine the choice between the sentence locative and the pure locative.

For instance, among the 75 examples where a verb can be provided by the modifier, a bread-room is

A room for or containing bread (Pure Locative)

but a coffee-house can be

A house that someone drinks coffee in.
(Sentence Locative)

A teapot is

A pot for or containing tea,

but a mixing-pot is

A pot[1] that something or someone mixes in.

Factory and shop can be used as modifiers to denote the source of goods (e.g. shop cakes) although a factory chimney is unlikely to denote

A chimney that someone makes in a factory.

Thus the 29 examples wrongly given a sentence interpretation cannot easily be excluded. The sentence interpretation is allowed together with the Pure Locative interpretation and the Annex interpretation[12] (which in any case precedes the Sentence interpretation). The Pure Locative interpretation is often the correct one.

Thus it is not advisable to make a rule excluding the second interpretations of Sunday coat and trench-coat:

A coat that someone wears in Sunday (in a trench);
A coat in or on Sunday (a trench).

Contrast bed-clothes:

Clothes in or on a bed.

In some cases both interpretations seem equally possible, e.g. savings-bank[2] (in the more recent interpretations):

A bank[2] for or containing savings;
A bank[2] that someone saves savings in.

There is a slight correspondence between the Pure Locative interpretation and the denotation **as** Locative of a small vessel (e.g. box, pot). A finer analysis might be achieved by distinguishing between larger locatives and vessels. However, filing box and mixing pot display the vessel as the sentence locative, so this distinction is not a clear one. With respect to covert verbs: in the case of bonnet-box, where bonnet has the covert verb wears, the pure locative interpretation is given first.

9. Should a covert verb be activated when in the modifier?

The inspection of the 280 examples yielding more than one Locative interpretation suggested that the use of a covert verb from the modifier to construct a sentence might be suspect. It is clear that the noun-verb in pushchair must form a sentence, but need we use the verb implicit in supper in cases where time or place is not concerned? Of the 61 examples inspected where the modifier provided a covert verb, 29 were found to be satisfactorily analyzed, e.g. supper-time:

A time that someone eats a supper or suppers in;

newspaper:

Paper that someone publishes news in.

In some cases the program was found to fill the slots wrongly, but a sentence was still needed: toll-gate:

*A gate that pays a toll.
(Cf. A gate that someone pays a toll in.)

The covert verb in the modifier is needed in analyses other than Locative ones, and the inanimate Subject is permissible outside the range of Locative expressions, even if it is to be forbidden within that range: tea-things (instrument), three-guinea shirt (costs or is worth).

Just as school hour and dipping-hole ought perhaps to place the head in the Locative slot before placing it as the Object, so we might wish to delay the production of the Object in the procedures which construct the sentences, in non-locative cases like draught ox. Although the program wrongly yielded

An ox that someone draws

before

An ox that draws something,

the ordering would be correct in the case of draught cider.[13] In fact, the program has been amended, to yield a somewhat better interpretation in such cases:

An ox that draws;
An ox that someone draws.

10. Noun + time with and without sentence interpretations

Plane[2] time, where plane[2] denotes the tree, is interpreted as

A time containing a plane[2].

This is clearly wrong. Lilac time has similar features and is perfectly acceptable:[14]

The time when lilacs bloom.

The difference is that lilac time is related to blooms. One wonders whether to put a reference on lilac to the verb blooms, or simply have a new feature 'temporary'. The program used to offer a Pure Locative interpretation of plane[2] time. The interpretation of plane[2] time has now been relegated to the end of the interpretations. There has also been an improvement where overt and covert verbs are concerned. (Plane[2] is a homograph where plane[1] (aeroplane) time is the correct version.)

Chocolate time[15] (denoting the evening time when one drinks a chocolate drink) and seed-time[16] (when one sows the seed) are both related to fixed or short passages of time.

The interpretations of this kind have been improved: dinner-time used to yield

A time for or containing a dinner or dinners.

Now it yields:

A time that someone dines in,[17]

which is correct because it includes a verb. Time as a head will probably always require a verb.[18] The old writing-time, similarly, now yields:

A time that someone writes in.

11. Conclusion from the 280 examples

The 'animate' or 'human' features do not disambiguate a Locative example with respect to its three possible relationships (Object, Sentence Locative and Pure Locative), but they have some correspondence with the Subject position in cases where the head is Locative and the verb is a covert one provided by the modifier.

The Locatives and the details from the 280 examples have now been dealt with.

(b) Examination of the performance and interaction of non-locative features

12. prize-book

Prize has the verb wins, but the interpretations are:

A book that a prize or prizes reads;

A book for or containing a prize or prizes.

This is an example of a verb (though covert) in the head over-riding the verb in the modifier (win - prize, read - book). In order to obtain the correct equative interpretation, one could add to the program a rule that two object nouns in combination allow an equative interpretation (a book that is a prize).

13. Metaphorical or fantastic interpretations

wood-walk has six interpretations. The correct one is last:

A walk in or on [a] wood.

The second interpretation is

The walk of [a] wood,

which is correct only in fiction or fantasy, e.g. in Macbeth where the wood walks to Dunsinane.

Examples like A wood walks can be excluded perhaps by confining certain verbs like walk to 'human' subjects. However, in literature many such verbs are used with inanimate subjects, e.g.

The wind shrieks;
The table groans.

Such a feature would have to be marked on verbs other than walks. Compare dream lover, where the same perils of metaphor and fantasy apply.

14. The 'illegal' extension of a feature.

(This is something about which I have not read among the users of features.)

coach-box at first failed to yield

The box of a coach.

In order to make it right, box had to be given the 'mechanical' feature %1. As a part of a mechanism, it yielded the correct interpretation. This is not a matter of 'rigging the results' since this association of 'container' words with mechanism is found in other examples of box outside the 'transport' area (squawk-box), and with other nouns (e.g. lorry cab).

Squawk-box switch therefore yielded (correctly):

The switch of a box that someone squawks in.

I have called this extension of area 'illegal' because on its own the word box would not be considered as a mechanism.[19]

One-horse palanquin exhibits the same extension. It occurs in Vanity Fair, when Joseph Sedley, on leave from India, is mocked by his father:

'"Joseph wants me to see if his - his <u>buggy</u> is at the door. What is a buggy, papa?"

"It is a one-horse palanquin," said the old gentleman.'[20]

Thus, in order to fit with <u>horse</u>, the <u>palanquin</u> (in fact a sort of sedan chair) is endowed with a 'mechanism' feature.

This shows how apparently anomalous examples and their treatment with the program and the dictionary may lead to more general solutions.

15. <u>The 'building' feature</u>

The 'building' feature, %7, is useful in several ways. For example, <u>hospital block</u> yielded in an early run of the program:

> A block that someone treats in a hospital or hospitals.

Now, with %7 added to <u>block</u>, it gives correctly

> A block that is a hospital.

16. <u>An interaction affecting the Fields and Material features</u>

<u>Stone</u>[1],[21] in Features, which has 3 (the Material feature), has also been given the Fields feature %7, i.e. 'part of a building'. The unfortunate result is that neither of the examples for which %7 was added to the definition has a better analysis: <u>door-stone</u> yields

Annex 4040	Stone[1] with a door or doors;
Material 6020	Stone[1] for doors or stone[1] in the form of a door;
Equative 5015	A stone[2] that is a door.

hearth-stone yields

Annex 4040	Stone[1] with a hearth or hearths;
Material 6020	Stone[1] for hearth or stone[1] in the form of a hearth;
Locative 3015	The kind of stone[2] found in or on a hearth.

All the interpretations of door-stone are wrong (it should be a step), and only the second interpretation of hearth-stone is correct. The second interpretation uses the 'material' feature of stone[1], so the Fields addition is irrelevant. An alteration in the size feature of stone[1], from # 3 to # 1, would give a first interpretation

Annex 4020 The stone of a hearth.

However, this is less correct than the Material interpretation (6020):

... stone in the form of a hearth.

At this stage it looks as if the 'building' feature ought to be omitted. There is some support for this in that brick has the 'material' feature but not the 'building' feature, and gives good interpretations of e.g. red-brick university:

A university of red bricks.

Finally, the 'building' feature on stone[1] causes three interpretations to be faulty:[22]

stone passage:

A passage to stone[1];

A passage that is stone[1].

stone step:

The step of stone[1] (Annex 4020, meaning that the step is part of a stone, like 'the tread of a stair').

stone wall:

The wall of stone[1] (Annex 4020).

In these last three cases, if the analysis procedure were to place the material modifier test before the semantic fields test, correct interpretations would be achieved. However, taking all the interpretations into account, I think that such a move is unnecessary: stone[1] would be better without its 'building' marker. Nearly all the examples just given would then be interpreted correctly at the first attempt.[23]

The general implication of this study is that an alteration to one feature can put in jeopardy several other interpretations of a word whose definition contains that feature. The fact that such alteration affects many different 'definitions' is actually a strength of the system (of the dictionary program and the interpretation program): it shows that the whole system acts together.

17. Interplay between features in hair-oil

Instead of treating hair as only a 'part of the body', the program recognizes the 'material' feature that was put on hair for its role in horse-hair sofa. Thus the interpretation reads

Oil of hair.

It would be difficult to mark oil with a verb or verbs, as its functions are so many; perhaps merely oils would suffice. Following the Material interpretation we would get a new and correct interpretation:

Something that someone oils hair with.

18. Interplay between verbs in shop-staff

As I have said at the beginning of this chapter, the original interpretation of shop-staff ran:

The staff that someone sells in a shop or shops.

This was corrected by adding the verb works to staff:

The staff that works in a shop or shops.

The alteration will then apply to railway staff, airport staff, bank staff, university staff, school staff,[24] etc. Contrast lift-man:

A man that is a lift;[25]
A man that a lift or lifts lifts;
A man that lives in or works in a lift.

The interpretation of shop-staff is corrected by adding to the head an overt verb which will override the covert verb in the modifier. By contrast, lift-man has an overt verb in the modifier which overrides the covert verbs in the head. This shows that to override a covert verb with an overt verb is not always correct. Boat-man displays a third pattern. Because the verb related to boat is covert, one of the verbs related to man is activated, giving a good first interpretation. Thus in shop-staff a covert verb is not enough, in lift-man an overt verb causes trouble, and in boat-man the interpretation with both nouns having covert verbs is satisfactory. In lift-man what appeared to be a useful verb was unsatisfactory, while the corrected version of shop-staff is satisfactory.

Compare boat-man:

A man that works [or operates] a boat or boats;

A man that lives in or works in a boat.

Ferry + man gets a similar interpretation.

19. Interplay of verbs resulting in redundancy

Certain nouns seem to call for related verbs, e.g. factory : makes; staff : works; book : reads. But the adding of such verbs often results in redundancy when the other noun also has a related verb.

By analogy with chair, a verb was added to the definition of bed. Chair has sits in, for e.g. "Conversation" chair:

A chair that someone sits in when someone converses.

However, lies does not lead to correct interpretations. It is not used in the first interpretations of bed-chamber, bedclothes, bedfellow, bedroom, bedside, bed-strings and bed-time. Some of these use it in their second interpretations, but these turn out to be wrong:

A chamber that lies in a bed or beds;
A fellow that lies in a bed or beds; etc.

Within the two examples that clearly call for verbs, lies is found not to be the right verb, or else to be redundant:

childbed:
A bed that a child or childs lies in.

deathbed:
A bed that someone lies in when someone dies.

Being in childbed denotes the late stage of pregnancy, so 'lies' is inappropriate;[26] deathbed would fare better without 'lies':

A bed that someone dies in.

My conclusion is that *lies*, although plausible as a verb for *bed*, in fact leads to either (a) wrong interpretation, or (b) redundant interpretation.

The verb *makes* can also be redundant. *Makes* is used with *machine* and *factory*, the former as <14 (instrument) and the latter as <12 (location). However, it is sometimes used redundantly.

For *cigarette machine* the program rightly yields

> A machine that someone makes a cigarette or cigarettes with.

There is no redundancy there. However, *adding machine* and *sewing-machine* yield, with redundancy:

> A machine that someone makes that someone adds with;
> A machine that someone makes that someone sews with.

(Compare a better definition: a machine that someone sews with.) These interpretations are partially right because they resemble interpretations where the *that*-clause is the object:

dancing-master:

> A master that controls or teaches that someone dances.

This causality suggests that the maker of the adding machine is instrumental in the adding.

20. *Redundancy of fire in the head position*

I took the reference to *burns* away from *fire* so as to interpret *study fire* and *kitchen fire*. The interpretation was

> A fire that burns a kitchen or kitchens

but it now reads

A fire in or on a kitchen.

There seem to be few noun sequences that use burns with an Object covertly. For example, the noun sequences house fire and chimney fire are normally locative without having Objects of burns.

Again, what appeared to be a useful verb turned out to be unnecessary.

21. Institutionalization

Institutionalization is the historical process whereby a word or noun sequence acquires a special interpretation, which is usually[27] no longer in accordance with the rules of word or compound formation, e.g. childbed, bridegroom, rainbow, necklace. For example, at first, the program interpreted water-fall as

The fall in water,

deriving it from the underlying sentence

Someone falls in water.

I edited the verb procedures with this and similar examples in mind, and the program now yields

The fall of water

from Water falls

before The fall in water.

The institutionalization of the first meaning places the second as ludicrous and therefore very unlikely. The interpretations of some other examples cannot even be corrected in this way, e.g. childbed. Although in this case the fault could be corrected, institutionalization is likely to remain a hindrance to the success of the program.

22. Brick + layer: a homograph

This section shows an attempt to handle homography with respect to verb, 'material' and 'annex' features.

The example brick + layer shows homography. Layer[1] is someone that lays something; layer[2] is a stratum. The old interpretation yielded:

(Annex 4010)	The layer[2] of a brick;
(Sentence 1)	Someone that lays a brick or bricks;
(Locative 3011)	A layer[1] in or on a brick.

The program has been altered, but it still yields a faulty interpretation first:

(Material)	A layer[1][made] of bricks;
(Sentence)	Someone or something that lays a brick or bricks;
(Material)	A layer[2] of bricks;
(Annex)	The layer[2] of a brick.

The second interpretation is the most correct one in both cases; among the latest interpretations the third is also correct.

The Material solution is wrong for brick layer but correct for red-brick university. The first interpretation by the program in its earlier form was:

A university that someone studies a red-brick or red-bricks in.

The first interpretation in the present form is:

A university of red-bricks.

23. The treatment of fellow: reversal of the head and modifier

There are several examples with fellow as modifier,

e.g.

fellow-citizen	fellow-director
fellow-creature	fellow-martyr.

In order to interpret them, the program reverses the head and the modifier. I caused it to do this because the verb 'is also' implicit in _fellow_ behaves like a headword. I have not seen this attempted in any other system of analysis.

fellow-creature yields:

> Someone or something that is also a creature or creatures.

This strategy is marked as feature 18, and is used successfully also for _deputy_, _fake_, _dummy_ and _toy_.[28]

24. _Deliberate use of ambiguity in the relationships between the nouns_ 29

This section is concerned with the use of _toy_, mentioned in the preceding section. _Toy men_ is a pun. It appears on p.51 of Deighton (1968). In the context, two men own a company making toys. They fall for a confidence trick and lose all their money. Their cheque is put into a safe with a false back. Leaving by helicopter, one of the tricksters looks down:

> I looked for the Continuum building where those two little toy men were guarding the front of that false safe.

Toy men means _men who make toys_ and _men who are toys_. The program captures only one meaning: _toy man_:

> A toy that mimics a man or men.

The context implies _men who make toys_ but this interpretation depends too much on the context for the program to recognize it.

25. *Material versus verb*

Straw hat and *leather shoe* originally yielded

> A hat of straw;
> A shoe of leather;

(Material) followed by

> A hat that someone wears with straw;
> A shoe that someone wears with leather.

I suppressed the second interpretation, but my interference with the verb procedure resulted in another unwanted second interpretation in the present output:

> A hat that straw wears;
> A shoe that leather wears.

It illustrates the interplay between two functions of the slot-filling procedures called from the verb procedure. This problem is hard to solve.

26. *Interaction of features on control, involving the 'impo' feature*

Any verb entry in the dictionary can have features added when they occur in a new noun entry. This is a strong safeguard against a split between the entries in Features on individual nouns, and the entry for the verb itself. An interesting interaction arises because the entry for *master* has two related verbs. The feature <6 ('impo') is eventually marked on the verb *controls*.

On the noun control, the verb is marked 'transitive' but not 'impo'. On master there occur two verbs, teaches as well as controls. Teaches is marked 'impo' as well as 'transitive': this is clearly possible, e.g. He teaches in Lancaster. All the verb features marked on a two-verb entry must apply to both verbs, so the dictionary program gives the feature <6 to the verb entry for controls as well as the verb entry for teaches.

This seems infelicitous and could be avoided by having

master[1] controls ... and
master[2] teaches ...

However, we actually find the <6 useful in the interpretation of control column, where the object is unspecified. The best definition is first among four, and uses <6:

A column that someone controls with;
A column that someone controls;
A column that controls with a control or controls;
A column that someone controls with a control or controls.

Thus the interaction of features can lead to good results in an unforeseen way.

27. Interaction of features on tail, involving semantic fields

The features 'body part' (%3) and 'item of clothing' (%8) interact on tail-coat. As well as yielding correctly

A coat with a tail or tails,

the latest version of the program has been unable to avoid the second and third interpretations:

A coat that someone wears in a tail or tails;

A coat in or on a tail.

Tail acts as a Locative because it is marked as a body part (for e.g. tail-end). Waist + coat, foot-mantle and knee-breeches exhibit the pattern body part + clothing, marked with to so that they can mean

A coat [reaching] to a waist,
A mantle to a foot,
Breeches to a knee.

Head-clothes shows the opposite problem to tail-coat.[30] I do not see an easy solution to the problem of tail-coat: perhaps tail could be divided into tail[1], animal, and tail[2], part of an item of clothing.

28. The 'impo' verb and transitivity

It is difficult to get the best interpretation of shooting party[31] first among the interpretations, mainly because party is a homograph. The best one comes fourth:

A party[2] that shoots.

Here the implicit object is quite clear (game animals and birds). However, the fifth interpretation fills in the Object, with the result:

A party[2] that someone shoots.

This is reminiscent of Peacock's words earlier on the same page as the noun sequence:

He was an excellent sportsman, and almost always killed his game; but now and then he killed his dog.

One cannot make shoot intransitive so I do not see how this problem is to be solved.

29. We have now looked at the presence and interrelationships of various features, showing how the program constructs interpretations to knit together a picture of the world implicit in noun sequences. It is evident that a good many problems of interpretation still call for solutions.

Footnotes to Chapter 5

1 Katz (1972), e.g. pp. 259, 369.

2 Fillmore (1968), especially p.27.

3 Leech (1969), p.104. A few of my features resemble those of Leech:

3. 'Material' implies +CONC.
4. 'Human' matches +HUM.
6. 'Exists physically' matches +CONC.
7. 'Animal but not Human' matches -HUM.
12. 'Locative of Time' matches -PERI and +PERI.

My 9 'Plural' matches the +PLUR in Leech's next diagram (of the system of countability, p.105).

My 10 'Does not normally take the indefinite article nor become plural' matches Leech's -COU in the same diagram.

4 E.g. Object: church-warden: a warden that looks after a church or churches. Sentence Locative: Modley bus: a bus that travels to Modley. Pure Locative: bedroom: a room for or containing a bed or beds.

5 A few changes have been made to the data since these statistics were obtained, but the changes are not significant.

6 Feature 7 ('animal') is placed on e.g. pig, dog; but I am here concerned with the difference between 'human' and 'inanimate'. (Feature 7 is not to be confused with Feature $\langle 7$.)

7 L.A. Zadeh, in the foreword to Kaufmann (1975), p. ix.

8 Place card is not in the present data.

9 Warren (1978), p. 24.

10 In fact the interpretations are reversed in the latest version of the program.

11 Not in the present data.

12 Of examples such as factory chimney:

The chimney of a factory.

13 Not included in the present data.

14 Lilac Time is the title of a musical drama. It is not included in the present data.

15 Not included in the present data.

16 Not included in the present data.

17 Here, in includes at.

18 Except for equative examples like summer-time, which can also be partitive.

19 The box nowadays sometimes denotes, in slang, a television set.

20 Thackeray (1847), 1954 ed., p.35.

21 Stone[1] is the material; stone[2] is the kernel of a pulpy fruit.

22 Ignoring the interpretations involving stone[2], which are wrong here.

23 There are also tombstone, touchstone and whinstone: these are not affected by the 'building' feature. Tomb has only 2 (locative), not a 'building' marker.

24 These examples are outside the data.

25 This kind of Equative interpretation is correct for fisher + man.

26 Though it may be appropriate for the mother. Fortuitously, lies is close to lying in, which Nuttall's dictionary defines childbed as.

27 The definition of institutionalization given above is strict, and that is why I modify it with the word usually. Some institutionalized examples are formed in accordance with present-day rules; e.g. necklace and washing-machine. In its earliest appearance in the corpus, necklace already denotes something which is not a kind of lace: Richardson (1740): 'two yards of black ribbon for my shift sleeves, and to serve as a necklace'. But the relationship between the parts is almost exactly the same as neck string, Deighton (1968), p. 19: 'library-style spectacles around my neck on a neck string'. Similarly, Lyons (1977), p. 542, gives washing-machine as an institutionalized example. This is formed in accordance with present-day rules, but is called institutionalized because clothes is implied: Lyons points out that the term could not be used of a dish-washer.

28 Unfortunately (not because of the reversal of roles), the 'Subject' feature on director and martyr causes the verb procedure to output an Equative interpretation before the 'is also' interpretation: fellow-director:

A fellow that is a director;
Someone or something that is also a director
or directors.

Thus an unhappy interplay of features is seen.

29 I am not here speaking of homography.

30 I.e. the desired interpretation is given second:

Clothes with a head or heads;
Clothes that someone wears in [on] a head or heads.

This happens because head has an Annex feature (5) for e.g. pin-head (not in the present data).

31 Peacock (1965 ed.), p. 73.

CHAPTER 6

WHAT HAS BEEN ACHIEVED IN THE COMPOSITION AND OPERATION OF THE PROGRAM

This chapter enumerates what I believe to be the most interesting and the most useful aspects of the program.

<u>General Properties of the Dictionary Program and the Interpretation Program</u>

The interpretation program, together with the Features list and the dictionary program, provides a working model of a small but significant area of the English language.

I should like to mention briefly four of the more interesting aspects of Features and the dictionary program:

(i) The Feature list can be written by the linguist with no knowledge of the computer.

(ii) If the linguist wishes to enter a homograph when he has previously entered a word, he may do so, and the Dictionary will treat the entries as separate words.

(iii) The separate entry for a verb which the dictionary program sets up is given new features (e.g.⟨6, the 'impo' feature) when they are encountered on new entries, as mentioned in the last chapter. This makes for generality as well as independence of the entries.

(iv) In view of the last point, the Dictionary could be adapted to take, also, parts of speech other than nouns and verbs, and thus become a small general dictionary.

As I say at the beginning of Chapter 1, my rules are interpretive rather than productive (such as those of Lees (1960), for example). Lees forms noun sequences from sentences; I form phrases and sentences from noun sequences.

I often use a phrasal interpretation, e.g. parlour stair:

A stair to a parlour.

In this, I work in contrast to some transformational grammarians, who trace all expressions back to sentences.

I work from a corpus. Among the precursors cited in Chapter 1, those using a corpus are Laffal (1973), Downing (1977), and Warren (with a huge selection) (1978).

With a corpus, a study is more objective, and can make generalizations more safely.

Warren uses an American corpus and I use a British one, but our classification is broadly similar.

Schwartz (1970) and Downing are the only linguistic precursors who study the interpretation of the noun sequence rather than its formation. The computer precursors generally interpret rather than compose sections of language, but except for Van Overbeke (1971) they do not study noun sequences as such.

The use of the computer in my work means that the grammar can be tested objectively on a large set of data.

In Chapter 1 I discuss Jespersen (1942) as the earliest of the grammarians I have consulted. He inspired me to objectivize an interpretation system, by making me aware of the hearer's role in the linguistic process.

However, even Jespersen is misleading when he says 'Compounds express a relation between two objects or notions, but say nothing of the way in which the relation is to be understood'.[1] The semantic relationship can often be gathered from the entries for the nouns. The program examines compounds (or sequences) out of context, and still gets 76% of them right. This is because the Dictionary is used. The program would, admittedly, be unable to make the distinction between homesickness and seasickness, but it would work quite well on the compounds in <u>gold</u> which Jespersen cites as not conforming to rules.[2]

Typology

With respect to the classification of noun sequences, the program offers eight groups of types, which break down into 27 types altogether.[3] These are used to classify noun sequences according to the semantic (and sometimes syntactic) relationships between the two or more nouns. Lees (1960), Marchand (1960, 1969), Adams (1973) and several others have offered typolcgies of noun sequences. I am not claiming that mine is better than all these, but it does work reasonably well under totally objective conditions on the computer.

My typology can most usefully be compared with that of Beatrice Warren.[4] Despite many minor differences, our typologies are very similar. This fact gives me more confidence in my classification, which is so different from those of Lees and Marchand. Though my examples are far fewer than Warren's, I should like to think that my typology supports hers.

The program largely validates the typology of noun sequences offered at the beginning of this book. This typology, much of which was devised without the computer in mind,[5] works well on the computer (with 76% correct interpretations).

The relationship between the two nouns is studied in my data for over 250 years. The data include evidence useful to writers about word-formation such as Adams (1973). Though much pioneering computer work has been done on early texts, mine is the only work I know of to take for examination by computer a selection of data from over 250 years of modern English.

The program sometimes produces interpretations that I have not envisaged even though they are acceptable, e.g. the two meanings of <u>council house</u>.

The program is practical and complementary to theory. For example, where Katz, working with features, offers theories,[6] I put into practice similar hypotheses. The proposed output from Katz's projection rules is a symbolic representation of the meaning, whereas my program yields (together with a type number) a paraphrase in English. The entries in my dictionary are much smaller than those he proposes,[7] and some of the features are different, but my dictionary is reasonably adequate for the analysis of noun sequences. If some different rules of grammar were added the entries could be expanded if it were to be used not only on noun sequences but on the sentence as a whole.

Aspects of Interest in the Program

With respect to grammar, the program has the advantage that the main ordering of the rules can easily be changed, and the rules can be tested in various orders.

The final form of the program displays a probabilistic structure, unlike the clear-cut rules often seen in expositions of syntax. This means that part of the output is often redundant, in the sense that many more interpretations are yielded than are likely to arise in practice. The main procedure, the analysis, has been tried with a sequence of clear-cut 'on/off' rules. However, it has been found that the analysis ought to inspect an example with respect to almost all the main groups of types. These are therefore placed in the order of probability.

One feature that I have not seen elsewhere is that in order to analyze examples where the modifier is fellow, e.g. fellow-creature, I exchange the head and the modifier and continue the rest of the analysis in the normal way. This successfully yields

Someone that is also a creature.

Another feature that I believe to be unusual is the structure of the dictionary entries for man and horse, which store references to more than one verb and allow the analysis procedure to choose the verb according to the features of the other noun in the sequence, e.g. barm-man:

A man that sells barm;

and one of the meanings of bird + man:

A man that looks after a bird or birds.

The construction of sentences from noun sequences, with the use of the slots and references in the Nest in cases of subordination, is I believe a worthwhile contribution to the storage of linguistic structures. The use of a procedure to output sentence interpretations is another contribution to linguistic programming, embodying as it does grammatical tests and strategies.

The procedure which sets up sentences, given nouns and related verbs, is unique in my experience. It shows that the same procedure can, when making a sentence, serve several different types of verb, yielding one or two sentences as required by the type of verb, and bringing together all the strands of verbs for the act of setting up the sentence.

The list of Features and its embodiment in the Dictionary, the dictionary and interpretation programs, and the output of interpretations, all form a closed system which is working reasonably well. (The data cannot be called part of a closed system: firstly, they are taken objectively from novels spanning 250 years, and, secondly, they can be increased as much as the linguist desires, provided the constituent nouns are placed in a Features list.) The system can be expanded, but it must be done carefully, as one new grammatical rule may touch on several other rules in the same program.

Some Possible Uses of the Program

The interpretation program displays in a small compass the whole of my syntax and much of my semantics of noun sequences. It is compact and reference is easily made from one part to another. Therefore it constitutes a good form for a grammar.

The dictionary and interpretation programs are not restricted to English. Provided that the examples are split into their component parts,[8] any Germanic noun sequence can be placed in a Features list (and from there into a dictionary) and interpreted by the program. Possibly other languages could be dealt with in a similar way.

The computer language Algol 60 is international and therefore the grammatical rules can be studied by anyone familiar with the computer language (although the features and types would have to be translated).

The program could be useful in translation, as part of a larger program, with, for example, the input consisting of English noun sequences and the output being French phrases or sentences.[9] It could also be useful to the human translator.

The program is an algorithm of a linguistic process. Neurologists may possibly find it useful. The aspects that I have in mind are the binary choices which the program makes, the storage systems of packed binary features, the semantic fields (including the comparative sizes of the members of those fields), and, finally, the order of interpretation.

To come to a more immediately practical use, Van Overbeke (1971) might find the program helpful in his splitting of compounds.

Winograd (1972) would find the program useful to fill a gap in his system. He requests a solution to the problem of parsing such expressions as

'an aluminum soup pot cover clearance sale'.[10]

In the same place, he recognizes the need for a great deal of semantic information, which for the program signifies the Dictionary as well as certain matching-processes in the program itself.

In the program, I am fulfilling the request by Winograd,[11] 'to use both the semantic markers and complex deductions to find the real relationships' [between the parts of noun sequences].

Final Note

I hope that the reader will have enjoyed the foregoing pages. In this study which bridges the two disciplines of linguistics and computing I also hope I will be forgiven for over-simplifying on the one hand and writing convoluted prose with insufficient examples on the other. As time goes on, I trust that there will be much more integration of the two disciplines, and I humbly offer this study towards the day when we will each be at ease in the other's language.

Footnotes to Chapter 6

1 Jespersen (1942), Part VI, p.137.

2 *Op.cit.*, Part VI, p.137.

3 Counting E1 as one type.

4 Warren (1978).

5 In Leonard (1968).

6 Katz (1972), *passim*.

7 Katz (1972), pp. 68 ff.

8 And provided that linking morphemes or inflexions are dealt with, either in the preparation of the data or in one of the programs.

9 The sentence procedures would require alteration, especially because French has no equivalent to our relative pronoun *that*.

10 Winograd (1972), p.157.

11 *Op.cit.*, p.157.

APPENDIX I

SAMPLES OF DATA

Introduction to Data

The following points show how the data are chosen. A sample of the data follows.

1. A noun sequence is an expression consisting of two or more nouns in sequence, fulfilling the function of a noun, without an overt syntactic link. It may be spelt as two words, hyphenated or spelt as one word, e.g. boot button, bonnet-box, bedroom. Grammarians have used the term compound to include these structures, but some noun sequences are used without the intention of forming a permanent compound, e.g. night attack, token gesture. Hence I use the term noun sequence rather than nominal compound.

2. Nested sequences are also included, e.g. (bed + room) window, (pig + skin)(document case), (front(drawing-room)) twilight.[1]

3. Agents, gerunds and nouns that can also be verbs are included as nouns, e.g. book + maker, book-keeping, manufacturing system, day + break.

4. Plural heads are made singular (e.g. boot button from boot buttons), except in the case of e.g. trousers.

5. Coordinated structures are excluded. They are noun sequences, but the program is not intended to deal with them, e.g. coal <and> iron field, stone pedestal or socket.

6. Nouns used in apposition are excluded, e.g. my son John. Some borderline cases such as sister kingdom are included.

7. N + one is excluded: 'I bought two flannel undercoats, not so good as my swan-skin and fine linen ones.' (Richardson, p.33)

8. N + N + ed is included, e.g. cream-colour<ed>; but

N + ed + N is excluded, e.g. cream-colour<ed> stuff, wissen-heart<ed> stick.

9. Dialect words and pronunciations are included, e.g. Flanders mear, Scots for mare (Scott). Bible aith (from a Scots speaker) and Pible oath (Peacock) (from a Welsh speaker) are included. Such a difference of spelling, however, does not cause these sequences to be reckoned as two examples: in the marking of the Interpretations, Pible oath is treated as a repetition of Bible aith. In one case, where the meaning of the dialect word is not easily deducible, its verb is glossed: rouping-wife: a wife that roups (sells). Horse-graith denotes part of the trappings of a horse, but it is not harness (offered by NED) as harness is coordinated with it in context.

10. Early spelling is preserved, e.g. cabbin-door, wast + coat (Defoe). As above, wast + coat is treated as another occurrence of waist + coat.

11. Nouns + street (or road etc.) are excluded, e.g. Cyprus Avenue, Eagle Road.

12. Noun sequences involving one or two proper nouns are included if one of the nouns has the force of a common noun, e.g. Portugal captain, Casting Committee. Locatives with initial capitals are also included: Calcutta ball, December morning, Dufton Locarno (a dance hall in Dufton). Water-port is listed as water-port.

13. Initials are included where they represent nouns, e.g. HQ Squadron, i.e. Headquarters; DDS tablets, i.e. di-amino diphenyl sulphone.

14. Numbers are allowed as premodifiers <in angle brackets> but not as nouns, not even half, hundred, million,

which can take the and behave in some ways like nouns. Excluded from the data are: quarter million additional participation; thirty or forty thousand livres; 78 per cent profit.

15. Four kinds of unit are included as nouns:

Units of weight, e.g. tun : <120> tun burthen.

Units of measurement, e.g. inch, foot, pint : <two> feet distance; < half->pint bumper.

Units of time, e.g. hour, second : play-hour, <sweep-> second hand.

Monetary units, e.g. dollar, £, shilling : <five> dollar bill, £5,000/a/year man, <seven->shilling piece.

16. Possessive nouns are excluded from the data, e.g. bird's nest, (though they can be registered as premodifiers : <cow's->skin trunk).

17. There are several examples where inspection has shown that the modifier may be a noun or an adjective. Some of these have been marked

OMIT AS ADJECTIVE,

e.g. <second->hand Austin Seven . Others, according to consultation of the NED and Webster,[2] have been given the benefit of the doubt, e.g. <next> door office, (Sheraton-type) furniture, (library-style) spectacles. Though these gave analysis problems, it was thought better to include them.

18. Footnotes in the novels are excluded from the data.

19. Noun sequences in passages of poetry in the novels are excluded.

20. Page numbers are given with a nought at the end. If a noun sequence occurs twice on one page, the 0 will become a 1. Such occurrences are not included in the data for this book.

21. The page numbers refer to the later edition. In the list of data, after the page number, there are a few occurrences of 1st, L. This indicates a noun sequence that occurs in the first edition but not the later edition, with the page number that it would have had if it had occurred in the later edition. 1st ED refers to the page number in the first edition. E.g. Thackeray has a passage about thieves in the first edition, which yields

THACKERAY 0440 1ST,L PEWTER ROOM

It was excised from a later edition. It would have occurred on p. 44 of the later edition used here.

22. The hyphenation is according to either the first edition or the later edition (specified in 'The Corpus', at the beginning of this book).

Bracketing

The data are bracketed with curved brackets where one noun sequence nests inside another. This is done by hand before the interpretation program is run on the data. E.g.

(bed + room) corridor
Sunday (tail-coat)
(front (drawing-room)) twilight
(pig + skin)(document case).

Only one caveat is necessary: in the case of examples deriving from sentences, e.g.

(fruit-preserving) season
(towel disposal) bin

it could be argued that all the nouns are at the highest level of realization. However, the program interprets these correctly when they are bracketed (and not otherwise).

In a few cases the bracketing seems odd at first sight:

(stewardess call)-button
Aston-(Martin tourer)
(hackney coach) + man.

Even though call-button, Aston-Martin and coachman seem integral wholes, a relationship exists between stewardess and call:

Someone calls a stewardess or stewardesses

and button fits into the sentence as an Instrument:

Someone calls a stewardess or stewardesses with a button.

If the program were to start the sentence with call-button, button would appear as the Object.

The Aston-Martin tourer is a car built by a Mr. Martin. The prototype Aston-Martin was tested on a hill called Aston. Thus there is no relationship between Aston and Martin: both relate directly to the tourer.

Though the sequence coachman was at one time very familiar, the hackney with coach denotes plying for hire and would become attached to man rather than coach if the bracketing were different.

Footnotes to Appendix I

1 (a) The plus sign is used to mark the nexus between two nouns spelt as one word, e.g. bed + room, book + maker.
(b) The equals sign is used where the example is hyphened at the end of a line, so that it might be intended to be one word, e.g. Fielding p.79: chair = man.
(c) Angle brackets are used to indicate words and morphemes in noun sequences that are not nouns, e.g. <stationary-> train noise; vinegar-face<d>.
(d) * before a noun indicates a capital letter, e.g. *LINCOLN = Lincoln.
(e) In some cases one of the nouns is complex in a way where premodification or postmodification is not really relevant. A hyphen would normally be used, but a hyphen makes the program expect the head-noun of a noun sequence. So a slash is used in these cases: Design/for/Living humour (the kind of humour found in the play Design for Living); Wu/Tao/tzu scroll (a scroll painted by Wu Tao-tzu).

2 Full details of the dictionaries are given in the Bibliography.

MARSH	0300	<">*CONVERSATION<"> CHAIR
DEIGHTON	0340	<*AMALGAMATED> *MINERALS CHEQUE
DEIGHTON	0290	<*BAY> *STREET FRIEND
BRAINE	0400	<*BULLDOG >*DRUMMOND TYPE
FIELDING	0790	<*COVENT->*GARDEN CHURCH
THACKERAY	0360	<*EAST >*INDIA *REGISTER
BRAINE	0200	<*FAIR >*ISLE CARDIGAN
RICHARDSON	0240	<ANOTHER->GUISE SORT <OF HEART>
DEIGHTON	0130	<ARMOURED> CAR COMPANY
DEIGHTON	0510	<ARTIFICIAL> SILK SCARF
BRAINE	0340	<BARBED >WIRE FENCE
SCOTT	0510	<BEND->LEATHER-GUN
BENNETT	0220	<BLACK->CURRANT JAM
DEIGHTON	0500	<BROWN> PAPER BUNDLE
BRAINE	0070	<CARBONATED->WATER SENSATION
RADCLIFFE	0200	<COMMON->PLACE REMARK
THACKERAY	0250	<COW'S->SKIN TRUNK
BENNETT	0050	<EVERY>DAY CROCKERY
BRONTE	0540	<EVERY >DAY COUNTENANCE
THACKERAY	0540	<EVERY->DAY LIFE
BENNETT	0260	<FIRST->FLOOR CORRIDOR
SCOTT	0560	<FIRST->RATE MAN/OF/WAR
LAWRENCE	0160	<FIRST->RATE PREACHER
BRAINE	0200	<FIRST->RATE TAILORING
BRONTE	1000	<FIRST->RATE TREAT
DEIGHTON	0400	<FIVE> DOLLAR BILL
BRAINE	0360	(*LAMPTON-*LUFFORD) *REPORT
LAWRENCE	0100	(*LION *WALLACE) BOOTH
DEIGHTON	0350	(*SECURITY *GUARD) CAP <AND> (GUN BELT)
DEIGHTON	0350	(*SECURITY *GUARD) COAT
BRAINE	0190	(*SHERATON-TYPE) FURNITURE
MARSH	0370	(SCHOOL-GIRL) *FRENCH
BRAINE	0350	(SCHOOL+ROOM) SMELL
DEIGHTON	0180	(SECURITY GUARD) <PEAKED> CAP
DEIGHTON	0170	(SECURITY GUARD) CAP
DEIGHTON	0130	(SECURITY GUARD) UNIFORM
MARSH	0390	(SHARK+SKIN) TROUSERS
BRAINE	0360	(SHOULDER-LENGTH) HAIR
BENNETT	0150	(SHOW+ROOM) DOOR
BENNETT	0210	(SHOW+ROOM) STAIR
DEIGHTON	0490	(SILK SCARF) MAP
MARSH	0260	(SLEEPING-CAR) ATTENDANT
GREENE	0120	(SODA-WATER) SIPHON
DEIGHTON	0410	(SQUAWK BOX) SWITCH
BENNETT	0400	(STAIR+CASE)-DOOR
DEIGHTON	0480	(STEWARDESS CALL)-BUTTON
MARSH	0110	(STRAW+BERRY) JAM
THACKERAY	0600	(TIGER-HUNTING) STORY

PEACOCK	0920	(TOLL-GATE) KEEPER
BRAINE	0440	(TOOTH+BRUSH) MOUSTACHE
DEIGHTON	0440	(TOP-SPEED) WAY
DEIGHTON	0500	(TOWEL DISPOSAL) BIN
BENNETT	0140	(WOOL+WORK) BUNCH
BECKFORD	2290	(WORMWOOD-COLOUR) FLY
BRAINE	0370	*GRADE/*THREE WIFE
BRONTE	0880	*GRANGE LIGHT
FIELDING	0880	*GUILD-HALL
DEFOE	0590	*GUINEA GRAIN
DEFOE	0400	*GUINEY TRADER
BRAINE	0070	*GUISELEY (SAND+STONE)
DEIGHTON	0450	*H*Q *SQUADRON
BRAINE	0360	*HAMILTON WATCH
THACKERAY	0250	*HAMMERSMITH *SEMIRAMIS
GREENE	0150	*HEINZ BEAN<S>
DEIGHTON	0110	*HEPPLEWHITE (BOOK+CASE)
BRAINE	0170	*HEYWOOD FLAVOUR
SCOTT	0260	*HIGHLAND GLEN
RICHARDSON	0320	*HOLLAND LINEN
PEACOCK	0070	*HOLYHEAD MAIL
PEACOCK	0200	*HOLYHEAD ROAD
BRAINE	0090	*HOME *COUNTY
BENNETT	0190	*HOWE (SEWING-MACHINE)
THACKERAY	0430	*INDIA PATTERN
SCOTT	0500	*KELSO RACE
THACKERAY	0320	*KENSINGTON TURNPIKE
DEIGHTON	0390	*KLEENEX TISSUE
SCOTT	0410	*KNIGHT *TEMPLAR
DEIGHTON	0110	*KNOLL DESK
BRAINE	0340	*LABOUR *M.*P.
GREENE	0560	*LAKE POET
THACKERAY	0520	*LATIN *GRAMMAR
THACKERAY	0320	*LIFE *GUARD
DEIGHTON	0190	*LINCOLN (HIRE-CAR)
RICHARDSON	0160	*LINCOLNSHIRE ESTATE
SCOTT	0370	*LOCHABER-AXE
RADCLIFFE	0140	*LOMBARDY POPLAR
DEIGHTON	0490	*LONDON (AIR+PORT)
DEIGHTON	0400	*LONDON FLIGHT
SCOTT	0290	*MADEIRA NEGUS
BRAINE	0260	*MARKET *SQUARE
BRAINE	0280	*MARTIN TOURER
BENNETT	0380	*MAY MORNING
BRAINE	0120	*MEDICI REPRODUCTION
THACKERAY	0570	*MIDSUMMER EXAMINATION
MARSH	0450	*MING VASE
GREENE	0090	*MISSISSIPPI (PADDLE-STEAMER)

BRAINE	0230		*MODLEY BUS
BRAINE	0410		*MONDAY DRABNESS
DEIGHTON	0420		*MONDAY MORNING
LAWRENCE	0680		*MONDAY NIGHT
GREENE	0110		*MONGO LANGUAGE
MARSH	0610		*MONTE/*CARLO RALLY
BRAINE	0370		*N*A*L*G*O <*NATIONAL >*CHARTER
MARSH	0120		*NARCOTICS *BUREAU
BRAINE	0360		*NASH *AIRFLYTE <*EIGHT>
LAWRENCE	0110		MOSS=ROSE
THACKERAY	0270		MOTHER-TONGUE
PEACOCK	0590		MOUNTAIN-(MOON+LIGHT)
PEACOCK	0570		MOUNTAIN-ASH
PEACOCK	0720		MOUNTAIN-CATARACT
PEACOCK	0800		MOUNTAIN CHAPEL
PEACOCK	0650		MOUNTAIN-FRAME
PEACOCK	0920		MOUNTAIN RECESS
PEACOCK	0930		MOUNTAIN ROAD
DEIGHTON	0350		MOUNTAIN TOP
RADCLIFFE	0420		MOUNTAIN VISTA
RADCLIFFE	0280		MOUNTAINEER CHILD
LAWRENCE	0150		MOUSE-COLOUR
RADCLIFFE	0330		MUD FLOOR
BRAINE	0280		MUD+GUARD
GREENE	0200		MUD HUT
GREENE	0480		MUD KITCHEN
BENNETT	0040		MULE-TRACK
PEACOCK	0270		MUSIC-ROOM
THACKERAY	0590		MUSLIN FROCK
RICHARDSON	0420		MUSLIN TUCKER
DEFOE	0490		MUSQUET-BORE
BENNETT	0090		MUSTARD-TINT<ED>
THACKERAY	0520		MUTTON-CANDLE
FIELDING	0760		NAME+SAKE
LAWRENCE	0500		NAVEL STRING
THACKERAY	0340		NECK+CLOTH
RICHARDSON	0330		NECK+LACE
DEIGHTON	0190		NECK STRING
DEIGHTON	0420		NECK+TIE
THACKERAY	0220		NEEDLE+WORK
DEFOE	0580		NEGRO SLAVE
SCOTT	0480		NEIGHBOUR *PLUMDAMAS
MARSH	0250		NET BAG
DEIGHTON	0110		NEWS+PAPER
THACKERAY	0430	1ST, L	NIGHT ATTACK
THACKERAY	0430		NIGHT-CAP
BRAINE	0350		NIGHT CLUB
MARSH	0380		NIGHT+DRESS

RADCLIFFE	0490	NIGHT-FALL
MARSH	0480	NIGHT+GOWN
DEIGHTON	0330	NIGHT SKY
DEIGHTON	0290	NOMINEE BID
DEIGHTON	0320	NOMINEE COMPANY
DEIGHTON	0190	NOTE+BOOK
DEIGHTON	0130	NOVELTY COMPANY
GREENE	0400	NOVICE MASTER
BRONTE	0610	OAK CASE
BRONTE	0660	OAK CLOSET
BRONTE	0470	OAK DRESSER

**#

APPENDIX II

SEMANTIC FEATURES

MANNER 14
£5,000/A/YEAR 1 6 9 <2 EARNS <5 <12
£600 5 6 9
£78.50 5 6 9
*AIRFLYTE 1 TRAVELS 6 <2 %1 #4 <11 <13
*ALLEYN 4 6 10
*ALNASCHAR 4 6 10
*AM 4 6 %2 #3 10
*AMALGAMIN 4 6 10 %2 #3
*APRIL 2 12 10
*ARMS 13 6 2 %7 #4
*ARNISTON 2 6 10
*ARTILLERY 1 <2 <11 SHOOTS %2 #3 6 13
*ASTON 6 2 10
*AUGUST 2 12 10
*AUSTIN 4 6 10 1 TRAVELS <2 %1 %2 #4 <11 <13
*AXMINSTER 6 10 2
*BAHAMAS 2 6 13 9
*BAINES 4 6 10
*BAYONNE 6 10 2
*BENGAL 2 6 10
*BESTWOOD 2 6 10
*BIBLE 13 6 2
*BITEM 2 6 10
*BOLOGNA 2 6 10
*BOTTOMS 2 6 13 9
*BOWL 2 6
*BREUGHEL 4 6 10
*BUBBLEBURGH 2 6 10
*BUILDING 6 2 %7 #4
*BUREAU 1 DEALS%WITH 2 4 6 <2 %2 %6 #3 <5 <11
*CAERNARVONSHIRE 2 6 10
*CALCUTTA 2 6 10
*CANNON 4 6
*CASH 10 6 1 <2 PAYS%FOR <5 <14
*CASHMERE 2 6 10
*CASTING 1 <1 CASTS <5 <4
*CERTIFICATE 6 1 <1 CERTIFIES <5 <16 <10
*CHARTER 6 1 <2 GRANTS <5 <16 <14
*CHEMICAL 3 6 10
*CHIEF 1 <2 RULES <5 <11 4 6 <6
*CHISWICK 2 6 10
*CHORUS 1 SING%TOGETHER 4 6 <2 %2 #3 <11
*CHRIST 4 6 10
*CHRISTMAS 2 12 10
*CHRYSLER 4 %2 #3 6 10
*CHURCH 4 %2 #3 2 6
*CITY 2 6 13 %2 #5

```
*CLUB 1 %2 #3 2 6 <2 MEETS <11
*CO/OP 2 %2 %7 #4 6 13
*COCK 2 %7 #4 6 13
*COMMITTEE %2 #2 1 <2 DEALS%WITH <5 <11 <16 6
*COMPANY %2 #3 MAKES USES 1 <2 <5 <11 6
*CONTINUUM 4 %2 #3 10
*CONTRACT 1 <2 <0 AGREES%WITH OR AGREES%ON <5 <6 <16 6
*CONVERSATION 1 CONVERSES <0 <1
*CORPORATION 4 6 %2 #3
*COUNCIL 4 %2 #3 6
*COUNTRY 2 6 13
*COUNTY 2 6 13
*COURIER 1 <2 13 2 6 PUBLISHES <5 <12
*COURT 1 JUDGES 2 4 6 %2 %7 #3 <2 <11 <13
*CRISP 4 6
*D.*D.*S. 3 6 10
*D.*D.*T. 3 6 10
*DECEMBER 2 12 10
*DEMERARA 2 6 10
*DEPOSIT 6 1 <1 DEPOSITS <5 <8
*DESIGN/FOR/*LIVING 2
*DIRECTOR 1 DIRECTS 4 6 <1 <3 <5
*DRAMA 1 <2 PERFORMS <12
*DRUMMOND 4 10
*DUFTON 2 6 10
*EASTER 10 2 12
*EDINBURGH 2 6 10
*ENGLAND 2 6 10
*ETON 2 6 1 <2 TEACHES <5 <13 10
*EXCHANGE 13 2 6 1 <1 EXCHANGES <5 <22
*FLANDERS 2 6 10
*FOOD 1 <2 EATS <12 <5 10 6 <6 %5 #4
*FRENCH 10 1 <2 SPEAKS 14 %2 #5
*FRIDAY 10 2 12
*FUNFUNN 4 6 %2 #3 10
*G.*B. 2 6 10
*GARBEL 4 6 10
*GARDEN 2 6
*GIMMERTON 2 6 10
*GOGH 4 6 10
*GOVERNMENT 4 6 %2 #3 13 1 GOVERNS <5 <6 <1 <3
*GRADE/*FOUR 2 10
*GRADE/*ONE 2 10
*GRADE/*SEVEN 2 10
*GRADE/*SIX 2 10
*GRADE/*TEN 2 10
*GRADE/*THREE 2 10
*GRAMMAR 10 5
```

*GRANGE 2 %7 #4 13 6
*GRASS 6 %4 %5 #4 10
*GUARD 1 GUARDS 4 6 <1 <3 <5 <6 <16 %2 #3
*GUILD 13 4 6 %2 #3
*GUINEA 2 6 10
*GUINEY 2 6 10
*GUISELEY 2 6 10
*H*Q 2 6
*HALL 2 13 6 %7 #4
*HALLOW 4 2 12
*HAMILTON 4 6 10
*HAMMERSMITH 2 6 10
*HEINZ 4 6 10 %2 #5
*HEPPLEWHITE 4 6 10
*HEYWOOD 4 6 10
*HIGHLAND 2 6 13
*HOLLAND 2 6 10
*HOLYHEAD 2 6 10
*HOME 2 6 10
*HORSE 6 7 11 1 <2 PULLS CARRIES <5 <11
*HOUSE 2 6 13 %7 #4
*HOWE 4 6 10 %2 #4
*INDIA 2 6 10
*ISLE 2 6 10
*JOE 4 6 10
*KELSO 2 6 10
*KENSINGTON 2 6 10
*KLEENEX 4 6 10 %2 #3
*KNIGHT 4 6
*KNOLL 4 6 10
*LABOUR 4 6 10 %2 #3
*LADD 4 10 6
*LAKE 2 13 6
*LAKE [2] 4 6 10
*LAMPTON 4 6 10
*LATIN 10 1 <2 SPEAKS 14
*LAWN 3 6 10
*LIBRARY 13 1 READS 2 6 <2 %2 %7 #4 <13
*LIFE 1 <1 <0 LIVES 10
*LINCOLN 4 6 10 %2 #4
*LINCOLNSHIRE 2 6 10
*LION 6 7
*LOCARNO 6 13 2
*LOCHABER 2 6 10
*LOMBARDY 2 6 10
*LONDON 2 6 10
*LUFFORD 4 6 10
*M.*P. 4 6 %2 #1

```
*MADEIRA 2 6 10
*MARKET 2 6 13 1 SELLS <2 <13 %2 #3
*MARTIN 4 6 10
*MAY 2 12 10
*MEDICI 13 4 6 %2 #3
*MIDSUMMER 2 12 10
*MINERALS 3 4 6 9 10
*MING 4 6 10 %2 #3
*MISS 4 6
*MISSISSIPPI 2 6 13
*MODLEY 2 6 10
*MONDAY 2 12 10
*MONGO 4 6 %2 #5 13
*MONTE/*CARLO 2 6 10
*MUMMY 4 6 10
*N*A*L*G*O 4 6 %2 #3 10
*NARCOTICS 1 DRUGS 6 9 <2 <5 <6 <14
*NASH 4 6 10
*NASSAU 2 6 10
*NEWARK 2 6 10
*O'*REILLY 4 6 10
*OBSERVER 2 6 1 <2 PUBLISHES <5 <12 13
*OCTOBER 2 12 10
*OFFICE 6 1 DEALS%WITH <2 <5 <13 2 4 %2 %7 #3 13
*OPERATION 1 OPERATES <1 <5 <9 <0
*OPERATION [2] 1 OPERATES%ON <1 <5 <0
*ORCHESTRA 1 PLAYS 6 <2 %2 #3 <11
*OSBORNE 2 6 10
*OTRACO 4 %2 #3 10
*OYSTER 6 %1 %5 #2 7
*PALMERSTON 2 %7 #4 6 13
*PANAMA 2 6 10
*PARLIAMENT 4 6 %2 #3 10
*PENTAGON 2 6 13 %2 #3
*PERCALE 3 10
*PIBLE 6 2 13
*PLAYBOY 6 4
*PLUMDAMAS 4 6 10
*POLLYWOG 4 6 10
*PORTUGAL 2 6 10
*PROP 6 <14
*PUNCH 6 1 <2 DRINKS <5 <12 10
*R.*A.*F. 4 %2 #4 13 6
*RECEPTION 1 RECEIVES <0 6 <1 <5 <7 <22
*REGISTER 13 6 2
*REPORT 1 <1 REPORTS <5 <16 <22 13 6
*RHINE 2 6 13
*RIVIERA 2 6 13
```

```
*ROHE 4 6 10
*ROLEX 4 6 10
*ROOM 2 6 13
*ROQUEVILLE 2 6 10
*SARACEN 4 6
*SATURDAY 2 12 10
*SCHIRAZ 2 6 10
*SCHOOL 1 STUDIES 6 <2 %2 %7 #4 <13 13
*SCRIPTURE 2 10
*SECURITY 10 14
*SEMIRAMIS 4 6 10
*SEPTEMBER 2 12 10
*SEX 10
*SHEET 6
*SHERATON 4 6 10
*SIGNAL 2 6 1 <2 PUBLISHES <5 <12 13
*SOCIETY 4 6 %2 #4
*SOUTHWELL 2 6 10
*SPIRIT 1 <2 6 10 DRINKS <5 <12 %4 #4
*SQUADRON %2 #3 4 6
*SQUARE 2 6 13
*STAFFORDSHIRE 2 6 10
*STATE 2 4 6 %2 #4
*STOCK 10 6
*STOCKHOLM 2 6 10
*STREET 2 6
*SUMMARY 1 6 <1 SUMMARIZES <5 <22
*SUN 2 %7 #4 6 13
*SUNDAY 2 12 10
*SUPPER 1 EATS 6 <2 <12 10
*SWISHTAIL 4 1 <2 CONTROLS OR TEACHES <5 6 <6 <11 <16
*TEMPLAR 4 6
*THESPIANS 4 6 9
*THRUSHCROSS 2 6 10
*THURSDAY 2 10 12
*TOLBOOTH 2 6 13
*TORY 4 %2 #1 6
*TOWN 2 6 %2 #5 13
*TREASURER 4 6 13 1 <2 IS%RESPONSIBLE%FOR%FUNDS <11
*TRIAL 13 1 <1 TRIES <16 <5 <6 <0
*TRUEBODY 4 6 10
*TUESDAY 2 12 10
*U*S 2 4 6 13 %2 #4
*V*I*P 4 6
*V.*I.*P. 4 6
*VAULTS 2 6 %7 #4 9
*VAUXHALL 2 6 10
*VICKERS 4 6 10
```

```
*VIENNA 2 6 10
*WAKES 2 12 1 <2 MAKES%MERRY <13
*WALLACE 6 4 7 10
*WALKER 4 6 10 %5 #4 1 <2 DRINKS <12 <5
*WARLEY 2 6 10
*WEDNESDAY 2 12 10
*WEEK 2 12
*WELLINGTON 4 6 10
*WHOLESALE 1 <2 SELLS%IN%BULK BUYS%IN%BULK <5 <6 <0
*WINDSOR 2 6 10
*WU/*TAO/TZU 4 6 10
*YARMOUTH 2 6 10
*YORK 2 6 10
*YORKSHIRE 2 6 10
*ZOMBIE 4 6 13
ACCENT 1 SPEAKS <2 14
ACCIDENT 1 HAPPENS <2 <11
ACCOUNT [1] 1 <2 DESCRIBES <0 <5 <16
ACCOUNT [2] 1 <2 KEEPS OR OWES <5 <12
ACHE 1 ACHES <1 <0
ACT 1 <1 <0 ACTS <5 <16
ACTOR 1 <1 <3 ACTS 4 6
ADDICT 1 IS%ADDICTED%TO 4 6 <1 <3 <5
ADDING 1 <4 10 <5 <1 ADDS <6
ADVERTISING 1 <1 <4 ADVERTISES <5 <6 10
AEROBATICS 1 PERFORMS 9 <2 <12
AFFAIR 1 <2 <0 IS%INVOLVED%WITH <5
AFTERNOON 2 12
AIR 2 6 10 13
AIR [2] 1 <2 FLIES OR LANDS <0
AITH 1 <2 <0 SWEARS
ALBINO 4 6 7 5
ALDER 8 6 %4 #4
ALE 10 6 1 <2 DRINKS <5 <12
AMATEUR 4 6 1 <2 PLAYS%FOR%LOVE <11
ANALYSIS 1 ANALYZES <1 <5 <0
ANCHOR 6 1 <1 ANCHORS <5 <6 <10
ANCHOVY 10 6 %5 #1 7
ANIMAL 6 7
APPARATUS 6 <14 10
APPENDIX %3 #1 5 6
APPLE 6 1 <2 EATS <5 <12 %4 %5 #2
APPLE/CHARLOTTE 1 6 <2 EATS <12 %4 %5 #4
APPRENTICE 4 6 1 <2 LEARNS <5 <6 <11 <16
APRON 6 %8 #3 1 <2 WEARS <5 <12
ARCH 6
ARCHETYPE
ARF 5
```

ARM 6 %3 #3 %6 %8
ARM [2] 6 %1 #4 1 <2 FIGHTS <14
ARSE 6 %3 #3
ARTILLERY 6 %2 #3 4 13 1 <2 SHOOTS <14
ASH %4 #4 6 8
ASH [2] 6 10 5
ASSISTANT 4 6 1 <1 ASSISTS <5 <6 <3
ATTACHMENT 5 6 1 <1 ATTACHES <8 <5
ATTACK <0 <1 1 ATTACKS <5 <6
ATTENDANT 1 ATTENDS%ON%OR%TO 4 6 <1 <3 <5
ATTIC 6 %7 #3
ATTIRE 6 10 1 <2 WEARS <5 <12 %8 #4
AUNT 4 6
AUTOGRAPH 1 <2 WRITES%ONESELF <5 <12 6
AVENUE 6 2
AXE 1 6 <2 CHOPS <14 %1 #2
BABY 4 6
BACILLUS 7 6 1 <2 INFECTS%WITH <5 <11
BACK 6 20 %3 #3
BAG 2 6
BAKER 4 6 1 <1 BAKES <5 <6 <3
BAKING 1 <1 BAKES <4 <8 6 10 %5 #4
BALANCE 6 1 <1 BALANCES <0 <9 <10
BALL [1] 6 1 <2 PLAYS <12 <14
BALL [2] 1 DANCES <0 <2
BALLET 1 DANCES 4 <2 <12 %2 #3
BAND [1] 1 ENCIRCLES 6 <2 <11 %8 #2
BAND [2] 1 PLAYS 4 6 <2 <11 %2 #3
BAND [3] 4 6 %2 #3
BANK [1] 2 6
BANK [2] 2 %2 %7 #4 6
BAR [1] 6 5
BAR [2] 1 <1 BARS <5 <3 6
BAR [3] %7 #3 2 6
BARGE 6 1 TRAVELS <2 <11 <13 %1 #4
BARM 6 10 %5 #2
BARN %7 #4 6
BARREL 6 2
BARRIER 6 1 <1 BARS <5 <6 <3
BASIN 2 6
BASKET 6
BAT [1] 6 7
BAT [2] 6 1 <2 HITS <5 <6 <14
BATH 1 BATHES 6 <1 <22
BATHING 1 BATHES <1 <4 10
BATTER 6 %5 #2 3 10
BATTLE 1 <2 <0 FIGHTS <5 <6
BAY [1] 6 2

```
BAY [2] 6 %4 #4
BEAM [1] 6 %1 %7 #2
BEAM [2] 1 <2 SHINES <0
BEAN 6 %4 %5 #1
BEAR 6 7
BED 1 LIES 6 <2 <13 %6 #4
BEE 6 7
BEECH 6 %4 #4
BEER 10 6 1 <2 DRINKS <12 <5 %5 #4
BELL 1 RINGS OR SUMMONS 6 <2 %1 #2 <11
BELT 1 ENCIRCLES 6 <2 %8 #2 <11
BENCH 6 1 <2 SITS <13 %6 #2
BERRY 6 %4 %5 #2
BEST 6 13 1 <2 WEARS <12 <5
BID 1 BIDS <1 <0 <5 <6
BILL [1] 6 %3 #1
BILL [2] 1 PAYS OR PAYS%FOR OR ADVERTIZES <2 <5 <14 <16 6
BIN 2 6
BIRD 6 7
BIRTH 1 <1 IS%BORN <0
BISCUIT 6 %5 #4
BIT 6 5
BITCH 6 7
BITE 1 <1 BITES <0 <5 <6 <22 6
BLADE 1 CUTS 6 <2 <5 <6 <14 %1 #1
BLANK 5
BLIND 1 PREVENTS%LIGHT%FROM%ENTERING 6 <2 <5 %1 #3 <11
BLOCK 6 %7 #4
BLOOD 6 10 %3 #2
BLOTTING 1 <1 BLOTS <5 <6 <4
BLUE 5
BOARD [1] 6 4 %2 #3 1 <2 RULES <5 <6 <11
BOARD [2] 2 3 6
BOARDER 6 4 1 <1 BOARDS <3
BOAT 6 19 1 <2 TRAVELS <11 <13 %1 #4
BODY %3 #4 6
BOLT 1 6 SHOOTS <2 <12 %1 %7 #1
BONE 3 6 10 %3 #2 %5
BONNET 6 1 <2 WEARS <5 <12 %8 #4
BOOBY 4 6
BOOK 6 1 2 16 <2 READS <5 <6 <12 <16
BOOT 6 %8 #3 1 <2 WEARS <12
BOOTH 6 2 %7 #4
BORDER 5 6
BORE [1] 5 1 <1 <0 BORES <5
BORE [2] 1 <1 BORES <3 4 6
BOSOM 2 6 %3 #3
BOTTLE 2 6
```

```
BOTTOM 6 20 %3 #2
BOUGH %4 #3 6
BOW [1] %8 #1 6
BOW [2] 1 <1 <0 BOWS
BOW [3] %1 #4 6
BOWL 2 6
BOWLER [1] 4 6 1 <1 BOWLS <3
BOWLER [2] 6 %8 #4
BOWLING 1 <1 BOWLS <4 10
BOX 2 6 %1 #2
BOXING 1 <1 BOXES <4 10
BOY 4 6
BRACELET 6 1 <2 WEARS <12 %8 #2
BRAID 1 BINDS 6 <2 <14 %8 #1
BRAIN 1 THINKS 6 <2 %3 #3 <11 <19
BRANCH %4 #3 6
BRAND [1] 1 6 <2 BURNS <12
BRAND [2] 5 1 <1 BRANDS <5 <10
BRAND [3] 17
BRANDY 6 %5 #1
BRASS 6 3 10
BRAT 4 6
BREAD 6 10 1 <2 EATS <12 %5 #4
BREAK 1 <1 BREAKS <5 <9 <0
BREAKFAST 1 6 BREAKFASTS <1 <0 %5 #4
BREAST %3 #3 6
BREECHES %8 #4 1 <2 WEARS <5 <12 6 9
BREEZE 1 BLOWS <2 <5 <6 <11
BRICK 6 3
BRIDE 4 6 1 <2 MARRIES <5 <12
BRIDGE 6 1 <2 CARRIES%OVER <5 <6 <11 2 %7 #4
BRIM 5 6
BROCADE 6 3 10
BROKER 4 6 1 <2 DEALS%IN <5 <11
BROOCH 6
BROOK 6
BROTHER 4 6
BROW 5 6 %3 #1
BRUSH 1 BRUSHES 6 7 <1 <5 <10
BUCK 6 7
BUCKLE %8 #1 6
BUFF 3 6 7 10 %3 #1
BUILDING 1 BUILDS 2 6 <1 <4 <5 <8 %7 #4
BULK 6 5
BULL 6 7
BUMPER 6
BUNCH 17 6
BUNDLE 17 6
```

BURGHER 4 6
BURNER 6 1 <1 <3 BURNS <5
BURTHEN 6 1 <2 WEIGHS <5 <6 <11
BUS 1 19 TRAVELS %1 #4 6 <2 <11 <13
BUSH 6 %4 #4 2
BUSINESS 1 TRANSACTS <2 10 <12
BUTTER 6 %5 #1 10
BUTTON 6 %1 %8 #1 <14
BUTTY 4 6
BUZZ 1 BUZZES <0 <1
CAB [1] 6 %1 #3
CAB [2] 1 TRAVELS 6 <2 %1 #4 <11 <13
CABBIN 2 6 %7 #3
CABIN 6 2 %7 #3
CABINET [1] 2 6 %6 #3
CABINET [2] 6 %2 #3
CADDY 2 6
CAKE 6 %5 #4 1 <2 EATS <12 <5
CALENDAR 6 1 <2 GIVES%DATES <11
CALF 6 7
CALICO 6 3 10
CALL 1 CALLS <0 <1 <5 <6 <7 <19
CAMBLET 6 3 10
CAMBRIC 6 3 10
CAMEL 6 7
CAMEO 6
CAMERA 6 %1 #4 1 <2 PHOTOGRAPHS <5 <14
CAMP 2 6 1 <1 CAMPS <22
CANARY 2 6 7
CANDIDATE 4 6 1 <2 STANDS%FOR%OFFICE <11
CANDLE 6
CANE 6 <14 3
CANISTER 2 6
CANON [1] 6 4
CANON [2] 2
CAP 1 <2 WEARS <5 <12 6 %8 #2
CAPTAIN 4 6 1 <2 COMMANDS <5 <11
CAR 1 TRAVELS 6 <2 %1 #4 <11 <13
CARD 1 PLAYS OR INDICATES 3 6 <2 <14
CARDIGAN 6 %8 #4
CARGO 6 1 <2 CARRIES <5 <12
CARNATION 6 8 %4 #3
CAROL 1 <2 SINGS <5 <6 <12
CARPET 6 2
CARRIAGE 1 19 TRAVELS 6 <2 %1 #4 <11 <13
CART 1 TRAVELS 6 <2 %1 #4 <11 <13
CARVING 6 1 <1 CARVES <4 <5 <6 <8
CASE 2 6

CASH 1 PAYS 6 10 <2 <14
CASINO 1 GAMBLES 2 6 <2 %7 #4 <13
CAST 1 <1 CASTS <5 <6 <0 6 <8
CASTOR [1] 3 6
CASTOR [2] 1 RUNS%ON 6 <2 %1 #1 <12
CAT 6 7
CATALOGUE 6 2
CATARACT 6 1 <2 FALLS <11
CATCH 6 1 <1 CATCHES <5 <0
CATHEDRAL 2 6 %7 #4
CAVALRY 6 13 %2 #3
CAVE 6 2
CAVERN 6 2
CAYENNE 10 2 6
CELLAR 6 2 %7 #3
CEMENT 3 6 10
CENTURY 2 12
CEREMONY 1 <2 <0 TAKES%PLACE
CHAIN 1 HOLDS 6 <2 <11
CHAIR [1] 1 SITS%IN 6 <2 <5 <12 %6 #4
CHAIR [2] 1 TRAVELS%IN OR CARRIES 6 <2 <5 <12
CHAISE 1 TRAVELS <2 6 <11 <13 %1 #4
CHALK 3 10
CHAMBER 6 2 %7 #3
CHANT 1 <1 CHANTS <0 <5 <6 <8
CHAPEL 6 2 %7 #3
CHARCOAL 6 3 10
CHARGE 1 CHARGES <1 <5 <8
CHARLOTTE 4 6 10
CHEEK 6 %3 #2
CHEMICAL 3 6 10
CHEQUE 1 PAYS%FOR 6 <2 <5 <14
CHERRY 6 %4 %5 #2
CHEST [1] 6 %3 #3
CHEST [2] 6 CONTAINS 1 <2 <11 <5
CHESTNUT 5 6 %4 %5 #1
CHEVAL 5 6
CHICKEN 6 7 %5 #6
CHIEF 4 6 1 <2 RULES <5 <6 <11
CHIELD 4 6
CHILD 4 6
CHILDHOOD 2 10 12
CHILDT 4 6
CHIMNEY 6 %7 #2
CHINA 3 6 10
CHIP 1 CHIPS 5 6 <2 <5 <8
CHOCOLATE 3 6 %5 #3 10
CHOIR 6 4 %2 #3 1 <2 SINGS <6 <5 <11

CHRISTMAS 2 12
CHROMIUM 10 3 6
CHRYSTAL 6 3 10
CHURCH %2 %7 #4 2 6
CIGARETTE 6 1 <2 SMOKES <12 <5 <6
CIRCLE 17
CISTERN 2 6 %1 #3
CITIZEN 4 6
CITRON 6 %4 %5 #2
CITY 2 6 %2 #5
CLASS 17 4 %2 #3 6 2
CLAW 6 %3 #3
CLAY 3 6 10
CLEARANCE 1 <1 <0 <5 <6 CLEARS
CLEARING 2 1 <1 CLEARS <5 <4 <6 <8 6
CLERGY 13 6 %2 #4
CLERK 1 WRITES 6 <2 <5 <6 <11 <20
CLOAK %8 #4 6
CLOCK %1 #4 6
CLOSE [1] 2 6
CLOSE [2] 1 <1 <0 CLOSES <5 <9
CLOSET 2 %7 #3 6
CLOTH 6 3 10 1 <2 WIPES OR COVERS OR LINES <5 <14
CLOTHES 6 9 %8 #4 1 <2 WEARS <5 <12
CLOTHING 6 10 %8 #4 1 <2 WEARS <5 <12
CLUB 1 2 6 <2 BELONGS%TO JOINS <11 %2 #3
CLUCKING 1 CLUCKS 7 <1 <4
CLUMP 17 6 %4 #5
COACH 1 TRAVELS 6 19 <2 %1 #4 <11 <13
COAL 3 6 10
COAST 5 6
COAT 1 6 <2 WEARS <12 %8 #4
COCK 6 7
COCOA 10 6 1 <2 DRINKS <12 <5 %5 #4
COCONUT 6 %4 %5 #2
COFFEE 6 %4 %5 #3 10 1 <2 DRINKS <5 <6 <12
COLLAR 6 %8 #2
COLLIER 4 6 1 <2 DIGS%COAL <11
COLLONEL 4 6
COLOUR 5 6
COLUMN 6 %1 %7 #3
COMB 6 1 <1 COMBS <5 <10
COMEDY 1 <2 AMUSES <5 <6 <11
COMMENTARY 1 <1 COMMENTS%ON <0 <5
COMPANY 4 6 %2 #3 1 <2 MAKES USES <5 <11
COMPARISON 1 COMPARES <1 <5 <0 <6 <10 <16
COMPLAINT <0 1 <1 COMPLAINS%OF <5 <6
COMPUTER 1 COMPUTES 6 <1 <3 <5 <6 %1 #4

CONCENTRATION 1 <1 CONCENTRATES <0 <5 <6
CONCERT 1 <2 ENTERTAINS <5 <6 <11 15
CONCOURSE 6 %2 #3 1 <2 MEETS <11 <0 <13
CONCRETE 6 3 10
CONE 6 %4 #1
CONFECTIONER 4 6 1 <2 MAKES%CAKES <11
CONFIDENCE 1 TRUSTS <0 <2
CONJUROR 4 6 1 <1 CONJURES <3
CONTRACT 1 <2 <0 AGREES <5 <6 <14 <16 6
CONTROL 1 <1 CONTROLS <5 <0 <10
COOKER 6 1 <1 COOKS <5 <10 <9 %1 #4
COOKING 1 <1 COOKS <4 <5 <9 10
COPE %8 %7 #3 6
COPPER 10 6 3
COPTER %1 #4 1 19 <2 TRAVELS <11 <13 6
COPY 6 1 <1 COPIES <5 <6 <8
CORAL 6 10 3
CORK 3 6 8 %4 #4 10
CORN 2 6 10 %4 %5 #3
CORNELIAN 6 3
CORNER 2 20 6
CORPORATION 4 %2 #3
CORPS %2 #3 4 6
CORRIDOR 2 6 19 %7 #3
COSTUME 10 6 1 <2 WEARS <5 <12 %8 #4
COT 2 6 %6 #2
COTE 2 6 %7 #4
COTTAGE 2 6 %7 #4
COTTON 3 6 10
COUNCIL 4 %2 #3 6
COUNTENANCE 4 6 %3 #2
COUNTER [1] 2 6 %6 %7 #3
COUNTER [2] 1 <1 COUNTS <5 <6 <10 <3
COUNTRY [1] 2 6 13
COUNTRY [2] 2 4 6 %2 #5
COURSE [1] 1 <2 RUNS <0 <13
COURSE [2] 1 <2 TEACHES <5 <13
COURT [1] 2 6 %7 #3
COURT [2] 1 JUDGES 6 <2 %2 %7 #3 <11 <13 <16
COUSIN 4 6
COVERING 1 COVERS 6 <1 <4 <5 <10
CRAFT [1] 5 1 <2 KNOWS <5 <12
CRAFT [2] 1 <2 <0 PERFORMS <5 <12
CRAFT [3] 6 1 <2 SAILS <5 <12
CRAKE 6 7 1 <1 CRAKES <0 <3
CREAM 6 10 %5 #2
CREATURE 6 7
CRESCENT 6

CREW 4 %2 #3 6
CRICKET 1 10 <2 <5 <12 PLAYS
CRIER 4 6 1 <1 CRIES <3
CRITIC 6 4 1 <1 CRITICIZES <5 <6 <3
CRITICISM 1 <1 CRITICIZES <5 <6 <0
CROCKERY 10 6 1 <2 EATS <14
CROCODILE 6 7
CROSS 6
CROWN 5 6 1 <2 WEARS <12
CRUST 5 %5 #1
CRYSTAL 6 10 3
CUFF 6 %8 #2 1 <2 SURROUNDS <5 <11
CULLENDER 6 1 <2 STRAINS <5 <6 <14
CUP 2 6 1 <2 DRINKS EATS <14 <6 <5
CUPBOARD 2 6 %6 #3
CURL 1 <1 CURLS <3 6 %3 #1
CURRANT 6 %4 %5 #1
CURTAIN 6 %6 #1 1 <2 COVERS OR REVEALS <11 <5
CUSHION 6
CUTTER 6 1 <1 CUTS <5 <6 <3 <10
CUTTING 1 CUTS 6 <1 <4 <5 <8 2 5
CUTTING/OUT 1 CUTS%OUT <1 <4 <5 <6
CYCLE 1 <1 CYCLES <10 6 %1 #4
DAIRY 2 6 %7 #4
DANCER 1 DANCES 4 6 <1 <3 <5 <6
DANCING 1 <1 DANCES <4 10
DARLING 6 4
DAWN 2 13 12
DAY 2 12
DEADPAN 6 %3 #2
DEAL [1] 1 <1 DEALS OR DEALS%IN <5 <0
DEAL [2] 6 3 10
DEATH 1 <1 <0 DIES 10
DEBT 1 <2 <0 <12 OWES
DECISION 1 DECIDES <1 <5 <6 <16 <19 <0
DECK 6 2 %1 #2
DELF 10 6
DEMAND 1 <1 DEMANDS <5 <0 <16
DEPARTMENT 2 6 %2 #3 1 <2 DEALS%WITH <5 <11 <16
DEPUTY 1 <1 DEPUTIZES%FOR <5 <3 6 18
DESIGN 1 DESIGNS 6 <1 <5 <8 <6 <16 <0
DESK 2 6 %6 #3
DIAMOND 3 6
DIFFERENCE 1 <1 DIFFERS 14
DINING 1 <1 DINES <4 10
DINNER 1 6 <1 DINES <0 %5 #4
DIPPING 1 <1 DIPS <5 <9 <4 10
DIRECTOR 1 DIRECTS 4 6 <1 <3 <5

DIRECTORY 1 INDICATES 6 <2 <5 <14
DIRT 3 10 6
DISAGREEMENT <1 10 1 <0 DISAGREES
DISH 2 6
DISPENSARY 6 %7 #4 1 <1 DISPENSES <5 <6 <22
DISPOSAL 1 <1 <0 DISPOSES%OF <5 10
DISTANCE 20
DISTILLERY 1 DISTILS <22 6 <1 <5 %7 #4
DITTY 1 <2 SINGS <5 <12 <16 <0
DIVAN 6 1 <2 LIES <13 %6 #4
DIVINER 6 4 1 <1 DIVINES <5 <3
DIVISION 5 6 %2 #3 1 <1 DIVIDES <0 <5
DO 1 <1 DOES <0 <5
DOCK 2 6
DOCUMENT 2 6
DOG 6 7 1 <2 WORKS <11
DOING 1 <1 DOES <5 <4 10
DOLLAR 6 1 <2 COSTS IS%WORTH <5 <12
DOMAIN 6 2
DOMINO 6
DOOR 6 19 %1 %6 %7 #2
DORMER 6 %1 %7 #2
DOVE 6 7
DRABNESS 5 10
DRAM 6
DRAMA 1 <2 PERFORMS <12 10
DRAUGHT 1 <1 <0 DRAWS
DRAWER 6 %6 #2 2
DRAWER [2] 1 <1 DRAWS <5 <3 6
DRAWING 1 DRAWS 6 <1 <4 <5 <6 <8
DRAWING [2] 1 WITHDRAWS <1 <4
DREAM 1 <1 DREAMS <0
DRESS 6 %8 #4 1 <2 WEARS <5 <12
DRESSER 6 %6 #4
DRESSER [2] 1 4 <1 DRESSES <5 <6 <3 6
DRESSING 1 6 DRESSES <1 <4 <5 <6 <7 <10
DRILL 1 DRILLS 6 <1 <5 %1 #4 <10
DRIVER 1 DRIVES 4 6 <1 <3 <5 <6
DROP 6 5 1 <1 DROPS <3
DROPPER [1] 1 6 4 <1 DROPS <5 <6 <3
DROPPER [2] 1 6 %1 #2 <1 DROPS <5 <6 <10
DUMMY 1 6 18 SEEMS%TO%BE <2 <5 <11
DUN 10 5
DUST 10 6 5
DUTY 1 <2 DOES <5 <12
DWELLER 1 <1 DWELLS <3 6
DWELLING %7 #4 6 1 <1 DWELLS <4 <22
DYING 1 <1 DIES <4 10

EAR 1 HEARS <2 6 %3 #2 <14
EAVES 6 2 9 %7 #2
ECHO 1 <0 <1 ECHOES <5 <6
EDGE 5
EDUCATION 1 <1 <0 EDUCATES <5 <6 <7 10
EFFECT 1 <1 EFFECTS <5 <8 <0
EGG %3 #2 6 %5
ELDER 8 %4 #4 6
ELEVATOR 1 LIFTS 6 2 <2 <11 %7 <5 %1 #2
END 20 1 <1 ENDS <0 <5 <9
ENGINE 1 WORKS 6 <2 <11 %1 #3
ENTERTAINMENT 1 ENTERTAINS <1 <5 <6 <7 <0
ENTRANCE 1 ENTERS <22 <0 6 <1 <5 %7 #2
EPITAPH 1 <2 READS <12
ESTABLISHMENT 6 2
ESTATE 2 6
EVE 12 20 2
EVENING 2 12
EVIL 10
EXAMINATION 1 <1 EXAMINES <5 <6 <0
EXCISE 1 <2 CHARGES <5 <12 10
EXCURSION 1 <2 GOES%ON <12
EXECUTIVE 1 CARRIES%OUT 4 6 <2 <11 <5
EXHIBITION 1 <1 EXHIBITS <5 <6 <0
EXPEDITION 1 GOES%ON <2 <12
EXPRESS 6 1 <2 TRAVELS <11
EYE 6 %3 #2 1 <2 SEES <5 <6 <14
FACE 6 %3 #3
FACTORY 6 2 1 <2 MAKES <5 <13 %7 #4
FAINTING 1 <1 FAINTS <4
FAIR 1 <2 HOLDS <12
FAIRY 4
FAKE 1 6 18 SEEMS%TO%BE <2 <5 <11 <16
FALL 1 <1 FALLS <0
FAMILY 6 17 %2 #1
FANTASY 1 <2 IMAGINES <5 <0 10
FARE [1] 1 PAYS%FOR 6 19 <2 <5 <14 <16
FARE [2] 1 EATS 6 <2 <12
FARER 4 6 1 <2 TRAVELS <5 <6 <11
FARM 2 6
FARTHING 6 1 <2 COSTS IS%WORTH <5 <12
FASHION [1] 1 <2 WEARS <5 <12
FASHION [2] 14
FAT 10 6 %3 %5 #1
FATHER 4 6
FEATHER %3 #1 6 3
FEET [1] 9 %3 #3 6 1 <2 TRAVELS <14
FEET [2] 5 3 9

```
FELLOW 1 IS%ALSO 4 6 18 <1 <5 <11
FENCE 6 1 <2 SURROUNDS <11 <5
FERRY 1 %1 #4 <2 TRAVELS <11 <13
FEVER %9 #4 10
FIBRE 3 10 %4 #1 5 6
FIDDLE 6 1 <2 PLAYS <5 <12
FIELD 2 6
FIG %4 %5 6 #2
FIGHTER 1 <1 FIGHTS <5 <6 <3 6
FIGHTING 1 <1 FIGHTS <4 10
FILAGREE 5 3 10 6
FILING 5 1 6 <1 FILES <4 <5 <6 <8
FILLAGREEN 5 3 10 6
FILM 1 2 <2 DEPICTS <5 <16 <11 6
FINANCE 1 <0 <1 <5 <6 FINANCES
FINGER 6 1 INDICATES <2 <14 %3 #2
FIR %4 #4 6 8
FIRE 6
FIRING 1 <1 FIRES <4 <5 <6
FISH 6 %5 #3 7 10
FISHER 1 4 7 <1 FISHES <3 <5 <6 6
FISHING 1 <1 FISHES <4 <5 <6 10
FIT 1 <1 <0 FITS <5 <6
FIT [2] 1 <2 <0 SEIZES <5
FLAKE 5 6
FLANNEL 6 3 10
FLAP 6 5
FLASK 2 6
FLAVOUR 5
FLIGHT 1 <0 <1 FLIES 10 19
FLOCK 3 5 6 10
FLOCK [2] 6 17 7
FLOOR 2 6 %7 #2
FLOORING 6 10 %7 #2
FLOW 1 <1 FLOWS <0
FLOWER 1 6 %4 #3 GROWS <2 <5 <9 <11
FLY 7 1 6 <1 FLIES <0 <3
FOLIO 6 3
FOLK 9 6 4
FOOD 6 1 <2 EATS <5 <6 <12 %5 #4
FOOT [1] %3 #3 6 1 <2 TRAVELS <14
FOOT [2] 3 5
FOP 4 6
FOREST 6 17 %4 #5
FORESTRUCTURE 6 5
FORK 6 <14
FORM %2 #3 6
FORTUNE
```

FOUNDLING 4 6 1 <1 FINDS <5 <8
FOUNTAIN 6 %1 #2
FOWLING 1 <1 FOWLS <4 10
FR. 6 1 <2 COSTS IS%WORTH <5 <12
FRAME 1 FRAMES 6 <2 <5 <10
FREIGHT 1 CARRIES 6 <2 <12 10
FRIEND 4 6
FRIGHT 1 FEARS <0 <2
FRILL 5 %8 #1 6
FROCK 6 %8 #4
FROCK [2] 6 %8 #3
FRONT 6 20
FRUIT 10 %4 %5 #2 6
FRYING 1 <1 FRIES <5 <6 <4 10
FUELLING 6 3 10
FUNGUS %4 %5 6 10 1 GROWS <2 <5 <9 <11
FURNACE 6 1 <2 BURNS <11
FURNITURE 6 10 %6 #4 1 <1 FURNISHES <5 <10
GALLERY 6 2 %7 #3
GALLON 5
GALLOWS 13 1 <2 HANGS <5 <9 <13 6
GAME 1 <2 PLAYS <6 <5 <12
GARAGE 2 6 %7 #4
GARDEN 2 6
GARDENER 1 <1 GARDENS <3 4 6
GARMENT 6 1 <2 WEARS <12
GAS 6 13
GATE %7 #2 6 19
GEAR 6 10 %1 #1 <14
GENTLEMAN 4 6
GERANIUM %4 #2 6 8
GESTURE 1 <2 MAKES <5 <12
GIANT 4 6
GIFT 1 <1 GIVES <5 <8 6
GILLYFLOWER 6 %4 #2
GIN [1] 1 6 <2 WORKS <5 <9 <11 %1 #4
GIN [2] 6 %5 #4
GINGER 6 10 %4 %5 #1
GIPSY 4 6
GIRL 4 6
GLARE 1 <1 GLARES <0
GLASS 3 6 10 <14
GLASSES 6 9 1 <2 WEARS <5 <12
GLEN 2 6
GLOBE 6
GLOOM 2 5 10
GLOVE %8 #3 1 <2 WEARS <5 <12 6
GLOW 1 <1 GLOWS <0

GOAT 6 7
GOD 10 <14
GOING 1 19 <1 GOES <4
GOLD 3 6 10
GOLF 1 10 <1 GOLFS <0
GOODNESS
GOOSE 6 7
GOVERNMENT %2 #3 13 6 4 1 <1 GOVERNS <3 <5 <6
GOWN 6 %8 #4 1 <2 WEARS <5 <12
GRADING 1 <1 GRADES <4 <5 <6 10
GRAIN 10 %5 %4 #1 6
GRAITH 6 1 <2 ENCIRCLES <5 <11
GRAMMAR 5 14 10
GRAPE 6 %4 %5 #2
GRASS 6 13 %4 #3
GRATE 2 6 %7 #2
GRATING 6 1 <1 GRATES <4 <8 <9 %7 #1
GRAVE 2 6 1 <2 BURIES <5 <13
GRAVEL 10 6 3
GREEN 2 6
GROCERY 10 6
GROOM 6 4
GROUND 2 13 6
GROUP 6 17 %2 #3
GROVE 2 6 %4 #5
GUARD 1 GUARDS 4 6 <1 <3 <5 <6 <16 %2 #3
GUESS 1 5 <1 <0 GUESSES <5
GUINEA 1 <2 COSTS IS%WORTH <5 <12
GUISE 14 5
GUN 1 SHOOTS 6 <2 <14 %1 #3
HABIT [1] 1 <2 <0 TENDS%TO <5 <16 <19
HABIT [2] 1 <2 WEARS <5 <12 %8 #4 6
HACKNEY 1 <2 HIRES <5 <12 6 %1 7 #4
HAFT 5 6
HAIR 3 6 %3 #1 10
HAIRDO 1 <1 <0 DOES%HAIR
HALF 5
HALL 6 2 %7 #3
HAM %5 %3 #2 6
HAND 1 INDICATES WORKS 6 <2 <5 %3 #3 <14
HANDKERCHIEF 6
HANDLE 5 6
HAPPINESS 10 1 <2 IS%HAPPY <0
HARBOUR 2 6
HARDBOARD 3 6
HARE 6 7 %5 #3
HAREM 1 ENJOYS 2 4 6 <2 %2 %7 #4 <12
HAT 1 6 WEARS <2 <12 %8 #4

HAY 10 %4 %5 #4 6
HAZEL %4 %5 #4 6
HEAD 1 THINKS OR RULES 5 6 <2 %3 %1 #3 <11
HEART 6 %3 #2
HEARTH 2 6 %7 #2
HEAT 5 14 10
HEATH 2 6
HEDGE 2 6 17 %4 #5
HEEL %3 %8 #2 6
HELICOPTER %1 #4 1 <2 TRAVELS <11 <13 6
HELMET 6 1 <2 WEARS <12 %8 #3
HELP 1 <0 <1 HELPS <5 <6 <3 <7 10
HERB %4 %5 #4 6
HERD 1 <1 HERDS <5 <3 4 6
HERD [2] 7 17 6
HEROIN 1 6 10 DRUGS <2 <5 <6 <14
HIDING HIDES 1 <1 <5 <9 <4 10
HIGHWAY 2 6
HILL 2 6
HIRE 1 <1 HIRES <5 <0 10
HISSING 1 HISSES <1 <4 10
HIVE 2 6
HOBBY 1 <2 PLAYS%WITH <0 <5 <12
HOLD 4 6 1 <1 <0 HOLDS <5
HOLDER 1 HOLDS 4 6 <1 <3 <5 <10
HOLE 2
HOLIDAY 2 12
HOLLA 1 <1 <0 HOLLAS
HOME 2 6
HONEY %5 #3 10 6
HORN 1 BLOWS 3 6 <2 %1 %3 #1 2 <12
HORROR 1 <1 HORRIFIES <5 <6 <0 <7
HORSE 6 7 11 1 <2 PULLS CARRIES <5 <11
HOSE 6 1 9 <2 WEARS <12 %8 #3
HOSPITAL 1 TREATS <13 <5 <6 4 6 <2 %7 #4
HOTEL 2 6 %7 #4
HOUR 2 12
HOUSE 2 6 %7 #4
HOUSEHOLD 4 6 %2 #3
HUMOUR 1 <1 AMUSES <5 <6 <7 <11 10
HUMP 5
HUNDRED 5
HUNT 1 <1 HUNTS <5 <6 <0 <3
HUNTING 1 HUNTS <1 <4 <5 <6 10
HUSBAND 4 6
HUT %7 #4 2 6
HYMN 1 <2 SINGS <5 <12
HYPO 6 3 10

```
ICE 10 6 3 %5 #1
IGNITION 1 <1 IGNITES <9 <0 10
IMPROVER 1 <1 IMPROVES <5 <9 <3
INCH 3 5
INCLINATION 1 <1 INCLINES%TO <0 <5 <16
INCOME 1 <2 RECEIVES <5 <12 10
INCREASE 1 <1 INCREASES <9 <5 <0
INDIARUBBER 3 6 10
INFANTRY 6 10 %2 #4
INK 3 6 10
INN 2 6 %7 #4
INSTRUMENT 6 %1 #3 <14
INTELLIGENCE 1 <2 <0 UNDERSTANDS OR INVESTIGATES <5 <6 10
INTEREST 1 <1 INTERESTS <3 <5
INTEREST [2] 1 <2 PAYS <12 10
INTIMATION 1 <1 INTIMATES <0 <5 <6 <16
IRON 3 6 10 <14
ISLAND 2 6
IVORY 3 6 10
IVY %4 #4 10 6
JACINTH 6 %4 #4
JACK 4 6
JACKET 6 %8 #3 1 <2 WEARS <5 <12
JAIL 2 %7 #4 6
JAM 1 SQUEEZES 6 <2 %5 #3 10 <12 <0
JERK [1] 1 JERKS <1 <0 <9
JERK [2] 4 6
JET 1 19 TRAVELS <2 6 %1 #4 <11 <13
JET [2] 1 6 FLOWS <2 <11 %1 #2
JET [3] 3 10 6
JOG 1 JOGS <1 <5 <9 <0
JOURNEY 1 TRAVELS <2 <0
JOURNEYMAN 4 6
JUG 2 6
JUICE 5 %5 #1 10
JUMPER [1] 1 <1 JUMPS <3 <5 <6 6
JUMPER [2] 6 %8 #3 1 <2 WEARS <5 <12
JUNGLE 2 6
KEEPER 1 <1 KEEPS <3 <5 6 4
KEEPING 1 <1 KEEPS <4 10
KENNEL 2 %7 #4 6
KEY 6 1 <2 LOCKS <5 <14 <16
KHAKI 6 3 10
KID [1] 3 6 10
KID [2] 4 6 7
KIN 4 1 <0 <2 IS%RELATED <11
KIND 17
KINGDOM 2 6
```

KITCHEN 6 %7 #3 2
KNEE 6 21 %3 #2
KNIFE 6 1 <2 CUTS <5 <6 <14
KNIGHT 4 6
KNOB 5 6 %6 #1
KNOT 1 6 <2 TIES <5 <12
LABEL 5 6
LACE 10 6 3 1 <2 WEARS <5 <12
LACQUER 1 DECORATES 6 <2 10 <14
LAD 4 6
LADY 4 6 1 <2 RULES <5 <6 <11 <16
LAMP 6 1 <2 ILLUMINATES <5 <6 <14
LAND 2 6
LANDING [1] 1 <1 LANDS <5 <9 <4 10
LANDING [2] 2 %7 #2 6
LANDSCAPE 2 6
LANGUAGE 1 <2 SPEAKS <5 <12
LAP 2 6 %3 #2
LAP [2] 6 %8 #2
LAP [3] 1 <2 TRAVELS <13
LARK 6 7
LASH 1 <1 LASHES <0 <3 <10 <5 6
LASS 4 6
LATCH %1 #1 %7 6
LATIN 10 1 <2 SPEAKS 14
LAUDANUM 1 6 10 DRUGS <2 <5 <6 <14
LAUREL 6 #4 %4
LAW 1 <2 RULES <5 <6 <14
LAWN [1] 6 %8 #4
LAWN [2] 2 6 %4 #4
LAYER [1] 1 <1 LAYS <3 <5 6
LAYER [2] 5 6
LEADING 1 <1 LEADS <4 <5 <6 10
LEAF 6 %4 %6 #2
LEATHER 3 6 10
LEAVE 1 <2 PERMITS%TO%GO <0 <5 10
LECTURE 1 <1 LECTURES <0
LEDGE 5
LEG 6 %3 %6 %8 #3
LEISURE 1 10 <2 <0 IS%AT%LEISURE
LEMON 6 %4 %5 #2
LENDER 4 6 1 <1 LENDS <3 <5
LENGTH 5
LEPER 4 6 %9 #4
LEPROSY 10 %9 #4
LESSON 1 <2 <0 TEACHES <5 <6 <16
LETTER 1 6 19 WRITES <5 <12 <13 <2 <16 <19 16
LETTERING 1 LETTERS 6 <1 <4 <8 10

LEVEL 1 LEVELS 6 <2 <10 5
LIBERTY 1 <2 <0 IS%FREE
LIBRARY 1 2 READS 6 <2 %2 %7 #4 <13 <5 <6
LID 5 6
LIEUTENANT 4 6
LIFE 1 LIVES <2 10 <0
LIFT 1 LIFTS 2 6 <1 <5 %1 %7 #2 <3
LIGHT 1 SHINES 6 <2 10 <0
LIGHTER 1 <1 LIGHTS <5 <3 <10 6
LIMB 6 %3 #3
LIME [1] 6 3 10
LIME [2] 6 %4 %5 #2
LINE 6 %1 #1
LINE [2] 1 <2 TRACES <12
LINEN 10 6 3
LINING 1 <1 LINES <3 <4 <5 <6 6 5
LINK 1 6 <1 LINKS <5 <10 <3
LINSEY 10 6 3
LION 6 7
LIP 6 %3 #1
LIVER [1] 1 <1 LIVES <3 4 7 6
LIVER [2] 6 %3 #2 %5
LIVING 1 <1 LIVES <4 10
LOADING 1 <1 LOADS <4 <5 <6 10
LOCK 1 LOCKS 6 <1 <5 <9 %1 %6 %7 #1 <10
LOCKNIT 3 6 10
LOOK 1 LOOKS <1 <0
LOOKING 1 <1 LOOKS <4 10
LORD 4 6 1 <2 RULES <5 <6 <11 <16
LOTION 6 1 <2 WASHES <14
LOVE 1 LOVES <1 <5 <7 10 <0
LOVER 1 <1 LOVES <5 <6 <3 4 6
LUNCH 6 %5 #4 1 <2 EATS <5 <12 10
LUST 1 LUSTS%FOR <1 10 <0 <5 <6
LYING/IN 1 LIES%IN <1 <4 10
MACHINE 1 MAKES 6 <2 <5 %1 #4 <14
MAGAZINE 6 2
MAGENTA 5 6 10
MAHOGANY 10 6 3
MAID 4 6 1 <2 WORKS <11
MAIDEN 4 6
MAIL [1] 1 19 <2 DELIVERS <5 <12 10 6
MAIL [2] 1 <2 WEARS <5 <12 10 %8 #4 6
MAIL [3] 1 6 19 TRAVELS <2 <11 <13 %1 #4
MAKER 1 <1 MAKES <3 <5 <16 4 6
MAKING 1 <1 MAKES <4 10
MALLOW 6 %4 #4
MAMMY 6 4

MAN 4 6 11 1 <2 MAKES WORKS SELLS LOOKS%AFTER RIDES <11 <5
MAN/OF/WAR %7 #4 6 1 <2 SAILS FIGHTS <11
MANAGER 1 <1 MANAGES <5 <3 4 6
MANNER 14
MANSION 6 2 %7 #4
MANTEL %7 #2 6
MANTLE 6 %8 #4 1 <2 WEARS <5 <12 19
MANUFACTORY %7 #4 6 2 1 <1 MANUFACTURES <5 <6 <22
MANUFACTURER 1 <1 MANUFACTURES <5 <3 4 6
MANUFACTURING 1 <1 MANUFACTURES <4 10
MAP 2 6
MARBLE 3 6 10
MARK 1 <1 MARKS <5 <6 <3
MARKET 1 2 SELLS 6 <2 <5 %2 #3 <13
MARRIAGE 1 <1 MARRIES <0
MARSH 2 6
MARTYR 4 6 1 <2 DIES%FOR%FAITH <11
MAST 6 %1 #2
MASTER 1 CONTROLS OR TEACHES 4 6 <2 <5 <6 <11 <16
MAT 2 6
MATCH 1 <2 PLAYS <12
MATCH [2] 1 <1 MATCHES <0 <9
MATCH [3] 1 <2 <14 LIGHTS 6 <5
MATE 1 <2 ACCOMPANIES <5 <7 <11 4 6
MATTER 6
MATTER/OF/FACT
MATTRESS 6 %6 #2
MEAL %5 #4 6 1 <2 EATS <12
MEAL [2] %5 #4 10 6
MEAR 6 7
MEASURE 1 <1 MEASURES <10 <5 <6
MEDICO 1 TREATS 4 6 <2 <11
MEMORIAL 6 1 <2 COMMEMORATES <5 <6 <14
MEMORY 1 REMEMBERS <2 <5 <6 <0 <14
MERCHANT 1 <2 TRADES%IN <5 <11 4 6
MESS [1] 1 <2 EATS <13 <0 6
MESS [2]
MESSAGE 1 SENDS <2 <12 <0 <16 16
METAL 3 6 10
MIDDAY 2 12 10
MIDNIGHT 2 12 10
MILE 2 3 20
MILK 10 6 %5 #3
MILL %1 %7 #4 1 <1 MILLS <5 <6 <22 6
MILLINERY %8 #4 6 10
MILLION 5
MIND 1 THINKS 6 <2 %3 #3 <11 <19
MINE 1 MINES 2 6 <1 <5 <6 <22

MINER 4 6 1 <1 MINES <5 <6 <3
MINERAL 3 6
MINIATURE 6
MINING 1 MINES 6 <1 <4 <5 <6 10
MINUTE 2 12
MIST 10 6
MISTRESS 4 6 1 <2 TEACHES CONTROLS <5 <6 <11
MIXING 1 MIXES <1 <5 <9 <4 10
MOLE 6 7
MONEY 1 BUYS <2 <5 <6 6 10 <14 <16
MOON 6 13
MOOR 2 6
MOPUS 10 6
MORNING 2 12
MOROCCO 2 6 10
MORTAL 4 6
MORTGAGE 1 <1 MORTGAGES <5 <6 <0
MOSQUITO 6 7
MOSS 6 %4 #1
MOTHER 1 NOURISHES 4 6 <2 <5 <6 <11
MOULD 1 <1 MOULDS <10 <5 6
MOUNTAIN 2 6
MOUNTAINEER 4 6 1 <2 LIVES%IN%MOUNTAINS CLIMBS%MOUNTAINS <11
MOUSE 6 7
MOUSTACHE 6 %3 #1
MOUTH 6 %3 #2 5
MUD 3 6 10
MUG 2 6
MULE 6 7
MURDER 1 <1 MURDERS <5 <6 <0 10
MUSEUM 2 %7 #4 6
MUSIC 1 <2 PLAYS <5 <12 2 10
MUSLIN 3 6 10
MUSQUET 1 <2 SHOOTS <5 <6 <14 6
MUSTARD 10 6 %5 #1
MUTTON 3 10 6 %5 #3
NACELLE %1 #2 6
NAIL 1 ATTACHES 6 <2 <5 %1 %3 #1 <14
NAME 5
NAVEL 6 %3 #1
NECK 6 %3 %8 #2
NECKERCHIEF %8 #4 6
NECKLACE %8 #4 6
NEEDLE 1 <2 SEWS <14 6
NEGRO 4 6
NEGUS 10 6 %5 #4
NEIGHBOUR 4 6
NERVE 6 %3 #1

NET 1 CATCHES CONFINES 3 6 10 <2 <5 <14
NEWS 10 1 <2 PUBLISHES <12 <5
NIGHT 2 12
NOG 10 6 %5 #4
NOISE 1 HEARS <2 10 <12
NOMINEE 1 NOMINATES 4 6 <1 <5 <7 <8
NONCHALANCE 14 10
NOTE 1 WRITES <5 <12 16 6 <2
NOVELTY 6
NOVICE 4 6 1 <2 LEARNS <19 <16 <5 <11
NUMBER 5
NUT 6 %4 %5 #1 %1
OAK %4 #4 3 6 8 10
OAT %5 %4 #2 6
OATH 1 <2 SWEARS <0
OFFICE 1 DEALS%WITH <13 <5 2 6 <2 %2 %7 #4
OFFICER 4 6
OIL 3 6 10
OLIVE 6 8 %4 %5 #3
OPERA 1 <2 SINGS <12 10
OPERATING 1 OPERATES <1 <4 <5 <9 10
OPERATION 1 OPERATES <1 <5 <9 <0
OPERATION [2] 1 <1 OPERATES%ON <5 <0
ORANGE 5 %4 %5 #2 6
ORCHESTRA 1 PLAYS 6 <2 %2 #3 <11
ORDER 1 ORDERS <1 <5 <16 <0 14
ORE 6 10
ORGANIZATION 1 <1 ORGANIZES <0 <8 %2 #4
ORPHAN 4 6
OSIER 3 %4 #4 6
OSTRICH 6 7
OUTING 1 <2 GOES%OUT <0
OVEN 6 1 <2 COOKS <5 <9 <14
OVERCOAT 6 %8 #4
OX 6 7
PACKER 6 4 1 <1 PACKS <5 <6 <3
PACKET 2 6
PACKING 1 10 <1 PACKS <5 <6 <4
PAD 6
PAD [2] 1 4 <2 ROBS <5 <6 <11
PADDLE 6 1 <1 PADDLES <5 <10 #2 %1
PAINT 1 PAINTS <1 6 10 <5 <6 <10
PAINTER 1 PAINTS 4 6 <1 <3 <5 <6
PAINTING 1 PAINTS 6 <1 <4 <5 <6 <16
PALANQUIN 6 %1 #4 1 <2 TRAVELS <11 <13
PALLET 1 <2 LIES <13 6 %6 #4
PALM 6 8 %3 %4 #4
PAN 2 6 1 <2 COOKS <13

PANE %7 #1 6
PANEL 2 6 %6 %7 #1
PANIC 1 PANICS <2 <0
PANTRY %7 #3 2 6
PANTS 6 9 %8 #4 1 <2 WEARS <5 <12
PAPER 2 3 6 10
PAPIER/MACHE 3 6 10
PARAFFIN 10 6 3
PARENT 4 6 1 <2 FATHERS%OR%MOTHERS <5 <6 <11
PARISH 2 6 %2 #3
PARK 2 6
PARLIAMENT %2 #3 1 <2 RULES <5 <6 <11 10
PARLOUR 2 %7 #3 6
PARQUET 3 6 10
PARSLEY 6 10 %4 %5 #4
PART 5
PARTICIPATION 1 PARTICIPATES <1 <10 <0 10
PARTING 1 <1 PARTS <9 <5 <4 10
PARTITION 1 DIVIDES 6 <2 <11 <0 <5 <6 %7 #2
PARTY [1] 1 <2 ENTERTAINS <5 <6 <0
PARTY [2] 4 6 %2 #3
PASSAGE 1 19 PASSES <0 <22 6 <2 %7 #3
PASSENGER 1 CARRIES 4 6 <2 <5 <12
PASSING 1 <1 PASSES <4 <5 <9 10
PASTE 10 3 6 %5 #4
PASTRY 10 6 %5 #3
PASTURE 2 1 <2 FEEDS%ON <5 <12 10 6
PATH 2 6 19
PATTERN 5
PAY 1 <1 PAYS IS%PAID <0 <8
PEA 6 8 %4 %5 #1
PEDAL 6 %1 #2
PEDESTAL 2 5 6
PEEP 1 <1 PEEPS <0
PEN [1] 1 WRITES 6 <2 <14 %1 #4
PEN [2] 2 6
PENCE 1 9 10 <2 COSTS IS%WORTH <5 <12 <6
PENCIL 6 1 <2 WRITES <14
PENNY 1 <2 COSTS IS%WORTH <5 <12 6
PENTHOUSE 2 6 %7 #4
PEOPLE 4 6 9
PEP 10 1 <1 PEPS%UP <5 <7 <3 <0
PEPPER 6 10 %4 %5 #1
PERIODICAL 2 6
PERRIWIG 6 %8 #4
PERSON 4 6
PERSPECTIVE 1 <2 VIEWS 14
PET 4 6 7

PETTICOAT 6 %8 #4
PEW 2 6
PEWTER 6 3 10
PHILOSOPHER 4 6 1 <2 LOVES%WISDOM <11
PHONE 1 TRANSMITS 6 <2 <5 <6 <16 <14 %1 #2
PHOTO 1 DEPICTS <2 <5 <6 <11 6
PHRASE 1 <2 SAYS <12 <5
PIANO 1 <2 PLAYS <12 <14 %1 %6 #4 6
PIANOFORTE 1 <2 PLAYS <12 <14 %1 %6 #4 6
PICK 1 <1 PICKS <5 <6 <10 6
PICTURE 1 DEPICTS 6 <2 <5 <6 <11
PIE 6 %5 #4
PIECE 6 5 <14
PIG 6 7
PIGEON 6 7
PILL 6 %5 #4 1 <2 TREATS <5 <14
PILOT 4 6 1 <2 GUIDES <11
PIN 1 SECURES OR PINS 6 <2 <5 <14
PINE 8 6 %4 #4
PINT 5
PIPE 6 1 <2 CONVEYS <11 <5
PISTOL 1 <2 SHOOTS <14 6
PIT 2 6
PIT [2] 6 %3 #1
PITCH [1] 3 6 10 %4 #1
PITCH [2] 5 2 1 <1 PITCHES <0
PLACE 2 6
PLAID 10 6 3 %8 #4
PLANE 1 19 TRAVELS 2 6 <2 %1 #4 <11 <13
PLANE [2] 6 8 %4 #4
PLANE [3] 5
PLANE [4] 6 1 PLANES <1 <5 <6 <10 %1 #4
PLANTATION 17 %4 #5 6
PLANTER 4 6 1 <1 PLANTS <3 <5 <6
PLASTER 6 3
PLATE 2 6
PLAY 1 <1 PLAYS <0 <5 <6
PLEA 1 <1 <0 PLEADS
PLEASURE 1 <2 TAKES%PLEASURE <0 10
PLOP
PLOUGH 1 PLOUGHS 6 <5 <6 <10 <1 %1 #4
PLUG 1 <2 PLUGS OR CONNECTS <5 <14 6
PLUM 6 8 %4 %5 #2 1 <2 EATS <12 <5
POACHING 1 10 <1 POACHES <4 <5 <6
POCKET 2 6 %8 #2
POET 4 6 1 <2 WRITES <5 <6 <11
POINT 5 2 12
POINTER 6 7 1 <1 POINTS <3

POISONING 1 POISONS <1 <4 <5 <7 <15 10
POKER 1 <1 POKES <5 <6 <10 6
POKER [2] 1 <2 PLAYS <12
POLICE 4 6 %2 #3
POLICY [1] 14
POLICY [2] 1 <2 PROVES <5 <14
POLISH 1 <1 POLISHES <5 <6 <10 6 10
POLITICS 9
POND 2 6
POP 1 <0 POPS <5 <9
POPLAR 8 %4 #4 6
POPPY %4 #2 6
PORCELAIN 3 10 6
PORCH 2 %7 #3 6
PORK 6 10 %5 #4
PORT 2 6
PORT [2] %5 #4 10 6
PORT [3] 6 %7 #3
POST [1] 6 %7 #1
POST [2] 1 CONVEYS 6 <2 <5 <14
POSTER 1 PUBLICIZES 2 6 <2 <5 <16 <11
POSTERN %7 #2 6
POT 2 6 3
POT [2] 3 6 10
POUCH 2 6
POWDER 10 6 <14
POWDER [2] 1 6 10 <2 MAKES%UP <5 <6 <14
POWER 5 14 10
PRAYER 1 <1 PRAYS <16 <19 <0
PREACHER 1 <1 PREACHES <3 6 4
PRESENT 6 1 <1 <5 PRESENTS <8
PRESERVING 1 <1 PRESERVES <5 <4 10
PRESS [1] 1 <2 PUBLISHES <5 <6 <11 13 %1 #4
PRESS [2] 1 2 PRESSES <1 <5 <22 %6 #4 6
PRESSURE 1 <1 PRESSES <5 <6 <10 5 10
PRICK 1 <1 PRICKS <5 <6 <0
PRINCE 4 6
PRINT 6 1 <1 PRINTS <0 <8 <5 <6
PRISON 2 %7 #4
PRISONER 1 <1 IMPRISONS <8 4 6
PRIVET 6 10 %4 #4
PRIZE 1 <2 WINS <12 6
PRO 1 PLAYS%FOR%MONEY 4 6 <2 <11
PROCESS 1 PROCESSES <2 <0 <5
PROFILE 5
PROFIT 1 <1 PROFITS <10
PROPERTY 1 <2 OWNS <12 10 6
PUDDING 6 %5 #4

PUMP 1 <1 PUMPS <5 <10 6
PUMP [2] 6 1 <2 WEARS <12 %8 #4
PUNCH 1 PUNCHES <1 <5 <0
PUNCH [2] 6 10 %5 #4
PUPPY 6 7
PURCHASING 1 <1 PURCHASES <4 <5 <6
PURSE 2 6
PURT
PUSHER 1 PUSHES 4 6 <1 <3 <5 <15
PUZZLE 1 PUZZLES <1 <5 <3
QUADRILLE 1 <2 DANCES <5 <6 <12
QUESTION 1 QUESTIONS <1 <5 <0
QUILT 6
RACE 1 <1 RACES <0 <9
RACING 1 RACES <1 <9 <4 10
RACKETING 1 RACKETS <1 <4
RADIO 1 TRANSMITS 6 %1 #3 <2 <5 <6 <14 <16
RAG 3 6
RAIL 6 2
RAIN 1 6 10 RAINS <0 <1 <3
RAKE 6 RAKES 1 <1 <10 <5
RALLY 1 <1 RALLIES <0 <5 <6 <9
RAMBLING 1 <1 RAMBLES <4 10
RANGE %7 #3 2 6
RASPBERRY 6 %5 %4 #2
RATE [1] 5 14
RATE [2] 1 <2 PAYS <5 <12 6 <0
RAYON 3 6 10
RAZOR %1 #4 6 1 <2 SHAVES <5 <6 <14
READING 1 <1 READS <5 <6 <4 10
RECEPTION 1 13 RECEIVES <0 6 <1 <5 <22 %7 #3
RECESS 5 2 6
RECORD 1 RECORDS 6 <1 <0 <5 <6 <16 <22
RED 5 10
REGIMENT 6 %2 #3
REHEARSAL 1 <1 REHEARSES <5 <6 <0
REMARK 1 <1 REMARKS <0 <16
RENT 1 <2 PAYS <5 <12 10
REP [1] 1 <2 PLAYS 14 10
REP [2] 3 10 6
REPEATER 1 <1 REPEATS <3 <9 6
REPRODUCTION 6 1 <1 REPRODUCES <5 <9 <8 <0 <3
RESIDENCE 1 <1 RESIDES <0 <22 6 10
RESORT 1 <1 RESORTS%TO <8 <5 6
RETAIL <14
REVENUE 1 <2 COLLECTS <5 <12 10 6
RHUBARB 10 6 %4 %5 #4
RIDING 1 <1 RIDES <4 <5 <6 10

RIM 5 6
RING [1] 1 WEARS 6 <2 <5 <12
RING [2] 2 6
RING [3] 1 SOUNDS <2 <11
RINGLET 6 %3 #1
RISE 1 <1 RISES <0 10
RITE 1 PERFORMS <2 <5 <12 <16 <0
RIVER 6 2
ROAD 2 6 19
ROADS 9 6 2
ROBBERY 1 <1 ROBS <5 <6 <0
ROCK 2 3 10 6
ROCKING 1 <1 ROCKS <9 <4 10
ROD <14 6
ROLL 1 6 ROLLS <1 <5 <8 <9 <0
ROLL [2] 6 %2 #3
ROLL [3] 6 %5 #4
ROLLER 1 <1 ROLLS <3 <10 6
ROOF 2 6 %7 #3
ROOM 2 6 %7 #3
ROPE 5 6
ROSE 6 %4 #2
ROUPING 1 <1 ROUPS(SELLS) <5 <6 <4 10
ROUT 1 2 12 <2 ENJOYS <5 <12
ROUTE 2 6
ROUTINE 14
RUBBER 3 6 8 %4 #3 10
RUDDER %1 #2 1 <2 STEERS <5 <6 <14 6
RUG 6 %6 #2 1 <2 COVERS <14
RULE [1] 1 RULES <1 <5 <0
RULE [2] 1 MEASURES <2 <14 %1 #2
RUM 10 %5 #4 6
RUMBLING 1 <1 RUMBLES <4
RUNNING 1 RUNS <1 <4 10 <16
RUSH 6 %4 #3 3
RUSK 6 %5 #4
RYE 10 6 %4 %5 #3
SADDLE 6 1 <2 SITS <13
SAFE 2 6 %6 %7 #3
SAFETY 1 <2 MAKES%SAFE <5 <6 10 14
SAFFRON 5 10
SAIL 6 1 <1 SAILS <0 <9 <10
SAILING 1 SAILS <1 <4 <5 <9 10
SAILOR 4 6 1 <1 SAILS <3
SAINT 4 6
SAKE 5
SALARY 1 <2 EARNS <5 <12
SALE 1 <1 SELLS <0 <5 <9

SALOON 6 2 %7 #3 %1
SALT 3 6 10 %5 #1
SALUTE 1 <1 SALUTES <0 <5 <6 <7
SAMPLE 1 SAMPLES 6 <1 <8
SANCTUS 1 <2 PRAYS <5 <12 13
SAND 6 2 10 3
SANDWICH 6 %5 #4
SATIN 6 10 3
SAUCE 10 6 %5 #4 1 <2 SEASONS <5 <11
SAUSAGE %5 #4 6
SAVING 1 6 SAVES <1 <4 <5 <6 <8 <16
SAVINGS 1 6 9 SAVES <1 <5 <8
SAVOUR 5
SAW 1 6 <1 SAWS <5 <6 <10
SAYING 1 <1 SAYS <5 <4 <8 <16 <19
SCALLOP 5 6 7
SCARF 6 %8 #2 1 <2 WEARS <12
SCENE 2 6
SCHEME 14
SCHOOL 1 2 STUDIES 6 <2 %2 %7 #4 <5 <6 <13
SCRAPER 1 SCRAPES 6 <1 <3 <5 <10
SCRAWL 6 1 <1 SCRAWLS <12
SCREEN 1 <1 SCREENS <5 <3 6 2
SCREW 1 FIXES TIGHTENS TURNS 6 <2 <5 <12 <14 %1 #1
SCRIPTURE 2 10
SCROLL 2 6
SCRUBBING 1 SCRUBS <1 <4 <5 <6 10
SCULLERY 2 6 %7 #3
SCUTTLE 2 6
SEA 2 6 13
SEAL [1] 6 7
SEAL [2] 1 SEALS <1 <5 <3 6
SEARCH 1 SEARCHES <1 <5 <0
SEASON 2 12
SEAT 1 <2 SITS%ON <5 <12 6 %6 #2
SECOND 2 12
SECRET 1 <2 CONCEALS <5 <12
SECTION 20
SECURITY 10 14
SEED 6 %4 %5 #1
SELLER 1 <1 SELLS <3 <5 <9 4 6
SENSATION 1 <2 FEELS <5 <0 <12 <16
SERVANT 1 SERVES 4 6 <1 <3 <5 <6 <7
SERVICE 1 <1 SERVES <0 <5 <6 <10 6 10
SET [1] 1 SETS <1 <0 <5 <9 <22
SET [2] 17 6 <14
SETTER 1 <1 SETS <5 <3
SEVENPENCE 9 1 <2 COSTS IS%WORTH <12

SEWING 1 <1 SEWS <5 <6 <4
SEX 10
SHAFT 2 6
SHAKE 1 <1 SHAKES <0 <8 <5 <9 6 10
SHAPE 5
SHARE 1 SHARES 6 <1 <5 <8
SHARE [2] 6 %1 #1
SHARK 6 7
SHAVING 1 <1 SHAVES <4 <5 <6 10
SHAWL 6 1 <2 WEARS <12
SHED %7 #4 2 6
SHEEP 6 7
SHEET 6 2
SHELL 5 %5 %3 #1 6
SHIFT [1] %8 #4 6
SHIFT [2] 1 <1 SHIFTS <5 <9 <0
SHILLIN' 1 <2 COSTS IS%WORTH <12 <5 6
SHILLING 1 <2 COSTS IS%WORTH <12 <5 6
SHINE 1 SHINES <1 <0
SHIP %7 #4 6 1 19 <2 SAILS <11
SHIRT 6 1 <2 WEARS <5 <12 %8 #4
SHIRTING 10 3 6
SHOAR 6 20
SHOE 1 <2 WEARS <5 <12 %8 #3 6
SHOOTING 1 <1 SHOOTS <4 <5 <6
SHOP 1 SELLS 6 <2 %7 #4 <5 <9 <13
SHOPPER 1 SHOPS 4 6 <1 <3
SHORE 20 6
SHORTAGE 1 <2 IS%SHORT <0
SHOT 1 SHOOTS <1 <5 <6 6 <0
SHOULDER 6 %3 #3
SHOULDER/OF/MUTTON 6 %3 %5 #3
SHOVEL SHOVELS 1 <1 <5 <10 6
SHOW 1 <1 SHOWS <5 <9 <0
SHOWER 1 <1 SHOWERS <0
SHRUB [1] 10 6 %5 #4
SHRUB [2] 6 %4 #4
SHUTTER [1] 1 6 <1 SHUTS <3 <5 <9
SHUTTER [2] 1 6 COVERS <2 <11 %7 #1
SICK 13 6 4
SICKNESS 1 <2 CAUSES <5 <16 %9 #4
SIDE 20 %3 #2
SIGHT 1 <1 SEES <0 <8 <10
SIGN 6 1 <1 SIGNIFIES <5 <3
SIGNET 1 <2 SEALS <14 <5 <6 6
SILK 3 6 10
SILL 6 %7 #1
SILVER 3 6 10

SINGER 1 <1 SINGS <5 <6 <3
SINGLET 1 6 <2 WEARS <12 %8 #4
SIPHON %1 #3 6 1 <1 SIPHONS <5 <10
SISTER 4 6
SITE 2 6
SITTING 1 <1 SITS <4 10
SIX 5
SIZE 5
SKATING 1 <1 SKATES <4 10
SKI 1 <1 SKIS <0 <10 6
SKIN 3 6 %3 #2
SKULL 6 %3 #3
SKY 2 6 13
SLAM 1 SLAMS <1 <5 <9 <0
SLATE 3 10 6
SLAVE 1 SERVES 4 6 <2 <11
SLEEPING 1 <1 SLEEPS <4
SLEEVE 6 %8 #3
SLIDE 1 SLIDES 6 <1 <5 <9 <3 <0 <22 %1 #1
SLIP [1] 1 <1 SLIPS <0
SLIP [2] 1 <2 WEARS <12 %8 #4
SLIPPER 6 %8 #3 1 <2 WEARS <12
SLOP 1 6 <1 SLOPS <9 <5 <6 <0
SMELL 1 <1 SMELLS <0
SMELLING 1 <1 SMELLS <9 <5 <4 10
SNAP 1 SNAPS <1 <8 <0
SNAP [2] 1 6 10 EATS <2 <12 %5 #4
SNIPE 6 10 7
SNOW 3 6 10
SOAP 10 6 1 <2 WASHES <14
SOCKET 1 HOLDS 6 <2 <11
SODA 10 6 %5 #3
SOFA 6 %6 #4
SON 4 6
SONATA 1 <2 PLAYS <12 <5
SONG 1 <1 SINGS <5 <6 <8
SOOT 6 3 10
SORT 17
SOUND 1 HEARS <0 <2 <5 <12
SOUP 10 6 %5 #4
SPECTACLES 6 9 1 <2 WEARS <5 <12
SPEECH 1 <1 SPEAKS <0 <5 <6
SPEED 14 10
SPELLING 1 <1 SPELLS <5 <6 <4 10
SPIKE 5 6
SPINNING 1 <1 SPINS <5 <6 <4 10
SPIRAL 1 WINDS 6 <2 <11
SPONGE 6 8 %4 #3

SPOON 6 1 <2 EATS STIRS <14
SPORT 1 <2 ENJOYS <12 <5 10 14
SPREAD 5 1 <1 SPREADS <0 <3 <8 <9 <5
SPRING [1] 2 12 13
SPRING [2] 1 RECOILS 6 <2 %1 #1 <11
SPRIT 5 6
SPRUCE 6 %4 #4
SQUAD 6 %2 #5
SQUAWK 1 SQUAWKS 7 <1 <0
SQUEEZER 1 6 <1 SQUEEZES <5 <3 <10
SQUIRE 4 6
STACK 17 1 <1 STACKS <22 <5 6
STAFF 1 4 <2 WORKS <11 %2 #3 13
STAGE 2 5 6
STAIR 2 6 19 %7 #2
STALK %4 #1 6
STAND 1 <1 STANDS <0 <22 6
STANDARD 2 5
STANE 3 6 10
STAR 1 6 <2 SHINES <11
STATE [1] 5
STATE [2] %2 #4 6
STATION 1 STANDS <13 6 <2 %7 #4
STATION [2] 2 6
STEAMER 6 %1 #4 1 <1 STEAMS <3
STEED 6 7 1 <2 CARRIES <5 <11
STEEL 3 6 10
STEERING 6 %1 #3 1 <1 STEERS <4 <5 <6
STEP %7 #1 6 1 <1 STEPS <22 <0
STEW 10 6 %5 #4
STEWARDESS 4 6 1 <2 LOOKS%AFTER <5 <11
STICK 5 6 <14
STICK [2] 6 4
STOCK 1 STORES 6 <2 <12 %1 #4
STOCKING 6 %8 #3 1 <2 WEARS <12
STONE 3 2 6 10 %7 #3
STONE [2] %5 #1 6 %4
STORE 1 <1 STORES <5 <22 6
STORM 1 BLOWS <2 <11 6
STORY 1 <2 NARRATES <5 <12 <16
STRAITS 2 6 9
STRANGER 4 6
STRAP %8 #2 6 1 <2 FASTENS OR RETAINS <5 <14
STRAW 3 6 10 %4 %5 #2
STREAM 6
STREET 2 6
STRETCHER 2 6 1 <1 STRETCHES <9 <3
STRING 3 6 10 5 <14

STRIPE 5 6
STRONGHOLD 1 PROTECTS <5 <13 6 <2
STRUCTURE 5 %7 #3
STUBBLE 6 5 %3 %4 #1
STUDY 1 2 <1 STUDIES <0 <22 <5 <6 6 %7 #3
STUFF 6 10
STUMP 5 6 <14
STYLE 5 14
SUEDE 3 10 6
SUGAR 6 10 %5 #3
SUIT 1 6 %8 #4 WEARS <2 <12
SUITE 2 6
SUMMARY 1 6 <1 SUMMARIZES <5 <22
SUMMER 2 10 12
SUN 13 6 1 <2 SHINES <11
SUPPER 1 <2 EATS <12 <5 %5 #4 6
SUPPLY 1 <1 SUPPLIES <0 <5 <8 13 6
SURFACE 6 2 20
SURGEON 4 6 1 <2 PRACTISES%SURGERY <11
SURPLUS 1 EXCEEDS 6 <2 <14
SWAIN 4 6 1 <2 RULES <11
SWAIN [2] 4 6
SWAMP 2 6
SWAN 6 7
SWEATER 6 %8 #4 1 <2 WEARS <12
SWEETHEART 4 6 1 <2 COURTS <5 <12
SWELL 1 <1 SWELLS <0
SWITCH %1 #1 1 <1 SWITCHES%ON <5 <10 6
SWIVEL 1 <1 SWIVELS <10 6
SYSTEM 14
TABLE 2 6 %6 #3
TABLET 6
TACKLE 6 <14 10
TAIL 6 %3 #2 %8
TAILORING 1 <1 TAILORS <5 <6 <4
TAKING 1 <1 TAKES <4 <5
TALK 1 <1 TALKS <0 10
TAN 1 5 <1 TANS <0 <5 <6
TANK [1] 2 6 %1 #3
TANK [2] 1 TRAVELS <2 6 <11 <13 %1 #4
TANKARD 2 6
TAP %1 #2 6
TAP [2] 1 <1 TAPS <5 <8 %8 #1
TAPE 5 3 10 6
TAPESTRY 2 3 6 10
TART %5 #4 6
TARTAN 3 6
TASSEL %8 #1

```
TAX 1 COLLECTS OR PAYS <2 <5 <12
TEA 6 8 1 <2 DRINKS EATS <5 <6 <12 %4 %5 #4 10
TEACHER 1 <1 TEACHES <5 <6 <3 <16 6
TEAK 3 6 8 %4 #4 10
TEAM 4 6 %2 #2
TEDDY 4 6
TELEGRAPH 1 <2 TRANSMITS <5 <6 <14 <16 %1 #2
TELEPHONE 1 TRANSMITS 6 <2 %1 #2 <5 <6 <14 <16
TELEPRINTER 1 TRANSMITS 6 <2 %1 #2 <5 <6 <14 <16
TELLER 1 <1 TELLS <5 4 6 <3
TENOR 1 SINGS 4 6 14 <2 <11
TENT 6 2
TEST 1 TESTS <1 <0 <5 <16
THEATRE 1 ACTS <13 6 <2 %7 #4
THING 6 <14
THORN 6 %4 #1
THOUGHT 1 <1 THINKS%ABOUT <0 <5 <16
THREAD %8 #1 10 6
THRUST 1 <1 THRUSTS <5 <6 <0 19
THUNDER 1 10 <1 THUNDERS <0
TICKET 1 ADMITS%TO OR INDICATES 6 <2 <5 <11 <16
TIE [1] 1 TIES 6 <1 <5 <8 <3 <0
TIE [2] 1 <2 WEARS <12 <5 6 %8 #2
TIGER 6 7
TIME 2 12
TIN 3 10 2 6
TINKLING 1 <1 TINKLES <4
TINT 5
TIP 5
TIP[2] 1 <2 GIVES <5 <12
TISSUE 3 6 %3 #2
TOAST 6 10 %5 #4
TOAST [2] 1 <2 DRINKS <12
TOASTING 1 <1 TOASTS <5 <6 <4 10
TOBACCO 10 6
TOE %3 #2 6
TOILET [1] 1 <2 PERFORMS <12 <5 13
TOILET [2] 2 6 13 1 <2 USES <12 %1 #4
TOKEN 1 <1 BETOKENS <5 <3 6
TOLL 1 <2 PAYS <12 <5
TOMB 2 6
TONE 1 <2 SPEAKS SINGS 14 <5 <6
TONGUE 6 %3 #2 1 <2 SPEAKS <14
TOOL 6 <14
TOOTH 6 %3 #1
TOP 20 6
TORCH 1 <2 LIGHTS <11 <5 <6 6
TOTAL 17 5
```

TOUCH 1 <1 TOUCHES <5 <0
TOURER 1 <1 TOURS <5 <6 <22 <3 %1 #4 6
TOWEL 6 1 <2 DRIES <5 <6 <14
TOWER 2 6 %7 #3
TOWN 2 6 %2 #5
TOXOPHILITE 4 6 1 <2 LOVES%ARCHERY <11
TOY 1 <2 MIMICS <11 <5 6 18
TRACK 1 <2 TRAVELS <13 6
TRADE 1 19 <1 TRADES <0
TRADER 1 19 <1 TRADES <3 4 6
TRADING 1 <1 TRADES <4 10
TRAFFIC [1] 1 10 TRADES%IN <2 <5 <0
TRAFFIC [2] 1 10 TRAVELS <2 6 <11 <13
TRAIN 1 TRAVELS 6 19 <2 <11 <13 %1 #4
TRAINING 1 <1 TRAINS <5 <6 <4 10
TRAITOR 4 6 1 <1 BETRAYS <5 <3
TRAM 1 <2 TRAVELS <11 <13 %1 #4 6 19
TRAP 1 <1 TRAPS <5 <10 %1 #2 6
TRAVEL 1 TRAVELS <1 <0 10
TRAVELLER 1 TRAVELS <1 <3 4 6
TRAVELLING 1 TRAVELS <1 <4 10
TRAY 2 6
TREAT 1 <1 TREATS <5 <6 <0
TREE 6 %4 #4
TRENCH 2 6
TRESTLE %6 #2 6
TRICK 1 DECEIVES <2 <0 <14
TRIP 1 <1 TRIPS <0
TROT 1 TROTS <1 <0
TROUSERS 6 9 1 <2 WEARS <5 <12 %8 #4
TRUCK 1 <2 TRAVELS <11 <13 6 %1 #4
TRUMP 6
TRUNK 2 6
TSETSE 6 7
TUB 2 6
TUCKER 6 %8 #2
TUN 5
TURN 1 TURNS 6 <1 <5 <9 <0 <22
TURNING/OUT 1 <1 TURNS%OUT <5 <6 <4 10
TURNPIKE 6 %1 #4
TURQUOISE 3 6
TWEED 3 10 6
TWILIGHT 12 2 10
TWINS 4 6 9
TWOPENNY 1 <2 COSTS IS%WORTH <12 <5 9
TYPE [1] 5 6
TYPE [2] 6 10 %1 #1 <14
UNDERCOAT 6 %8 #3

UNDERWEAR 6 10 %8 #3 1 <2 WEARS <5 <12
UNIFORM 6 %8 #4 1 <2 WEARS <5 <12
UNIVERSITY 1 <2 STUDIES <5 <6 <13 %7 %2 #3 6
URN 2 6
UTENSIL 1 6 <2 USES <12 <14
VAINQUEUR 4 6 1 <2 CONQUERS <5 <6 <11
VALLEY 2 6
VAMPIRE 4 7 6 1 <2 SUCKS%BLOOD <11
VANTAGE 1 <2 SURVEYS <5 <6 <13 <0 10
VASE 2 6
VAULT 2 6 %7 #3
VELVET 3 6 10
VESPER 2 12
VICUNA 3 6 7
VIEW 1 <0 <1 VIEWS <5 <6 <12
VILLA 2 6 %7 #4
VILLAGE 2 6 %2 %7 #5
VINE %4 #4 6
VINEGAR 6 10 %5 #4
VISION 1 <2 SEES <5 <6 <0 <12
VISTA 1 <2 SEES <0 <12
VOICE 1 <2 SPEAKS SINGS <5 <6 <14
VOLUME 5 6
WAGGER 1 <1 WAGS <3 <5 6
WAGON 1 TRAVELS 6 <2 %1 #4 <11 <13 19
WAINSCOTTING 2 6 10 %7 #1
WAIST 6 21 %3 %8 #1
WAITING 1 WAITS <1 <4 10
WAKES 1 <2 CELEBRATES <12 <5 13
WALK 1 6 <1 WALKS <0 <22
WALKING 1 <1 WALKS <4 10
WALL 1 SURROUNDS 2 6 <2 %7 #2 <11 <5
WALLET 2 6
WANDRING 1 <1 <4 WANDERS
WAR 1 <2 FIGHTS <12 <5
WARDEN 4 6 1 <2 LOOKS%AFTER <11 <5
WARDROBE 2 %6 #4 %8 6
WASH 1 <1 WASHES <0
WASHER [1] 1 <1 WASHES <3 %1 #4
WASHER [2] 6 %1 #1
WASHING 1 WASHES 6 <1 <4 <5 <6 <8 10
WAST 6 21 %3 %8 #1
WATCH [1] 1 WATCHES 4 6 <1 <3 <6 <5 %2 #3
WATCH [2] 6 %1 #4 1 <2 WEARS <5 <12
WATER 2 6 10 %5 #4
WATERING 1 <1 WATERS <5 <6 <4 10
WAX 3 6 10
WAY 2 6 14

```
WEATHER 10
WEAVER 1 <1 WEAVES <5 4 <3 6
WEDDING 1 WEDS <1 <4
WEEK 2 12
WEIGHT 5 6 1 <1 WEIGHS <0
WEIGHT [2] 6 1 <2 PRESSES <5 <11
WHEEL %1 #2 6
WHIN 6 10 3
WHIRL 1 <1 WHIRLS <0
WHISK 1 <1 WHISKS <5 <6 <0 <10
WHISKY 6 10 %5 #3
WHISTLE %1 #1 1 <1 WHISTLES <0 <10 6
WHISTLING 1 <1 WHISTLES <4
WICK 5 6
WIDOW 4 6
WIFE 4 6 11
WIND 1 <2 BLOWS <11 13
WINDOW 2 6 %1 %7 #2
WINE 10 6 %5 #4
WING 6 %3 #2
WINNER 1 <1 WINS <5 <6 <3 4 6
WIRE 3 10 %1 #1 5 6
WITCH 4 6
WITNESS 1 <1 WITNESSES <5 <6 <3 4 6
WOMAN 4 6 11 1 <2 MAKES WORKS SELLS LOOKS%AFTER RIDES <11
WOMEN 4 6 11 9 1 <2 MAKES WORKS SELLS LOOKS%AFTER RIDES <11
WOOD %4 #5 6 2 3 10
WOOL 3 6 10
WOOLSEY 3 10 6
WORK 1 WORKS 6 <1 <5 <9 <0 %1 #1
WORKING 1 <1 WORKS <4
WORM 6 7
WORMWOOD 6 10 %4 %5 #2
WORSTED 3 6 10
WRECK 1 <1 WRECKS <8 <0 <5 6
WRIGHT 1 <2 MAKES <5 <11 4 6
WRIST 6 %3 #2
WRITER 1 WRITES 4 6 <1 <3 <5 <6 <16
WRITING 1 WRITES 6 <1 <4 <5 <6 <8 <16
YARD 2 6 %7 #3
YOUTH 4 6 13
ZIPPER %8 #1 1 <1 ZIPS <10 <5 <6 6
**#
```

APPENDIX III

INDEX OF PROCEDURES

APPENDIX III

INDEX OF PROCEDURES IN THE INTERPRETATION PROGRAM

Prefatory Note

All the procedures in the program are given here. The reader may wish to compare the outlines of procedures given in Chapter 3. Or he may wish to trace the course of a noun sequence through the program, as I have done with council house.

There are some semantic patterns of noun sequences which are not represented in the data,[1] and others where the relationship between the nouns is not easily seen. In these cases, examples from outside the data are used in this Index without comment.

The number given on the same line as the name of a classifying procedure (e.g. C3 ... 3030) is the number which is used in the internal processes, and which is printed at the beginning of an interpretation using that procedure.

Many of the procedures have parameters in brackets, (roughly speaking) items which carry certain information into, and often out of, the procedure. For instance, the procedure Opbracket(c) is called with the parameter c having the value of a location on the card. If that location contains an opening bracket, Opbracket not only becomes 'true', but also adds one to c, and thus moves one place along the card. Similarly, Carderror (c) causes the computer to print the value of c, the location where an error on the card has been detected.

The procedures are given here in alphabetical order because (a) The reader may want to know where a procedure is called:

e.g. Opbracket is called from Nestfill, and
(b) The reader may want to know what other procedures are called by a given procedure.

Some Points about Procedures

Four points must be made about procedures.

1. Generally in computer programs procedures are used to avoid repetition. Some of my procedures are like this, for example the procedure Collate6, which embodies a process that is used, on average, 500 times in the search for each noun in the present dictionary. But others are written to encapsulate statements about grammatical structure, e.g. the procedure Findfields, which makes a group of comparisons between semantic features only once for each noun sequence. The advantage of embodying these rules in a procedure is that Findfields and the other seven comparable procedures can be arranged in various different orders until the most satisfactory order is reached.

2. An integer procedure, for the purposes of this book, is one that takes an integer value, i.e., roughly speaking, the value of a whole number, e.g. -1, 0, 1, 2. For example, the procedure Comp11 takes the value of the location in the dictionary at which a given noun is stored.

When it has taken this value, the procedure Lookup2 uses Comp11 to refer to the entry, and causes all the semantic features and relationship with verbs (e.g. paints for painting) to be copied into storage areas (in particular, the arrays Nouns and Feats) ready for the interpretation procedures (e.g. Analyze).

3. A boolean procedure is simply a procedure which takes the value 'true' or 'false'. For example, the procedure Opbracket is called from Nestfill to see whether the next character to be read from the card is an opening bracket. If

Opbracket becomes 'true', as in (*show + room*) *stair*, then *Nestfill* moves down to a lower level of the Nest to accommodate the nested sequence.

Some procedures have been made boolean not for such a specific purpose, but for the Mainprogram and the higher-level procedures (e.g. *Nestfill*, *Analyze*) to monitor that the analysis is taking place. For example, *Locfind* yields 'true' if a locative interpretation has been made. A 'false' result would not activate the procedure *Pset* and might even lead to an Equative interpretation.

4. A recursive procedure is one that calls itself. An example of recursion is found in the procedure *Anafledge*, which governs the procedure *Analyze*, the most important of all the procedures. *Anafledge* calls the procedure *Infledge*. *Infledge* operates to give a numerical value to the head and the modifier. The numbers identify the nouns, e.g. 1, 2 and 3 for (*bear + skin*) *rug*. These appear thus in the Nest:

← x →

1	2	y
rug	-2	-1
skin	bear	-2

← x →

1	2	y
3	-2	-1
2	1	-2

Infledge normally yields 1 and 2 (i.e. for a simple two-word sequence), and then the analysis takes place. When *Infledge* meets a negative number in the Nest, it calls *Anafledge*, which then analyzes e.g. *bear + skin* before coming up to perform an analysis at the level of *rug*. Thus *Anafledge* (indirectly) calls itself.

To cite another example of recursion, this time from the output procedures: *Fledge*, which rules the output of interpretations, calls *Phrasout* to output a phrase such as (for *council house*):

A house made by or belonging to a council.

Here <u>council</u> and <u>house</u>, being single nouns, are easily output by <u>Nounout</u> (under the instruction of <u>Phrasout</u>). Where nesting occurs, as in (<u>bear + skin) rug</u>, <u>Fledge</u> instructs <u>Phrasout</u> to yield a paraphrase of the noun sequence. <u>Nounout</u> yields <u>a rug</u>. However, when <u>Nounout</u> meets (<u>bear + skin</u>) it calls <u>Fledge</u> to paraphrase <u>bear + skin</u>:

A rug made of <u>the skin of a bear</u>.

In this case, <u>Fledge</u> ultimately calls itself.

Recursion can take place several times, as in the analysis of

(front (drawing-room)) twilight.

Another example (from outside the data) is

school ((foot + ball) game).

The computational recursions mentioned in this section reflect recursive patterns in the natural language being analyzed.

<u>A1</u>

This name is reserved for the wide range of sentence examples (excluding locative sentences): e.g. <u>car thief</u>, <u>sunrise</u>. In the Interpretation files, the underlying sentences of the <u>A1</u> type are given, e.g.

Someone steals a car
The sun rises.

They are referred to as <u>Sentence 1</u>, <u>Sentence 2</u> etc. The term <u>A1</u> does not, therefore, appear, but it is reserved in case it is

A1, cont'd.

needed for further study. It is mentioned here lest the reader, finding A2, A3 etc., should search for A1 as a type identifier.

A2 (y, z) boolean 1020

Called from Phrasout. Calls Phrase.

y and z denote axes of the Nest. These are necessary to locate the nouns denoted by the numbers.

Procedures A2 to A5 inclusive represent sentence types, the relationships denoting an activity.

A2 causes a paraphrase of the noun sequence to be printed out. Phrasout picks up from the Nest the number denoting the relationship. Phrase prints the two nouns on either side of the preposition or other expression which is provided by A2, e.g. paraffin cooker:

A cooker powered by paraffin.

The numbers offered as parameters for Phrase indicate what articles the nouns will require, and whether the modifier should be printed as plural. A2 becomes 'true' when the paraphrase has been printed.

A3 (y, z) boolean 1030

As for A2; e.g blackwater fever, train-fever:

A fever causing or caused by {black water / a train or trains}

A4 (y, z) boolean 1040

As for A2; e.g. Lincoln car:

A car made by or belonging to Lincoln.

A5

A5 (y, z) boolean 1050

As for A2; e.g. police truncheon:

A truncheon belonging to the police.

Addifind boolean

Called from Analyze. Calls Relate.

Where head and modifier are proper nouns and the sequence is hyphened, Addifind registers the Additive relationship, e.g. Lampton-Lufford in (Lampton-Lufford) report.

Addpref (lz)

Called from the Mainprogram.

Addpref is called when there is homography.

After the operation of Anafledge, the number of homographic variants is known, and Anafledge yields the figure of the last filled face on the z-vector of the Nest. lz (last z) takes the value of that figure. Addpref reads all the priority numbers from the Nest and adds up the nested ones. It gives weight to the higher numbers by squaring numbers before adding them. Weight is also added to the numbers of nested sequences, as the numbers of the non-nested sequence are not squared. Addpref stores the resultant priority numbers in the array Pref, to be used by the procedure, Order. The highest numbers rank as best.

Adject (b, n, OUT) boolean

Called from Nountr. Calls Carderror.

b denotes the location on the card where < occurs. n denotes the noun (e.g. boy) in connexion with which the adjective is to be stored. OUT denotes the label in Nountr to which to

Adject, cont'd.

jump if there is an error on the card.

Adject is called when an opening angle bracket (<) occurs on the card, e.g. *<little-> boy class*. Such a bracket usually indicates a premodifier.

When the premodifier is found, pointers to its first and last letters on the card are placed in the array Adj, and *Adject* becomes 'true'. *b* is moved to the beginning of the noun. If <and> or <or> is found, *Adject* yields 'false', and does not move *b*.

Adjp(n)

Called from *Nounp*. Calls *Printch*.

Adjp prints the adjective associated with the noun denoted by *n*. E.g. when *n* denotes *boy* in *little-boy class*, *Adjp* will print the word *little* before *boy*.

An (n)

Called from *Nounout* and *Slotout*. Calls *Printch* and *Writetext*. *An* is available to print the indefinite article before the noun denoted by *n*. E.g. the sentence output for *coal-rake* is

Someone rakes coal with a rake or rakes.

This illustrates how *An* suppresses the article when a noun does not take an indefinite article or is plural. If the noun denotes something unique, e.g. *sky*, *An* will print *the*. If the noun begins with a vowel, *an* is printed; if not, *a* is printed.

Anafledge (lfg, y, lz) boolean

Called from the Mainprogram and from *Infledge*. Calls *Analyze*, *Infledge*, *Newline*, *Print*, *Recover*, *Tidy* and *Writetext*.

Anafledge, cont'd.

Anafledge is an important recursive procedure to analyze noun sequences at each level in the Nest. It can be thought of as 'fledging' the relationship from the Nest. It puts the type numbers into the 'left-hand side' of the Nest (i.e. where x = -1 to -7). Each homography causes a new 'face'[2] on the z-axis to be set up, and any previous analysis to be copied into it. E.g. for (night-time) watch, where watch is ambiguous, meaning a mechanism or a person, night-time is analyzed in Nest [x, -2, 1], and when at the level Nest [x, -1, 1] the ambiguous watch is discovered, Anafledge copies into Nest [x, -2, 2] the analysis already made of night-time.

lfg denotes the 'last filled g': the last filled row of Slots. It is used as a parameter when Anafledge calls Analyze. lz denotes the last filled z-face of the Nest, for polysemy.

The variables head and mod in turn take the value of the procedure Infledge. Infledge takes the value of the noun in Nest [x, y, z]. If Nest [x, y, z] holds a negative number instead of a (positive) reference to a noun, Infledge calls Anafledge to analyze the nested sequence to which the number points downwards in the Nest.

The head and modifier (e.g. wall and stone in stone wall) activate Infledge, and take its integer value. Infledge yields, when it has traced a noun to its lowest level in the Nest, statements that the noun or nouns are at their lowest: headeepest and modeepest.

By acting recursively, through Infledge, Anafledge reaches the lowest nested noun sequence and analyzes it, gradually moving up the Nest until it has analyzed the highest noun sequence.

For the purpose of analysis, if the head or modifier is represented only by a pointer to its deepest level, the head or modifier from the deepest level is recovered. E.g. in (show + room) stair, after show + room has been analyzed, room is

Anafledge, cont'd.

recovered so that its relationship with stair can be determined.

Next, Anafledge deals with a minor matter which has to be settled here or in Analyze: the occurrence of fellow and similar words, as in fellow passenger. If fellow occurs as the head, any features denoting an overt verb in the head are made 'false'. If it occurs as the modifier, the contents of Nest [1, y, z] and Nest [2, y, z] are exchanged. Also the feature 'human' which may occur on the modifier is set 'false'.[3]

These changes in the features are to prevent erroneous analyses. Fellow passenger will now yield someone that is also a passenger.

The procedure Analyze is called. If the Nest overflows with the type numbers, a notification is printed.

If the head or modifier is not at its deepest level, the procedure Tidy is called to tidy the type numbers by eliminating type numbers which are not taken up by the relationships at higher levels.

Finally, Anafledge checks whether polysemy occurs, and if it does, Anafledge loops back and goes through all the same processes, this time with z denoting another 'face' of the Nest. Anafledge becomes 'true' when it has fulfilled its duties. It would be 'false' if an expected noun were absent from the Nest.

Analyze (head, mod, lfg, y, z, headeepest, modeepest, pol, OVER)

Called from Anafledge. Calls Addifind, Equifind, Findfields, Hasverb, Locfind, Matheadfind, Matmodfind, Pannexfind, Pset, Redupfind and Verbalfind.

This important procedure analyzes a noun sequence in the Nest. The head is in Nest [1, y, z] and the modifier is in Nest

Analyze, cont'd.

[2, y, z]. Let either of these numbers be n. A negative n gives the lower value of y. The -2 in Nest [2, -1, z] causes us to think of the row y = -2, where we find 1 and 2, representing show and room.

Headeepest and modeepest are 'true' when the head or modifier respectively is not nested more deeply. Analyze records type numbers in Nest [x, y, z] when x is a negative number (the 'left-hand side' of the Nest), and records priority numbers in Nest [3, y, z]. If either of the arrays Slots and Nest overflows, there is a jump out of this procedure, to the label OVER.

The parameters refer to the head and the modifier as described under Anafledge. lfg, y and z are as previously described in connexion with the arrays Slots and Nest. Pol is true when Anafledge has found polysemy.

Inside Analyze are nine procedures which identify the different types of relationships between the nouns. (Sometimes one relationship is found by two procedures, following different routes.) The procedures identifying the types are Addifind, Equifind, Findfields, Locfind, Matheadfind, Matmodfind, Pannexfind, Redupfind and Verbalfind. The types sought are:

Addifind	Additive	May-June
Equifind	Equative	baby boy
Findfields	Annex	laurel leaf
Locfind	Locative	garden path
Matheadfind	Material	sheet copper
Matmodfind	Material	stone wall
Pannexfind	Annex	table top
Redupfind	Reduplicative	chug-chug
Verbalfind	Verbal	car thief

Analyze is the procedure which contains the order in which the program inspects the noun sequences for the relationship or relationships between the two nouns. These relationships and

A Diagram of the Nest

The array Nest is the array in which the nouns are stored at the beginning of each analysis and the type numbers are stored at the end.

Its definition is Nest [-7:3, -4:-1, 1:12]. This means that it has eleven locations on the x-axis, four on the y-axis, and twelve on the z-axis. It can be pictured like this:

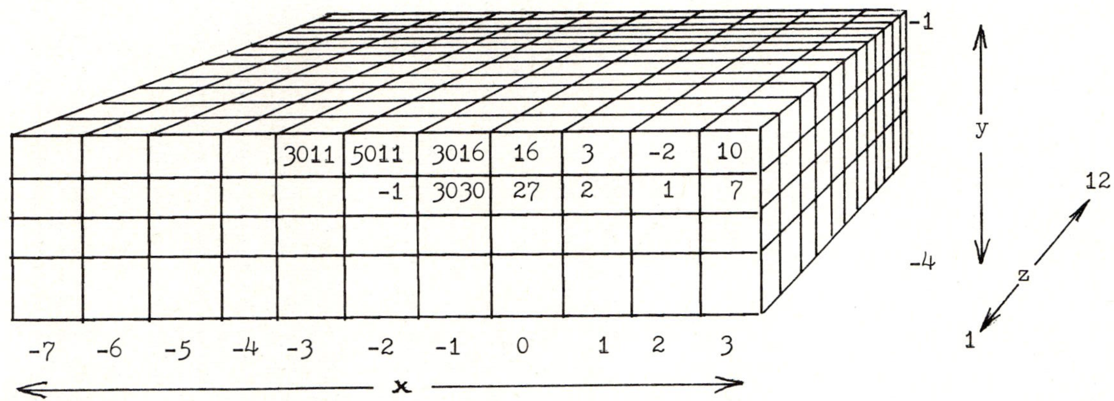

The numbers represent 3 meanings (one correct) of (bed + room) corridor.

Analyze, cont'd.

their order are mentioned elsewhere in this study. I ought to say that if there is homography, the order of inspection is somewhat different from the order where each noun has only one meaning. The latter and more commonly used order is:

Findfields
Matmodfind
Pannexfind
Verbalfind
Locfind
Matheadfind
Addifind
Redupfind
Equifind.

The procedure Pset places the priority number in column 3 of the Nest.

The importance of the procedure Analyze is that it calls the above procedures consecutively, so that I was easily able to shuffle them about when the order was shown, on application, to be wrong.

I found that for each noun sequence, access had to be allowed to most of the procedures, i.e. Analyze does not skip procedures except where, if Findfields is 'true', Analyze skips to the Verb and Locative procedures. None of the other procedures are skipped except the minor types Addifind and Redupfind, and Equifind when yielded by default.

For homography, the operation surrounding an Annex type, Findfields, causes a skip to procedures lower down the list. If more data is analyzed, it is possible that this 'skip' will have to be restrained.

The order of inspection is also the order for printing the paraphrases (which is done from another procedure, Fledge).

Attach (head, mod)

Called from Pannexfind.

Attach, cont'd.

In examples such as (table-top) polish, this procedure attaches the features of table to those of top. Top belongs to the category of the pure annex, and thus usually becomes locative when used as a modifier. When the analysis of (table-top) polish is made, after the annex relationship has been found for the nested table-top at the level where $y = -2$, the relationship at the level where $y = -1$ will be sought between top and polish. This would simply yield the locative top polish:

polish at the top

i.e. the top polish among other polishes, as described, for example, in an advertisement. But in (table-top) polish, we require top to have its annex meaning, not its locative meaning: and before the relationship between top and polish is sought, the features of table have to be attached to top.

B1

This name is reserved for a quite wide range of examples: the sentence examples containing locatives, e.g. towel disposal bin, birthday, pit-singlet. In the Interpretation files, the underlying sentences of the B1 type are given: e.g.

> Someone disposes of a towel or towels in a bin or bins;
> Someone is born in [= on] a day or days.

They are referred to as Sentence 1, Sentence 2 etc. The term B1 does not, therefore, appear.

The verb-locative examples span the distance between the purely verbal examples like headache and the purely locative examples like London house. Thus, the term B1 is reserved in case it is needed for further study. It is mentioned here lest

B1, cont'd.

the reader, finding C1, should search for B1 as a type identifier and not find it.

C1S1 (y, z) boolean 3011

Called from Phrasout. Calls Phrase.

y and z denote axes of the Nest, for locating the nouns denoted by the numbers.

Procedures C1S1 (i.e. C1 subtype 1) to C3 inclusive represent locative types.

C1S1 causes a paraphrase of the noun sequence to be printed out. Phrasout picks up from the Nest the number denoting the relationship. Phrase prints the two nouns on either side of the preposition, phrase or clause which is provided by C1S1; e.g. London house:

A house in or on London.

The numbers offered as parameters for Phrase indicate what articles the nouns will require, and whether the modifier should be printed as plural.

C1S1 becomes 'true' when the paraphrase has been printed.

C1S2 (y, z) boolean 3012

As for C1S1; e.g. Newark man:

A man that lives in or comes from Newark.

C1S3 (y, z) boolean 3013

As for C1S1; e.g. pit pony:

A pony that lives in or works in a pit.

C1S4 (y, z) boolean 3014

Calls Writetext as well as Phrase, for The kind of. Otherwise, as for C1S1; e.g. deckchair:

The kind of chair used in or on a deck.

C1S5 (y, z) boolean 3015

Calls Writetext as well as Phrase, for The kind of. Otherwise, as for C1S1; e.g. mountain ash:

The kind of ash found in or on a mountain.

C1S6 (y, z) boolean 3016

As for C1S1; e.g. parlour stair:

A stair to a parlour.

C2 (y, z) boolean 3020

As for C1S1; e.g. bottom drawer:

The drawer at the bottom.

C3 (y, z) boolean 3030

As for C1S1; e.g. art gallery:

A gallery for or containing art.

Carderror (c)

Called from Adject, Nestfill and Nountr. Calls Newline, Print and Writetext.

Carderror, cont'd.

c denotes a location on the card.

Carderror prints a warning when a simple error is found on the card, and gives the location. It operates, for example, when three successive nouns are found without bracketing, giving the location of the first letter of the third noun.

Cardin

Called from the Mainprogram. Calls Nextch, Readch and Skipch.

Cardin reads a line of 80 characters or less into the array Card. (The line may be shorter than 80 characters if tape or teletype input is used.)

Clobracket (c) boolean

Called from Nestfill.

This procedure deals with Card[c], i.e. the location c in the array Card. Clobracket becomes 'true' and adds 1 to c if Card[c] contains a closing round bracket, as for instance after room in

(show room) stair.

Code (c)

Called from Verbp and Verbinterp.

Code takes the value of the internal representation of character c, which may be any character in the set.

Codig

Called from Nountr. Calls Writetext.

Codig, cont'd.

When <and> or <or> is encountered in the noun sequence, Codig writes 'Card skipped because of coordinator or special modifier'.

Collate6 (Nar) integer

Called from Comp11.

Collate6 is a procedure for finding a noun in the dictionary.

Nar is an array to hold a noun. It is assumed that it holds a noun in location [1] to location [Nar [0]]: i.e. the number of the last filled location is stored in Nar [0].

The dictionary, similarly, stores the last location of the letters of the noun in Dict [g], where the noun begins in Dict [g + 1].

Collate6 assumes that there is a word in Nar [1] to Nar [Nar[0]]. It compares it with a word in Dict [g + 1] to Dict [g + Dict[g]]. It yields (i.e. as the integer value of Collate6) the location of the same noun in the dictionary. If the noun is not in the dictionary, it yields -7 (a number lower than the negative numbers usually encountered as pointers in the dictionary). It yields 3 if the word in Nar is lower than the word being inspected in the dictionary (i.e. earlier in the alphabet). It yields 2 if the word in Nar is higher (later in the alphabet) than the word in the dictionary. It yields 1 when the words are equivalent.

Comp11 (Nar) integer

Called from Lookup2. Calls Collate6.

Comp11 is a procedure for giving the location of a noun in the dictionary.

Nar is an array to hold a noun. It is assumed that it holds a noun in location [1] to location [Nar[0]]: i.e. the number of

Comp11, cont'd.

the last filled location is stored in Nar [0]. Using Collate6, Comp11 compares the noun in Nar with nouns in Dict [6: Dict [-6]]. It yields the location of the same noun in the dictionary: i.e. it takes the value of the integer location of the noun. If the noun is not in the dictionary, Comp11 yields -7 (a number lower than the negative numbers usually encountered in the dictionary).

The noun is in locations 1 to Nar [0] of Nar, and in locations [g + 1] to [g + Dict [g]] of the dictionary. (When used in connexion with the dictionary, g represents the first positive location of a word.)

Copy (g, lfg)

Called from Fitonoun.

g designates a row of the array Slots, which holds sentences. lfg denotes the latest row to be filled. This procedure copies row g of Slots into row lfg, e.g. when there are two interpretations for the noun being fitted into the sentence, one as object and the other as instrument:

Someone collects.
Someone collects cutters.
Someone collects [rose-hips] with cutters.

Copies are occasionally made unnecessarily, but unnecessary copies are not passed on to the paraphrases.

D1 (y, z) boolean 4010

Called from Phrasout. Calls Phrase.

y and z denote axes of the Nest, for locating the noun denoted by the numbers.

D1, cont'd.

Procedures D1 to D4 inclusive represent Annex types. D1 causes a paraphrase of the noun sequence to be printed out. Phrasout picks up from the Nest the number denoting the relationship. Phrase prints the two nouns on either side of the preposition which is provided by D1; e.g. hillside:

The side of a hill.

The numbers offered as parameters for Phrase indicate what articles the nouns will require, and whether the modifier should be printed as plural.

D1 becomes 'true' when the paraphrase has been printed.

D2 (y, z) boolean 4020

As for D1; e.g. apron strings:

The strings of an apron.

D3 (y, z) boolean 4030

As for D1; e.g. Army captain:

A captain in the Army.

D4 (y, z) boolean 4040

As for D1; e.g. armchair:

A chair with an arm or arms.

Defin (g, n)

Called from Lookup2 and Polyin. Calls Expand2.

Defin, cont'd.

Initially, g denotes the location in the dictionary of the noun being dealt with. n denotes the noun.

Defin puts definitions (composed of semantic and syntactic features) from the array Dict into the arrays Nouns and Feats. It puts the associated verbs into the array Verbs and their features into the array Vfeats.

Dict [g] identifies the word. Dict [g + Dict [g]] stores the end of the word.

The primary features from Dict [g + Dict [g] + 1] go into Feats [1, b, n] as bits (i.e. binary digits), which are thus set 'true'. The secondary features (those applicable to verbs) from Dict [g + Dict [g] + 2] go into Nouns [-2, n] as an integer and into Feats [2, b, n] as bits. The tertiary features (denoting semantic fields) from Dict [g + Dict [g] + 3] go into Nouns [-3, n] as an integer and into Feats [3, b, n] as bits. The size integer (in the fourth position among the features) goes from Dict [g + Dict [g] + 4] into Nouns [-4, n].

The total of verbs associated with this noun goes from Dict [g -4] into Nouns [-5, n]. The verbs themselves go into Verbs [letters, n, v]. Their features from Dict [vg + Dict [vg] + 2] go into Verbs [-1, n, v] as an integer and into Vfeats [n, b, v] as bits. The location g of the next homograph of the noun is taken from Dict [g -1] into Nouns [-1 , n]. If there is no homograph, g is -1.

E1 (y, z) boolean 5011-5015 This procedure is reached in six separate ways, but the equative paraphrase which is its output satisfies all six sources. These have been given in Chapter 1.

Called from Phrasout. Calls Phrase.

y and z denote axes of the Nest, for locating the nouns denoted by the numbers.

E1, cont'd.

Procedures E1 and E2 represent Equative types.

E1 causes a paraphrase of the noun sequence to be printed out.

Phrasout picks up from the Nest the number denoting the relationship.

Phrase prints the two nouns on either side of the clause which is provided by E1; e.g. baby boy:

A boy that is a baby.

The numbers offered as parameters for Phrases indicate what articles the nouns will require, and whether the modifier should be printed as plural. E1 becomes 'true' when the paraphrase has been printed.

E2 (y, z) boolean 5020

As for E1; e.g. divorce case:

A case of divorce.

(There is only one source for this, as opposed to E1.)

Equifind boolean

Called from Analyze. Calls Relate.

Equifind becomes 'true' when an Equative relationship has been found. Some equative relationships are detected during the operation of other procedures, e.g. the relationship in producer-director, which is detected during the operation of the procedure Verbinterp. But Equifind catches those examples that have slipped through the nets of the other typological procedures (i.e. Findfields etc.): the equative relationship is found by default. E.g. archetype orphan:

Equifind, cont'd.

An orphan that is an archetype.

The type number that Equifind yields is 5015.

Ergive (n)

Called from Fledge, Lower, Nounout, Record, Sentout, Slotout. Calls Writetext and Print.

Ergive uses Writetext to write Error number n encountered in analysis. n is printed as a number according to where Ergive has been called from, showing in which part of the analysis the error has occurred. For example, the procedure Fledge calls the procedure Slotout (for the printing of a clause), and Slotout may also call Fledge. In this case, two levels of the Slots are accessed. g is from the type number in the 'left-hand side' of the Nest. gg is a number held in Fledge. If they should become equal, Ergive is called, and prints a warning, as well as the number n (5) to show in which procedure the error was detected (in this case, the procedure Fledge).

Expand2 (bar, w, t, b, n)

Called from Defin.

Expand2 expands information, stored as bits (binary digits) in the computer word (unit of storage), into vector n of the array Bar. The bits are stored in the dictionary as parts of a (usually large) number.

In practice, Expand2 expands the features from the positions 0 to 22 in a computer word into a boolean array, Feats. w denotes the number stored in the word. In Feats they can easily be accessed without having to operate on the number which 'contains' the bits. The array Feats has the dimensions 1:t, 0:b and 1:m. t is the total of words to be expanded, in practice 3.

Expand2, cont'd.

b is 22: the highest used bit. n is the vector (of the array) into which the features of each noun are put. m is the highest permitted value of n, i.e. 7. Expand2 is also used to put the features of verbs into the array Vfeats.

Extend (z, lz)

Called from Polytest.

Normally the Nest is filled on only one 'face', i.e. it is used as a two-dimensional array, flat like a picture. Its dimensions are represented by x and y. But when there is polysemy, one or more 'faces' in the third dimension are brought into play, making it into a 3-dimensional box. The third axis is denoted by z. The analysis of the sequence with the second or subsequent meaning is carried out in the new z-face or z-faces. In a nested sequence, e.g. (canary-bird) bill, the polysemy may not be encountered until after the analysis of the nested nouns (canary and bird) has taken place. In this case the whole of the analysis hitherto done is copied into the z-face newly opened (for bill[2]).

F1 (y, z) boolean 6010

Called from Phrasout. Calls Phrase.

y and z denote axes of the Nest, for locating the nouns denoted by the numbers.

Procedures F1 to F4 inclusive represent Material types.

F1 calls for a paraphrase of a noun sequence to be printed out. Phrasout picks up from the Nest the number denoting the relationship. Phrase prints the two nouns on either side of the

F1, cont'd.

clause or preposition which is provided by F1; e.g. stone wall:

A wall of stone.

The clause containing made of is provided for the case where either (or both) of the sequences between which the F1 relationship exists is nested. Other types of relationship are expressed by of, e.g. D1, so when occurring with nesting, the F1 relationship is expressed more explicitly; e.g. mahogany (table top):

The top of a table made of mahogany.

The numbers offered as parameters for Phrase indicate what articles the noun will require, and whether a modifier should be printed as plural. F1 becomes 'true' when the paraphrase has been printed.

F2AND3 (y, z) boolean 6020 or 6030

Calls Phrase and Writetext.
As for F1; e.g. pipe-clay; sheet copper:

Clay for pipes;
Copper in the form of a sheet.

It is not possible to distinguish these two types by the use of features alone, and so F2 and F3 go to a common paraphrase which offers both types and meanings: pipe-clay:

Clay for pipes or clay in the form of a pipe.

F4 (y,z) boolean 6040, 6050

As for F1. Both the relationship numbers 6040 and 6050 lead

F4, cont'd.

to Type F4. 6040 and 6050 denote a relationship in which the head is a collective noun, e.g. 6040 haystack, 6050 tree-clump:

a stack of hay;
a clump of trees.

6040 is reached from the procedure Matmodfind, and 6050 from the procedure Findfields.

Fields (head, mod) boolean

Called from Findfields and Twoloc.

Fields inspects a noun sequence to see whether both its nouns belong to the same semantic field. The fields defined in this study are:

1. Mechanism, e.g. phone, car.
2. Human organization, e.g. clergy, police.
3. Part of the body, e.g. head, leg.
4. Plant or tree, or part of one, e.g. fruit, olive.
5. Food or drink, e.g. ham, beer.
6. Furniture, e.g. table, leg.
7. A building, or part of one, e.g. parlour, stair, house.
8. Clothing, e.g. button, collar.
9. Disease, e.g. fever, leprosy.

If one or more matches of fields occur, Fields becomes 'true'.

Findfields boolean

Called from Analyze. Calls Fields and Relate.

When the head and the modifier belong to the same semantic fields (which are listed above in the entry for the procedure Fields), several further steps are taken.

Findfields, cont'd.

If the head denotes a building or part of one, and also takes the preposition to (e.g. stair), Findfields yields the locative relationship 3016 (C1 subtype 6):

A stair to a parlour

rather than the Annex relationship 4010 (D1):

The stair of a parlour.

If the head is a collective noun, e.g. clump in tree-clump, a material relationship, 6050 (F5), is yielded:

A clump of trees.

Where the modifier is proportionally larger than the head, Type 4020 (D2) is yielded: fir-bough:

The bough of a fir.

Where the head is larger than the modifier, Type 4040 (D4) is yielded: cherry tree:

A tree with a cherry or cherries.

When both are the same size, Type 5011 (an Equative type) is yielded:

A tree that is a fir.

If Fields returns 'false', other ways of establishing a relationship through semantic fields are explored. If the head denotes a human being and the modifier a human organization, 4030 is yielded:

A man in the clergy.

<u>Findfields, cont'd</u>.

If the head denotes a part of the body and the modifier a human being or an animal, 4020 is yielded:

Hair of a horse.

If the modifier denotes a part of the body, and is itself modified (either by another noun or by an adjective), and if the head is human or animal, 4040 is yielded: <u>pudding-head Wilson</u>:

Wilson with a head that is a pudding.

If the head and modifier each denote a human being or an animal, provided that they are not agents of verbs, 5010 is yielded: <u>birdman</u> in one of its meanings:

A man that is a bird.

When any of the above relationships is yielded, <u>Findfields</u> is set 'true'.

<u>Fitonoun (f, g, lfg, lx, on, x, y, z, OLAB)</u> boolean

Called from <u>Setvnoun</u> and <u>Verbinterp</u>. Calls <u>Copy</u>, <u>Function</u>, <u>Hasverb</u>, <u>Lower</u>, <u>Record</u>, <u>Setrow</u>, <u>Tryitem</u>, <u>Trysent</u>.

When this procedure is called, a row of Slots has already been set up: e.g. <u>towel disposal</u> sets up a row with <u>dispose of</u> as the verb and <u>towel</u> as the object. <u>Fitonoun</u> tries to fit another noun, which we shall call <u>on</u>, into that row: e.g. with (<u>towel disposal) bin</u>, <u>bin</u> becomes the locative of place. <u>f</u> has the value of the function already filled by the noun with the verb: e.g. 2 (verb) for <u>disposal</u>, 3 (object) for <u>nominee</u>. <u>g</u> has a value on the <u>g</u>-axis of Slots (the vertical axis). <u>lfg</u> denotes the last filled <u>g</u>, i.e. the last filled row. <u>lx</u> denotes the latest value of <u>x</u> in the 'left-hand side' of the Nest, for

Fitonoun, cont'd.

use when the type number is recorded. *on* denotes the other noun, e.g. *bin*. *x*, *y* and *z* denote the axes of the Nest in use when the procedure is called. If *x* = 1 it is called to fit a head in; if 2, a modifier. OLAB is the label (outside *Fitonoun*) to jump to if Nest or Slots overflow.

When called for the modifier, *Fitonoun* may find that the modifier itself is associated with a verb: e.g. *riding* in *riding coat*. Another sentence is set up in Slots: *Someone rides*. Using the procedure *Trysent*, *Fitonoun* places in the row

Someone wears a coat

a negative number which is a reference to *lfg* + 1, the latest row:

Someone rides.

The procedure *Record* places in the Nest a reference to the higher sentence. When output, this line of Slots yields

A coat that someone wears when someone rides.

Certain checks are made before a subordinate clause is set up. The *on* (*riding*) must be the modifier: a nested sequence with only a pointer to the modifier is not dealt with here. And *riding* must be a verb: the other functions are not normally dealt with here. Features which permit a verb (the verb of the other noun) to form a subordinate clause are intransitivity, having an implicit object (*rides*: *rides a horse*), and causation (John *grows* flowers: the flowers *grow*).

If the verb provided by *on* is covert, the noun itself can be fitted in, and in this case we jump to NFIT for another interpretation. Similarly, even when the noun overtly denotes the action (*riding*), it may also fulfil another function, usually

Fitonoun, cont'd.

denoting a physical entity: *help*, as in *home help*, subject; *building* as in *computer building*,[4] object; *comparison* as in *comparison shopper*, instrument; *reception*, *drive*, as in *hotel reception*, *hotel drive*, locative of place. If such another function is found, we also jump to NFIT to fit the noun into the sentence. If the modifier is nested, e.g. *(fox-hunting) clothes*, and if its head denotes an action (*hunting*), we move down the Nest to where the modifier is stored (*fox-hunting*), and then to the 'left-hand side' of the Nest to pick up the analysis already made. We find a reference to the row of Slots in which *fox-hunting* appears as a sentence. The procedure *Trysent* then tries to fit the sentence set up by the modifier into the sentence set up by the head:

> Clothes that someone wears when someone hunts a fox or foxes.

When *Trysent* succeeds, *Fitonoun* places the reference to the modifier's row of Slots into the row set up by the head.

If the head of the modifier does not denote an action, *Fitonoun* treats it as a thing, and moves to the label NFIT.

NFIT also marks the point in *Fitonoun* where the procedure deals with examples in which the other noun is the head of the sequence, e.g. *dinner time*.

At NFIT, the procedure *Tryitem* is called, and a function (*of*) for the other noun is sought in the existing sentence. When the verb is not provided by the level of the Nest at which *Fitonoun* was called, the row of Slots is copied into another row. In either event, a reference to the other noun is put into the existing sentence. If the other noun is the head, a reference is also put into Slots [0, lfg, 1], where the output process will find it and begin the paraphrase with it: *towel disposal bin*:

Fitonoun, cont'd.

A bin that someone disposes of a towel or towels in.

If the function of the other noun is not one of activity, but is the locative of place, a check is made to see whether it should take to. This results in the output (for e.g. Modley bus) of

A bus that travels to Modley,

rather than

A bus that travels in or on Modley.

When the other noun has been fitted into a sentence, the procedure Record puts into the 'left-hand side' of the Nest the negative number which refers to the row of Slots holding the sentence, and Fitonoun becomes 'true'.

Fledge (gg, x, y, z) boolean

Called from Nounout, Slotout and the Mainprogram. Calls Ergive, Phrasout and Slotout.

This procedure 'fledges' noun sequences from the Nest. It is used to output the paraphrases of the noun sequences. When Fledge calls Slotout and Slotout calls Fledge it is acting recursively.

On the first use of Fledge, gg will be 0. x will be -1 and lower negative values (referring to the alternative interpretations in the 'left-hand side' of the Nest). y, an axis of the Nest, will be -1.

g holds the type number, or, where a sentence is involved, a reference to a row of Slots. z is a reference to the z-face of the Nest, which will be 1 unless there is polysemy, in which case it will have a value between 1 and 12 inclusive.

<u>Fledge, cont'd</u>.

For a simple noun sequence, e.g. <u>table top</u>, <u>Phrasout</u> is called and uses several procedures, including <u>Nounout</u>, to print

The top of a table.

If there is an underlying sentence, e.g. <u>fox hunting</u>, <u>Slotout</u> is called and uses several procedures, including <u>Nounout</u>, to print

The hunting of a fox.

Where nesting occurs, e.g. (<u>hall table) top</u>, the procedure <u>Nounout</u> halts in its printing and requires <u>hall table</u> to be Fledged, so that <u>Fledge</u> calls <u>Phrasout</u> again, and we get

The top of a <u>table in or on a hall</u>.

Sentence types are signified by a negative value of <u>g</u>. E.g. in <u>eating house</u>, <u>eating</u> has set up a row of Slots, and <u>house</u> has been fitted into it:

A house that someone eats in.

A more complex example is <u>riding-coat</u>, where two sentences are set up, to yield

A coat that someone wears when someone rides.

When <u>Fledge</u> is called from the Mainprogram, the values of its parameters are (<u>0, x, -1, z</u>). The first parameter will be used to carry either a type number or the number of a row of Slots. The value of <u>x</u> is changing, as we are in a loop, where <u>x</u> moves from -1 to -7. (We are also in a loop where <u>z</u> moves from 1 to <u>1z</u>.)

Five different instances of the use of <u>Fledge</u> will be given.

Fledge, cont'd.

(1) When only a phrase is needed: parlour stair. g becomes Nest [-1, -1, z], i.e. 3016. Phrasout is called with g and calls C1S6, which calls Phrase (which uses Nounout) to output

A stair to a parlour.

(2) In the case of a complex phrase, (bed + room) corridor, g becomes 3016. Phrasout, C1S6 and Phrase are called, as above. Nounout causes a corridor to be printed. Phrase prints to and calls Nounout again. This time Nounout finds that it is dealing with a nested sequence. It calls Fledge recursively: Fledge (0, -1, -2, z).

g becomes Nest [-1, -2, z], i.e. 3030. Phrasout is called with g and calls C3, which calls Phrase (which uses Nounout) to output

A room for or containing a bed or beds

(and another meaning). Thus the output for the whole sequence is

A corridor to a room for or containing a bed or beds.

(3) We can have a sentence set up by one noun, without nesting: fox-hunting. g becomes Nest [-1, -1, z], i.e. -1 (a reference to a row of Slots). Slotout (g) is called, and uses Sentout and Nounout to give

The hunting of a fox.

(4) We can also have a sentence set up by one noun, with nesting: (stewardess call)-button. g becomes Nest [-1, -1, z], i.e. in this case -3, referring to a row of Slots containing

Someone calls a stewardess or stewardesses
with a button or buttons.

Slotout (g) is called, and uses Sentout and Nounout to give

A button that someone calls a stewardess or
stewardesses with.

(5) We can have a phrase inside a sentence: (silk scarf) maker. g becomes Nest [-1, -1, z] i.e. -1 (a reference to a row of Slots). Slotout (g) is called, and causes Someone that to be printed. Then Sentout is called. It uses Verbp to print makes. Then it calls Nounout to print the object. Nounout finds that it is nested, and calls Fledge recursively: Fledge (-1, -1, -2, z) which causes a scarf of silk to be printed, giving:

Someone that makes a scarf of silk or scarfs of silk.

There are at least five other possible patterns that Fledge deals with:

(6) Sentence inside phrase: (dining-hall) door.

(7) Sentences set up by two nouns: riding-coat.

(8) Sentences set up by two nouns, one noun nested: (fox-hunting) clothes.

(9) Sentences set up by two nouns, both nouns nested: (fox-hunting) (horse-whip).

(10) Complex phrase with two sequences nested, one having a verb: (pig + skin)(document case).

These will not be pursued here, as the same principles apply to them as to the five patterns just described.

Fledge operates on a homographic example thus. The rows of noun numbers with their interpretation numbers are given according to their semantic priority. A clear example is

Fledge, cont'd.

lime + stone, where both nouns have two meanings. In this case, the likelihood of a lime (fruit) to have a stone causes the Annex interpretation to be given first. The correct interpretation comes only third. This example has been used because it indicates the meanings very clearly; a homographic example with a correct output first time is powder-chest. The output from lime + stone is as follows:

Homographic variant no. 4, preference no. 1
 Annex 4020
Homographic variant no. 1, preference no. 2
 Material 6010/Locative 3030
Homographic variant no. 3, preference no. 3
 Material 6010
Homographic variant no. 2, preference no. 4
 Locative 3030/Material 6020

Interpretation(s) in order of homographic preference:

The stone[2] of a lime[2].
Stone[1] of lime[1].
Stone[1] for or containing lime[1].
A stone [2] of lime [1].
Stone[1] for or containing a lime[2] or lime[2]s.
Stone[1] for lime[2]s or stone[1] in the form of a lime[2].

Fledge becomes 'true' when it has output at least one paraphrase.

Function (n, subject, action, object, instrument, place)

Called from Fitonoun and Verbinterp.

Function, cont'd.

This procedure is called when a noun has an associated verb. A boolean variable becomes 'true' if the noun represented by n fulfils that function. For example, the subject becomes 'true' if the noun is teacher, but the object becomes 'true' if the noun is passenger and its verb is carries. Both action and object become 'true' if the noun is washing.

G1 (y, z) boolean 7010

Called from Phrasout. Calls Phrase.

y and z denote axes of the Nest, for locating the nouns denoted by the numbers.

This procedure represents the Additive type. G1 calls for a paraphrase of a noun sequence to be printed out. Phrasout picks up from the Nest the number denoting the relationship (7010). Phrase prints the two nouns on either side of the and provided by G1; e.g. May-June:

May and June.

H1 (y, z) boolean 8010

Called from Phrasout. Calls Nounp and Writetext.

y and z are as for G1.

This procedure represents the Reduplicative type. H1 calls for a paraphrase of a noun sequence to be printed out. Phrasout picks up from the Nest the number denoting the relationship (8010). For e.g. chug-chug, H1 prints

A repeated sound of

and uses Nounp to print chug, giving

A repeated sound of chug.

Hasverb (n) boolean

Called from Analyze, Fitonoun, Matmodfind and Verbalfind.

n denotes a noun. Hasverb becomes 'true' if the noun has one or more associated verbs, whether overt or covert.

Horse (y) integer

Called from Verbinterp and Verbp.

y here represents a noun. This procedure selects a verb from the verbs associated with horse, e.g. pulls if the noun has a mechanical feature. It yields the number of the verb, or 0 if none is suitable. Horse follows or precedes the noun. E.g. in horse-tram, tram is the noun denoted by y. (The output is ultimately

A tram that a horse or horses pulls.)

Infledge (lfg, x, ndeepest, pol) integer

Called from Anafledge. Calls Anafledge, Polytest and Writetext.

lfg denotes the last filled row of Slots. x denotes a column of the Nest, and will be 1 (head) or 2 (modifier). ndeepest gives whether the noun being sought is at its deepest level or is nested. pol is 'true' when there is homography.

Infledge yields the number of the noun in Nest [x, y, z]. If this number is greater than 0, it represents a noun directly; if less, it refers to another sequence lower down in the Nest. In the former case, ndeepest is set 'true', as the noun is at its lowest level in the Nest; in the latter, ndeepest remains 'false' and Anafledge is called recursively to 'fledge' the sequence from lower down in the Nest.

Where ndeepest is 'true', Polytest is called, and pol becomes 'true' if the noun is homographic.

If Anafledge finds no noun in the expected place, a statement of the failure is printed.

Initslots

Called from the Mainprogram.

Initslots initializes all the Slots: i.e. it gives all the locations in the array Slots an initial value of, in this case, 0.

Locative (n) boolean

Called from Locfind.

This procedure inspects a noun's features for a locative feature, and becomes 'true' if it finds it.

Locfind boolean

Called from Analyze. Calls Locative, Modloc, Relate, Timeplace and Twoloc.

If the head is locative, several things are done. If the modifier has an overt verb and no material existence, e.g. dance hall, Locfind returns 'false' (these sequences are dealt with under Verbalfind). Otherwise, Locfind returns 'true', e.g. council house, Newark man.

If the modifier is also locative, Twoloc is normally called to perform an analysis. However, the head (or modifier) may denote a locative of time while the modifier (or head) denote a locative of place. In these cases the procedure Timeplace is called to perform an analysis. Both these procedures yield type numbers for the 'left-hand side' of the Nest, and Locfind

Locfind, cont'd.

normally returns 'true'. In addition, where the locative is the head, type 3030 (C3) is yielded, to give, e.g. for bread room

A room for or containing bread,

and Locfind returns 'true'.

Where the head and not the modifier is a locative of time, e.g. play hour, type 3030 is not yielded.

If the modifier and not the head is locative, the procedure Modloc is called, for e.g. sponge-bag, and Locfind normally returns 'true'. The exception to this occurs when the head has an overt verb and no material existence, e.g. (Town Hall) dance.

Lookup2 (n) boolean

Called from Nestfill. Calls Comp11, Defin, Notin2 and Polyin.

This procedure looks up a noun in the Dictionary, and yields 'true' if it finds it. The noun (obtained during Nestfill) is in the array Nouns. n is the number of the noun in the Nest.

The procedure does not alter n unless it finds polysemy. It yields 'false' if the noun is not in the dictionary, or if the definitions overflow the array Nouns. If the noun is in the dictionary, Lookup2 places its semantic features in the vector n of the array Feats. It discovers how many verbs the noun has, and places references to them in the array Nouns (in location [-5, n]). v takes the value of the number of verbs. The verbs are placed in the array Verbs (beginning after the location [letters, n, v]). The features of the verbs are placed in the array Vfeats. These features and the features denoting semantic fields also appear, packed (i.e. each set of features contained in one number), in Nouns [-2, n] and [-3, n]. The number denoting the comparative size of a member of a semantic field is

Lookup2, cont'd.

placed in Nouns [-4, n]. At first, Nouns [-1, n] holds Dict [g -1], which, if positive, indicates a homograph. The homograph is placed in Nouns [0:30, n+1], and a reference to n+1 is placed in Nouns [-1,n].

Lower (lfg, int) boolean

Called from Fitonoun, Setvnoun and Timeplace. Calls Ergive.

This procedure lowers lfg by one. lfg stands for last filled g, where g denotes a row of Slots. A row is then ready to hold a new sentence. Fourteen rows are allowed for. If Lower overflows the Slots, an error warning is printed, with a number (int) to show where the error occurs.

Man (x) integer

Called from Verbinterp and Verbp.

x here represents a noun. This procedure selects a verb from makes, works, sells, looks after and rides. It yields the number of the verb, or 0 if none of these is suitable, e.g. if an analysis using location or semantic fields is suitable. The word man follows the xth noun: e.g. in bread-man, bread is the xth noun. Because bread has a 'food' feature, Man selects sells, and the output is ultimately

A man that sells bread.

Material (n) boolean

Called from Pannexfind, Matheadfind and Matmodfind.

If the third primary feature (the material feature) is 'true', this procedure yields 'true': e.g. it is true for gold, mud and silk.

Matheadfind boolean

Called from Analyze. Calls Material and Relate.

If the head has a material feature, Matheadfind becomes 'true', provided that the modifier denotes something that has a physical existence and is a noun that takes an article.

Matheadfind is one of the eight procedures in Analyze which have been permuted during the preparation of the program.

Matmodfind boolean

Called from Analyze. Calls Hasverb, Material, Maybething and Relate.

This procedure is usually called when the modifier denotes a material. If the head denotes something collective, e.g. in hay + stack, and does not belong to a specific semantic field, type 6040 (F4) is yielded.

If the modifier denotes a material, several things can happen. Where the head has a physical existence, type 6010 (F1) is yielded.

If the 'physical' feature is not marked on the head, Maybething is called, to say whether a nested sequence may denote a thing. If so, 6010 (F1) is yielded. Where the head has an intransitive verb, metaphor can be encountered: silver laughter. Here again, 6010 is yielded.

Where the modifier denotes a human being and the head a human organization, 6050 (also leading to Type F4) is yielded.

Matmodfind is one of the eight procedures in Analyze which have been permuted during the preparation of the program.

Maybething (y, z) boolean

Called from Matmodfind.

This procedure tells from an earlier analysis whether a nested sequence may denote a thing (as distinct from, or as well as, an action). If so, it yields 'true'. E.g. gold (cigarette case).

When Maybething is called, y is Nest [1, y, z], i.e. -2. We look at the type numbers on this lower level. Cigarette case has the type number 3030 (C3). Since at least one of the type numbers is positive, Maybething is set 'true'.

Modloc (head, mod, lx, y, z, OVER)

Called from Locfind. Calls Relate.

This procedure deals with sequences where the modifier is locative. The following rules operate in order, and as soon as one set of conditions is found applicable, the rest of the rules are skipped.

If the head is human or animal, Type 3012 (C1 subtype 2) or 3013 (C1 subtype 3) is yielded, the former if the modifier is a proper noun. E.g. 3012:

A man that lives in or comes from Newark;

3013:

A pony that lives in or works in a pit.

If the modifier has a physical existence and the head denotes an item of furniture, Type 3014 is yielded; if a plant or part of one, Type 3015. E.g. 3014:

The kind of chair used in or on a deck;

3015:

The kind of ash found in or on a mountain.

Modloc, cont'd.

If the head takes to, Type 3016 is yielded:

A stair to a parlour.

When none of these has been identified, Modloc yields Type 3011:

A house in or on London.

If Type 3012 is found, Type 3011 is also yielded. If Type 3014 is found, Type 3015 is also yielded.

The procedure Relate places all the numbers in the 'left-hand side' of the Nest.

Nestfill (b) boolean

Called from the Mainprogram. Calls Carderror, Clobracket, Lookup2, Nexus, Nountr, Opbracket, Tail and Toosmall.

Nestfill is a major procedure whose function it is to transfer and store a noun sequence from a card, and to store relevant information from the dictionary. Nestfill assumes the presence of certain arrays which have been set up by the Mainprogram for storing words, features, etc. (The numbers given after the array names show the bounds of each array. Where an array has more than one dimension, two or more sets of bounds are given.) These arrays are:

Adj	[1:2, 1:7]
Card	[0:80]
Dict	[-6:i] where i stands for the upper bound of the particular dictionary read in.
Feats	[1:3, 0:22, 1:7]
Level	[-4:-1, 1:2]
Nar	[0:30]
Nest	[-7:3, -4:-1, 1:12]

Nestfill, cont'd.

Nouns [-5:30, 1:7]
Verbs [-1:30, 1:7, 1:5]
Vfeats [1:7, 0:22, 1:5]

Nestfill puts the nouns from the card into the array Nouns, beginning at Card [b]. In this study, *b* is 25: that is, each noun sequence begins in the 25th location on the card, allowing room for the author and page number in the earlier locations. *Nestfill* puts 'definitions' (sets of features) from the dictionary into the array Feats and into the negative part of Nouns. *Nestfill* then puts related verbs into the Verbs array, and their features into Vfeats. It puts the nexus (e.g. space, hyphen) into Nest [0, y, 1]. Into the array Adj (at the pointer to its noun) it puts pointers to the adjective on the card, e.g. *<stationary> train*.

Several possible meanings are yielded for (*bed +room*) *corridor*. The nested sequence *bed + room* is accommodated where *y* = -2 by the use of the array Level. A clearer (though a-typical) example is (*pig + skin*) (*document case*). Unlike (*bed + room*) *corridor*, this does not show diversity of meanings, but it does show another situation in which more than one level of the *y*-axis is used.

Nestfill places the references to the nouns in Nest [2,y,1] and Nest [1, y, 1]. Each nexus is placed in Nest [0, y, 1], where 16 denotes a space and 27 denotes a plus sign (for one-word examples). 1, 2, 3 and 4 denote *pig*, *skin*, *document* and *case*. -2 and -3 point to lower levels of the *y*-axis. In this procedure, *z* = 1.

Nestfill begins, after the label INIT, by initializing the arrays Adj, Level, Nest and Nouns to 0. Most of the variables, i.e. *i*, *j*, *l* and *n*, become 0. *c* takes the value of *b*, which is 25, as mentioned above. *nfy* denotes 'next free *y*', i.e. a value

Nestfill, cont'd.

for the y-axis where the next data are to be stored. It starts with the value -1.

At STEPDOWN, l becomes l-1. Level [l, 1] becomes 2, and Level [l,2] becomes nfy, which is here -1. nfy then becomes nfy -1, which is here -2. At MORESTEP, we meet the opening bracket before pigskin, and Nest [Level [l,1], Level [l,2],1] becomes nfy, i.e. Nest [-2, -1, 1] becomes -2. We then return to STEPDOWN. l becomes l - 1, i.e. -2. Level [l, 1] becomes 2 and Level [l,2] becomes nfy, here -2. nfy becomes nfy - 1, i.e. -3. At MORESTEP we do not meet another bracket, so we go on to perform Nountr, which transfers the noun into the array Nouns, deals with adjectives, and yields the number of the next location after the noun. At INNEST, Nestfill puts into the Nest a number designating the noun being dealt with, which is here 1 (for pig). It is put into the Nest at the location [Level [l,1], Level [l,2], 1], i.e. Nest [2, -2, 1]. Level [l, 1] then becomes Level [l, 1] -1. At SEEK, Nestfill calls Lookup2 to look up pig in the dictionary, and to place it and its associated verbs and features in arrays ready for use. At IFPAIR it is found that we do not yet have a pair of nouns. So the procedure Nexus is called to place a number in Nest [0, y, 1], denoting the + sign between pig and skin.

We return to MORESTEP. There is no nested opening bracket, so the second noun (skin), is transferred to the array Nouns, using Nountr. At INNEST, its number (2) is put into the Nest at Nest [Level [l, 1], Level [l, 2], 1], i.e. Nest [1, -2, 1]. Level [l, 1] then becomes Level [l, 1] -1. At SEEK, Nestfill calls Lookup2 to deal with skin. At IFPAIR, Level [l, 1] is found to be 0, showing that a pair of nouns is in the Nest. At STEPUP, Level [l, 2] becomes 0, and l becomes l + 1 (here -1). Clobracket shows that there is a closing bracket after skin, so that nested item has filled a modifier position. Level [l, 1]

Nestfill, cont'd.

becomes Level [1, 1] -1. We return to IFPAIR. Level [1, 1] is not 0 so we move down, and Nexus is called to place a number in Nest [0, y, 1] denoting a space, for the space between (pig + skin) and (document case). Now we return to MORESTEP. Opbracket finds an opening bracket. Nest [Level [1, 1], Level [1, 2], 1] becomes nfy, i.e. Nest [1, -1, 1] becomes -3. We go back to STEPDOWN. l becomes l -1, i.e. -2. Level [1, 1] becomes 2 and Level [1, 2] becomes nfy, here -3. nfy becomes nfy -1, i.e. -4. At MORESTEP we do not meet another bracket, so we go on to perform Nountr, which transfers the noun (document) into the array Nouns. At INNEST, Nestfill puts into the Nest a number designating the noun being dealt with, which is here 3 (for document). It is put into the Nest at the location [Level [1, 1], Level [1, 2], 1], i.e. Nest [2, -3, 1]. Level [1, 1] then becomes Level [1, 1] -1. At SEEK, Nestfill calls Lookup2 to deal with document. At IFPAIR it is found that we do not yet have a pair of nouns. So the procedure Nexus is called to place a number in Nest [0, y, 1], denoting the space between document and case.

We return to MORESTEP. There is no opening bracket, so the fourth noun (case) is transferred to the array Nouns, using Nountr. At INNEST, its number (4) is put into the Nest at Nest [Level [1, 1], Level [1, 2], 1], i.e. Nest [1, -3, 1]. Level [1, 1] then becomes Level [1, 1] -1. At SEEK, Nestfill calls Lookup2 to deal with case. At IFPAIR, Level [1, 1] is found to be 0, showing that a pair of nouns is in the nest. At STEPUP, Level [1, 2] becomes 0, and l becomes l + 1(here -1). Clobracket shows that there is a closing bracket for case, so that nested item has filled the position of a head. Level [1, 1] becomes Level [1, 1] -1. We return to IFPAIR. Level [1, 1] is 0, so a pair of noun sequences is in. At STEPUP, Level [1, 2] becomes 0. l becomes l + 1, i.e. 0. Since l is 0, all the nouns in

Nestfill, cont'd.

the sequence have been dealt with, so we move to DONE.

At DONE a check is made to see whether there is a 'tail' of further words or letters on the card. If so, an error warning is output. We are now near the end of Nestfill.

If at least one noun sequence has been read from the card, if the Nest is sufficiently large, and if the dictionary definitions have been collected, Nestfill becomes 'true' and, at OUT, comes to an end.

A simplified version of the working of Nestfill

The steps will be shown in connexion with the labels, which are given on the left. The example used is (pig+skin)(document case):

STEPDOWN	Level is altered.
MORESTEP	A reference to nested nouns enters the Nest.
STEPDOWN	Level is altered.
MORESTEP	Nountr transfers a noun (pig) into Nouns. (Also, Nountr always deals with any adjective, and yields the next location on the card.)
INNEST	The number 1 is put into the Nest for pig. Level is altered.
SEEK	Lookup2 for pig. Looks it up, and places it and its associated verbs and features into arrays ready for use.
IFPAIR	We do not yet have a pair of nouns. Nexus for + sign between pig and skin.
MORESTEP	Nountr transfers skin into Nouns.
INNEST	The number 2 is put into the Nest for skin. Level is altered.

Nestfill, cont'd.

SEEK	Lookup2 for skin. As above.
IFPAIR	A pair of nouns is in, i.e. pig + skin.
STEPUP	Level is altered.
IFPAIR	We do not yet have a pair of noun sequences. Nexus for the space between pig + skin and document case.
MORESTEP	A reference to nested nouns enters the Nest.
STEPDOWN	Level is altered.
MORESTEP	Nountr transfers document into Nouns.
INNEST	The number 3 is put into the Nest for document. Level is altered.
SEEK	Lookup2 for document. As above.
IFPAIR	We do not yet have a pair of nouns. Nexus for space between document and case.
MORESTEP	Nountr transfers case into Nouns.
INNEST	The number 4 is put into the Nest for case. Level is altered.
SEEK	Lookup2 for case. As above.
IFPAIR	A pair of nouns is in, i.e. document case.
STEPUP	Level is altered.
IFPAIR	A pair of noun sequences is in, i.e. (pig + skin) (document case).
STEPUP	Level is altered. All the nouns in the sequence have been dealt with.
DONE	A check is made for any further words on the card.
OUT	Nestfill ends.

When there is homography, just as with monosemic nouns, the analysis places type numbers in the negative part of the x-axis, and priority numbers in the locations on the x-axis where $x = 3$. Numbers representing the actual words go into the locations where $x = 1$ (the head) and $x = 2$ (the modifier).

Nestfill, cont'd.

Here, for example, is a two-noun sequence in which both nouns have at least two meanings:

lime + stone:

lime[1]: the substance
lime [2]: the fruit
stone[1]: the substance, also with a Locative feature.
stone[2]: the kernel of a pulpy fruit.

The Nest can be diagrammed thus:

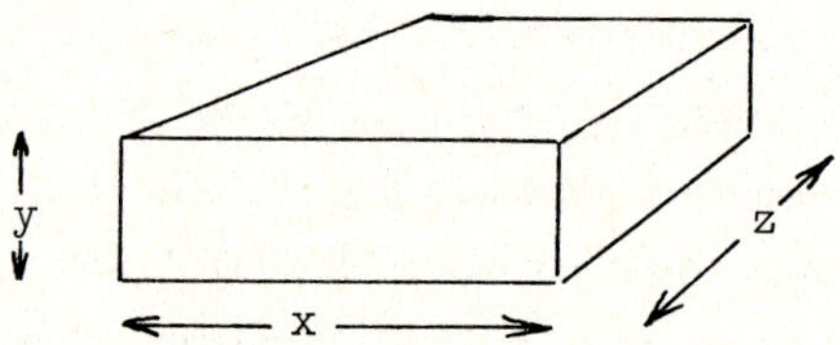

The part we are concerned with is the extension of the frontal analysis along the z-axis of the Nest.

Where x = 0 a plus sign is represented: lime + stone is one word. Where x = -1 and -2, Analyze has caused the type numbers to be put in (in this case, some material types, some locative and an annex). Where x = 3 the priority numbers have been placed by the procedure Pset. These priority numbers enable Anafledge to output the results in what is intended to be the order of likelihood.

A minor point which needs explanation is how the homography procedures deal with parts of the noun sequence that have already been analyzed when the homograph is encountered. A left-nested homographic example[5] is (Bursa[1] peach[2]) stone[3]. Bursa is a town famous for its peaches. The correct meaning of the noun sequence would be rendered thus by the program (type C1, subtype 5):

The stone[2] of the kind of peach found in or on Bursa.

Nestfill, cont'd.

At the stage when Bursa peach has just been analyzed, and stone is not yet brought into the analysis, there is only one dimension (or 'face') of the Nest in use.

Then, when the analysis of peach stone takes place, the homograph of stone is discovered. The whole of any work hitherto done is copied on to the next 'face' of the Nest, i.e. where $z = 2$. In this example, the important item is the 3015, signifying a C type. As 3 represents stone[1], the figure 4 is used for stone[2].

When stone [1] and stone [2] have been dealt with in the analyses, the interpretations are filled in where x is smaller than 0. The point being made, however, is that the results of an already-performed analysis (here, the figure 3015 where y = -2) are copied over into other rows on the z-face of the Nest whenever a homograph is encountered at a higher level (here, where y = -1).

Newline (n)

Called from Anafledge, Carderror, Notin2, Underout and the Mainprogram. Outputs n new lines.

Nextch integer

Called from Cardin and the Mainprogram.

Works like Readch but does not move the input stream. Reads one character but leaves the input stream positioned at that character. It enables the program to look ahead a little.

Nexus (c, y) boolean

Called from Nestfill.

Nexus, cont'd.

If it finds a nexus in Card [c], Nexus puts it into Nest [0, y, z] and yields 'true'. A nexus in any one of space, =, +, -. (The equals sign is used when there is a hyphen at the end of a line, which may not be a lexical separator.)

Notin2 (Nar)

Called from Lookup2. Calls Newline, Printch and Writetext.

Nar is the array containing a word which Lookup2 cannot find.

Notin2 prints the information that the word is not in the dictionary and that the card will therefore be skipped.

Nounout (art, g, pl, x, y, z) boolean

Called from Phrase and Sentout. Calls An, Ergive, Fledge, Nounp, The and Writetext.

Nounout outputs in graphic form a noun found in Nest [x, y, z]. The values of the parameters art and pl are: the = 1, an = 0, no article even if usual = -1. For the plural, plural = 2, singular = 0, either = 1. Thus the following is output, e.g. for (rose-water) style:

The style of water for or containing a rose or roses.

If Nest [x, y, z] contains a negative number, a nested sequence is being dealt with. The procedure Fledge is then called. (g is one of its parameters.)

Nounp (n)

Called from H1, Nounout and Slotout. Calls Adjp, Printch and Writetext.

Nounp, cont'd.

Nounp prints the noun numbered n, and any preceding adjective.

Nountr (b, n)

Called from Nestfill. Calls Adject, Carderror and Codig.

If it finds a word beginning in Card[b], Nountr adds 1 to n, puts the noun into the array Nouns [1:30, n], moves b to the first location after the word, and yields 'true'. It skips leading spaces. If it is called at a premodifier in brackets , it puts its pointers into the array Adj. If it is called at a coordinator, it gives a warning and skips the card. Any suffix, such as the ⟨ed⟩ in chocolate-colour⟨ed⟩, is put into the array Nouns but ignored in the total of letters put into Nouns [0, n]. The terminators of a word are space, -, =, +,) and the Newline symbol.

Opbracket (c) boolean

Called from Nestfill.

This procedure deals with Card [c], i.e. the location c in the array Card. Opbracket becomes 'true' and adds 1 to c if Card [c] contains an opening round bracket, as for instance before show in

(show + room) stair.

Order (z)

Called from the Mainprogram and Order. Calls Order.

This procedure determines the relative probability of homographic interpretations. It orders numbers from 1 to lz, in the array Pref [1, z]. These numbers are references to the axis z of

<u>Order, cont'd</u>.

the Nest. This procedure orders them according to the probability numbers in the array Pref [0, z]. The latter numbers give the total probability of the meanings of different noun sequences, composed of probabilities according to each homograph. This procedure uses the array Pref [0:1, 1:lz]. Pref [1, z] contains the preference numbers 1 to <u>lz</u>. Pref [0, z] contains the probability numbers. The highest number signifies the most probable relationship. Equal numbers are preserved.

In the Mainprogram, if there are six homographs the entries in the array Pref range from 1 to 6 in the six locations on the <u>y</u>-axis. If there are only two, the entries merely occupy the first two locations. <u>Addpref</u> is called, and then <u>Order</u>.

The sequence <u>(air+field) inspection</u> shows homography in <u>air</u>. Air[1] is the usual circumambient air. Air[2] is the air connected with flying.

The Nest will therefore contain two meanings. In the columns where x is 1 and 2, the three nouns are designated by numbers:

```
 1,2     3       4
(air + field) inspection
```

The numbers in column 0 denote each nexus between the nouns, here + and space. The numbers along the negative part of the <u>x</u>-axis are type numbers. Where <u>z</u> = 1, the Nest holds the first word meaning. Where <u>z</u> = 2, it holds the second word meaning. Where <u>z</u> = 1, the four relationships requested by the type numbers are:

The inspection $\left\{\begin{matrix}\text{in}\\ \text{of}\end{matrix}\right\}$ a field for or containing air[1], <u>field</u> locative, <u>field</u> object

Order, cont'd.

The inspection $\begin{Bmatrix}\text{in}\\\text{of}\end{Bmatrix}$ a field in or on air[1],
field locative, field object.

Where z = 2, they are:

The inspection $\begin{Bmatrix}\text{in}\\\text{of}\end{Bmatrix}$ a field that someone flies or lands in,
field locative, field object.

The inspection $\begin{Bmatrix}\text{in}\\\text{of}\end{Bmatrix}$ a field for or containing an air[2] or air[2]s,
field locative, field object.

An attempt is made to get the meanings into the correct order. As each analysis is performed, a number is placed in Nest [3, y, z] giving the probability of the interpretation. With a verb in the Head, sentence examples have a higher probability (7) than locative examples (6).

The probability numbers are accommodated in Nest [3, y, z]. So the -3 in Nest [-1, -2, 2], as it designates a sentence, causes a 7 to be put into Nest [3, -2, 2]. However, for the other homograph, 3030 and 3011 give only locative meanings, so a 6 is put into Nest [3, -2, 1]. It is this difference which causes

The inspection of a field that someone flies or lands in

to be output before

The inspection of a field for or containing air[1].

In Nest [3, -1, 1] and Nest [3, -1, 2] the number 7 is placed for the sentence interpretations given by -1, -2, -4 and -5 at the top level.

Order, cont'd.

The procedure Addpref, for each of the z-faces of the Nest, takes the number in Nest [3, y, z], squares it, and adds it to the number above. Thus for air[1] + field inspection, it squares 6 and adds it to 7, giving 43. For air[2] + field inspection, it squares 7 and adds it to 7, giving 56. These numbers are placed in Pref [0, z]. Thus the probabilities are weighted according to the inner interpretation.

The procedure Order exchanges the probability numbers and references to z-faces. If there are more than two probability numbers, Order carries on exchanging numbers where necessary all the way up the array. This is done by calling itself recursively. Finally the array is left holding the probability numbers and the values of z (references to the z-faces of the Nest), ready for their output in the preferable order:

The inspection of a field that someone flies or lands in.

The inspection of a field for or containing an air[2] or air[2]s.

The inspection of a field for or containing air[1].

The inspection of a field in or on air[1].

(In the above examples, for the sake of simplicity, the sense of inspection with an implicit object, leading to

An inspection in a field ...

is omitted.)

Pannexfind boolean

Called from Analyze. Calls Attach, Material and Relate.

This procedure seeks a pure annex, e.g. table top as opposed to the clover leaf sought by Findfields.

If the head has the Annex feature Feats [1, 5, head], e.g. rim in basin rim, Pannexfind yields the annex relationship 4010 (D1):

The rim of a basin.

When Feats [1, 20, mod] is 'true', then the modifier is a word like top or side, which is a pure annex in the head position but is a locative in the modifier position. In this case, if the modifier is not nested, has no preceding adjective and has no related verb, Pannexfind yields the locative relationship 3020 (C2): top table:

The table at the top.

If one or more of these conditions does not apply, the sequence with Feats [1, 20, mod] 'true' yields the annex relationship 4040 (D4): (baize-top) table:

A table with a top of baize.

When the modifier does not have Feats [1, 20, mod] but has the annex feature [1, 5, mod], e.g. edge-tool, Pannexfind yields Type 4040 (D4):

A tool with an edge or edges.

If the modifier has neither of the above-mentioned primary features, 5 or 20, the head is considered again. If it has the manner feature Feats [1, 14, head] (e.g. style) or the latent-locative annex feature Feats [1, 20, head] (e.g. top) and if the modifier has no overt verb, then type 4010 (D1) is yielded: (rose-water) style:

The style of water for or containing a rose or roses

Pannexfind, cont'd.

and table-top:

The top of a table.

If the example is nested, the procedure Attach is called. In examples such as (table-top) polish, this procedure attaches the features of table to those of top.

When any of the above types have been found, Pannexfind returns 'true'.

Pannexfind is one of the eight procedures in Analyze which have been permuted during the development of the program.

Phrase (hart, prep, quart, pl, y, z) boolean

Called from the procedures A2 to H1 which outline the phrases that are required to be printed, as specified in the entry for Phrasout. Calls Nounout, Printch and Writetext.

Phrase causes a phrase to be printed.

Let us take for example D1, which calls Phrase:

Phrase (1, '('OF')', 0, 0, y, z)

e.g. table-top:

The top of a table.

The preposition is specified by the procedure D1. The 1, also thus specified, requires the definite article to be printed. The first 0 requires the indefinite article. The second 0 requires the qualifier noun (table) to be given in the singular.

The various signifiers are:

Definite article:	1
Indefinite article:	0
No article desired even if usual for this noun:	-1

Phrase, cont'd.

Qualifier noun to be plural:	2
Qualifier noun to be singular:	0
Qualifier noun to be either singular or plural:	1

The paraphrases are printed by means of Nounout.

Phrasout (r, y, z) boolean

Called from Fledge. Calls the procedures A2 to H1 which outline the phrases that are required to be printed: A2, A3, A4, A5, C1 subtype 1, C1 subtype 2, C1 subtype 3, C1 subtype 4, C1 subtype 5, C1 subtype 6, C2, C3, D1, D2, D3, D4, E1, E2, F1, F2AND3, F4[6], G1, H1.

This procedure, during the printing of the output by Fledge, is called to translate type numbers (found in the 'left-hand side' of the Nest) into the procedures which will cause phrases to be printed. Sentence types involving the Slots are not dealt with here.

The values for each type number are given and the appropriate procedure called: e.g. for table top the figure 4010 taken from the Nest is translated into D1, which is the name of a procedure. That procedure causes

The top of a table

to be printed.

Of the parameters, r denotes the type number which signifies a relationship. y and z denote locations on the y-axis and z-axis of the Nest where r is found.

Polyin (g, n) boolean

Called from Lookup2. Calls Defin and Toosmall.

Polyin, cont'd.

This procedure is used when a noun has been found in the dictionary and proves to have one or more homographs, e.g. port[1], port[2]. It puts the homographs, and their features and related verbs, into the arrays Nouns, Feats, Verbs and Vfeats. It overwrites a suffix.[7] It yields 'true' unless the array Nouns overflows, in which case a warning is output. n denotes where the noun is placed in the array Nouns. g is the dictionary location of the next homograph of the noun.

Polytest (x, y, lz) boolean

Called from Infledge. Calls Extend and Writetext.

This procedure tests the current example for homography. It extends the accommodation in the Nest for all combinations of homography, and copies into it all the lower analysis hitherto made. E.g. port[1] is kept in Nest [x, y, 1]; port [2] will be put into Nest [x, y, lz] i.e. Nest [x, y, 2]. lz (the 'last filled z') will be greater than 0 when Polytest is called. For each homography, lz will be incremented, and a copy of each face of the nest (i.e. Nest [z, y, z]) for each filled z will be put into Nest [x, y, lz].

Print (i, m, n)

Called from Anafledge, Carderror, Ergive, Infledge, Typout and the Mainprogram.

In the program, Print prints the integer i, its format being determined by m and n: e.g. m and n determine how many spaces will be allowed for the number.

Printch (c)

Called from Adjp, An, Notin2, Nounp, Phrase, Typout, Verbp and the Mainprogram.

Printch prints a character, i.e. in the program anything that is not a number. It is used to output noun sequences, underlying sentences, paraphrases, error warnings and so on.

Pset (p, int)

Called from Analyze.

As the analysis proceeds, numbers denoting the probability of each interpretation are placed in Nest [3, y, z]. These are later used in cases of homography by the procedure Order. In the entry for Order will be found an account of the use of these probability numbers. What Pset ensures is that, among several possible values according to the several interpretations in the 'left-hand side' of the nest, p (the probability number) will always bear the highest possible value. E.g. for tent flap, the Annex type D1 (4010) is yielded:

The flap of a tent.

The probability number 8 is placed in Nest [3, -1, 1]. Next, the locative type C1S1 (3011) is yielded:

A flap in or on a tent.

The probability number for the locative type is here 7. If it were greater than 8, Analyze would cause it to overwrite 8; but as it is smaller, Pset prevents it from overwriting 8.

Record (tn, lx, y, z) boolean

Called from Fitonoun, Relate, Timeplace and Verbinterp. Calls Ergive.

This procedure records a type number in the 'left-hand side' of the Nest (i.e. where x is negative). tn is the type number; lx is the 'last filled x', i.e. the latest location on the x-axis to be used. If there is overflow, Ergive prints a warning.

Recover (x, y, z, pol) integer

Called from Anafledge.

This procedure is used where the head or modifier taking part in the analysis is nested: e.g. in (bed + room) corridor, room is recovered from the lower level to be analyzed with corridor, to give

A corridor to a room ...

Redupfind boolean

Called from Analyze. Calls Relate.

When the head and modifier are at the same level in the Nest and are identical nouns, the Reduplicative relationship H1 (8010) is yielded: e.g.

the chug-chug of the engine:
A repeated sound of chug.

(Examples such as compiler-compiler, which are not onomatopoeic but have a syntactic relationship, are picked up in Verbinterp, before Redupfind is activated.) When 8010 is yielded, Redupfind is set 'true'. Redupfind is one of the eight procedures in Analyze which have been permuted during the development of the program.

Relate (int, lx, y, z, OVERF)

Called from Equifind, Findfields, Locfind, Matheadfind, Matmodfind, Modloc, Pannexfind, Redupfind, Twoloc and Verbalfind. Calls Record.

Relate uses the procedure Record to record a type number in the 'left-hand side' of the Nest, i.e. where x is negative. It jumps to the label OVER in Anafledge if the Nest overflows. (On the call of the procedure, OVERF is replaced by OVER.)

Selectinput (n)

Called at the very beginning of the program.

Selectinput selects which input channel is to be used. In practice the file of the dictionary has been merged with the file of the data, so only one channel is selected.

Selectoutput (n)

Called at the very beginning of the program.

Selectoutput selects which output channel is to be used. In practice the program outputs to a single file which is later printed on the line-printer; so only one channel is selected.

Sentout (ff, g, vhead) boolean

Called from Sentout, Slotout and Underout. Calls Ergive, Nounout, Sentout, Verbp and Writetext.

This procedure prints a sentence from a row of the array Slots. Together with Slotout, it will also output an expression beginning with, e.g., the instrument, going to the end of the sentence and then returning to the beginning to print the subject, verb and object. This latter facility is used in the printing

Sentout, cont'd.

of relative clauses in the paraphrases:

(a) Someone cuts bread with a knife.

(b) (A knife that) someone cuts bread with.

Output by Slotout

ff is one less than the first function to be output: e.g. where the sentence is to be output in the normal order, ff is 0 (the subject is 1). f becomes ff. g denotes the row of slots to be output. If the head-noun denotes an activity, e.g. halt, vhead is 'true'.

At the label FUNCTION, f becomes f + 1. For the output of a normal sentence, f becomes in turn 1, 2, 3 and so on: e.g. (towel disposal) bin:

1	2		3		5	
Someone	disposes of	a	towel or towels	in	a bin or bins	

until the whole sentence is printed. Prepositions, such as in, are inserted before the locative and manner adjuncts are printed. Where a function is not used, a 0 will be found in its location, and it will be ignored. Where the head or modifier fulfils a function, 1 or 2 respectively will be found there, and the word is printed. In the subject and object functions, the figures 4 or 5 may be found. These have been placed there by Setrow and denote an unknown human or inanimate entity. Someone is printed for 4 and someone or something for 5.

If Slots [2, g, 1] = 1, i.e. if the head provides the verb of the sentence, then vhead is 'true'. When the f for the function reaches the value of 8, if vhead is 'true' the value of f is reduced to 0, and the sentence is begun again.

x takes the value of Slots [f, g, 1], where f is the current function. If x is 0 we return to FUNCTION. If x is a negative

Sentout, cont'd.

number, it is a reference to a sentence in another row of the Slots. In this case a relative pronoun or conjunction appropriate to the function is printed. Sentout is called recursively, and the result is, for example, where $f = 6$,

riding coat:
Someone wears a coat when someone rides.

Where f is a positive number, several conditions and the uses of various prepositions are encountered. Where $f = 1$ (for the subject), if the head provides the verb of the sentence, and if the subject slot contains a number (2) denoting the modifier, then if the object slot is empty, of is printed, e.g. fantasy story:

Someone narrates fantasy:
The story of fantasy.

If the object slot is filled, by is printed. If the subject slot contains a number denoting the head, the prepositions are not printed and we merely return to FUNCTION.

Where $f = 2$ (for the verb), if the verb slot contains the number 3 we jump to the label OUT, and Sentout is concluded. The number 3 will have been placed there by Slotout after the head has been found and just before it is printed.

If x is smaller than 3, it denotes a verb provided by a head (1) or modifier (2). y takes the value of Slots [2, g, 2] and the verb is printed. If x is greater than 3, we are dealing with two locations, of time and of place (as explained under Timeplace), and is is printed, for e.g. Autumn land:

The land as it is in the Autumn.

We then return to FUNCTION.

Sentout, cont'd.

Where f = 4, with is written: coal-rake:

Someone rakes coal with a rake or rakes.

When the head has already been output by Slotout:

Something that [8]

Sentout prints

someone rakes coal with.

Where f = 5 or 6, in is written, unless x is greater than 3, in which case to is written:

cooking-pot:
Someone cooks in a pot or pots.
home letter:
Someone writes a letter or letters to a home or homes.

Where f = 7 (for manner), if x = 3, in is written; otherwise like or in is written.

After the current value of f has been dealt with, we come to the printing of the noun. If x is 1 or 2 (denoting the head and the modifier), y takes the value of Slots [f, g, 2], and the noun is printed. If x is 4, someone is printed. If x is 5, something or someone is printed. We then return to FUNCTION, where a loop operates until f = 8. From there, Sentout comes to an end.

Setrow (f, g, x, y, z, tr)

Called from Fitonoun and Setvnoun.

This procedure is used to set up a row of Slots where the noun in Nest [x, y, z] provides the verb and its function is f.

Setrow, cont'd.

x is 1 or 2 as the head or the modifier provides a verb.

Slots [f, g, h] has the bounds [-1:7, -1:-14, 1:2].

E.g. for coal-rake, rake sets up a row of slots. Slots [0, -1, 1] contains a reference to the function of the noun which caused the row to be set up, e.g. 4 for the instrumental function. Slots [-1, -1, 1] contains the value of z.

Of the numbers in Slots [f, g, 1] when x = 1 to 4 inclusive, 4 denotes a human agent unspecified, 1 denotes the head, which is rake in the instrumental position, and 5 a non-human object unspecified. The numbers in Slots [f, g, 2] give values of y at the Nest. Coal is fitted into the row by Fitonoun, taking the object position, i.e. represented by 2 where x = 3. Noughts fill the slots where x = 5, 6 and 7.

For Stockholm Chief, a transitive row is set up, and also a row with an implicit object. In both rows where x = 1 and 2 Slots contains 1 denoting the head: in the first row there is also a 5 in the third (object) slot. In the first case, Fitonoun fits Stockholm into the object slot; in the latter, the slot of the locative of place (where x = 5).

x is 2 for cases like the riding of riding hour.

The row is set up by the modifier, riding, and Fitonoun fits hour into the 6th slot, the locative of time. In this case, the 2 showing that the verb is the head of the row will be overwritten by the reference (6) to the location of the head-noun. For riding-coat, where both nouns have verbs, rows of Slots are set up:

y = -1 Someone wears a coat : x[1:3]= 4, 1, 1.

y = -2 Someone rides: x[1:3]= 4, 2, 0.

A reference to the first sentence is later placed in the time location, a negative number. Thus we get Slots [6, -1,1] = -2:

Setvnoun

Someone wears a coat when someone rides.

Setvnoun (lfg, lx, on, vn, x, y, z, s, v, obj, inst, p, OLAB) boolean

Called from Verbinterp. Calls Fitonoun, Lower and Setrow.

Setvnoun (pronounced Setveenoun) sets up one or more rows of Slots for vn (the noun associated in the dictionary with the verb). Setvnoun yields 'true' if it fits on (the other noun) into at least one row. Rows of Slots are set up according to the function of the noun (vn) and the transitivity of the verb. lfg is the 'last filled g', i.e. the last filled row of Slots. lx is the last filled location in the 'left-hand side' of the Nest, where x is negative (i.e. the interpretation storage). x, y and z refer to axes of the Nest where x denotes a head or modifier. s, v, obj, inst and p refer to functions of the noun. OLAB is the label to go to if the sentences overflow the Slots.

In this procedure, many attributes of verbs are activated. Five verb valencies are recognized:

(1)	transitive	Stockholm chief toy maker
(2)	intransitive	sunrise, cave-dweller
(3)	can imply its own object (written as impo in Setvnoun)	Stockholm chief (as in (1); all impo verbs are transitive), comparison shopper
(4)	causative (or ergative)	Someone increases the salary; The salary increases
(5)	transmissive	Someone poisons the food; The food poisons someone.

An attribute of this procedure is that there is a loop (at the label CANTWICE) to enable two sentences to be set up (in the

Setvnoun, cont'd.

array Slots) where two paraphrases must be yielded, as for the impo verb:

The chief rules Stockholm;
The chief rules in Stockholm.

(1) We shall pursue the path of the purely transitive verb makes through Setvnoun, in the sequence toy maker. nbool becomes 'true' as maker is a subject. f becomes 1 for the subject. tr (for transitive) becomes 'true'. In the case of maker, impo becomes 'false'. The verb is in the head. After the label CANTWICE, a row of slots is anticipated by Lower and set up by Setrow:

1	2	3	4	5	6	7
S	V	O	Instr.	Loc.pl.	Loc.tm.	Manner
1	1	5	0	0	0	0

The 1 in the subject slot represents maker. The 5 requires an object. If the verb takes a human object, the object slot becomes free for a human object, taking the value 4 instead of 5.

The procedure Fitonoun is then called to fit the other noun (toy) into the Slots:

1	2	3	4	5	6	7
S	V	O	Instr.	Loc.pl.	Loc.tm.	Manner
1	1	2	0	0	0	0

The job is done, and we move back to the beginning of Setvnoun. nbool is 'false' for all the other functions maker might fulfil, and so we conclude Setvnoun, with

Someone that makes a toy or toys

in the Slots.

Setvnoun, cont'd.

In the next illustrations we shall usually give the entries where x = 1, 2 and 3: the slots for subject, verb and object. The instrument, place, time and manner slots are not filled in these illustrations.

(2a) Let us now pursue the path of the purely intransitive verb rises through Setvnoun, in the sequence sunrise. On its first round, testing for a subject in rise, nbool becomes 'false', but on its second round, testing for an 'activity' (i.e. a verb meaning) for rise, it becomes 'true'. Thus f becomes 2. tr (for transitive) becomes 'false'. impo becomes 'false'. The verb is in the head. If the modifier is a locative, its locative feature is cancelled. After CANTWICE, a row of Slots is anticipated by Lower and set up by Setrow:

1	2	3
S	V	O
4	1	0

The 1 in the verb slot represents rise. The 0 in the object slot (unlike its behaviour in the other slots) blocks the slot. Fitonoun allows sun to fill the subject slot as it has not the features to fill any of the other slots:

1	2	3
S	V	O
2	1	0

This job is done, and we move back to the beginning of Setvnoun. nbool is 'false' for all the other functions, so we conclude Setvnoun with

The rise of the sun

in the Slots.

Setvnoun, cont'd.

(2b) Let us now pursue the path of another purely intransitive verb, dwells, in the sequence cave-dweller. The principles on which the Slots are set up are the same as for sunrise, but this time the other noun (cave) fills a locative slot, not a subject slot.

nbool becomes 'true' as dweller is a subject. f becomes 1 for the subject. tr (for transitive) becomes 'false'. In the case of dweller, impo becomes 'false'. The verb is in the head. loc becomes 'true' and the locative feature of cave becomes 'false'. After a 'false' run, the locative feature is set 'true' again. After the label CANTWICE, a row of Slots is anticipated by Lower, and set up by Setrow:

1	2	3
S	V	0
1	1	0

The 1 in the subject slot represents dweller. The 0 in the object slot (unlike its behaviour in the other slots) blocks the slot. Fitonoun fits cave into the slot of the locative of place:

1	2	3	4	5	6	7
S	V	0	Instr.	Loc.pl.	Loc.tm.	Manner
1	1	0	0	2	0	0

When this job is done, we move back to the beginning of Setvnoun. nbool is 'false' for all the other functions, so we conclude Setvnoun with

A dweller in a cave

in the Slots.

(3a) Let us now pursue the path of a verb which can imply its own object, e.g. Stockholm chief, where one can say

Setvnoun, cont'd.

The chief rules

as well as

The chief rules Stockholm.

nbool becomes 'true' as *chief* is a subject. *f* becomes *1* for the subject. *tr* becomes 'true'. *impo* becomes 'true': i.e. *rules*, the verb related to *chief*, can imply its own object. The verb is in the head. After the label CANTWICE, a row of Slots is anticipated by *Lower* and set up by *Setrow*:

1	2	3
S	V	O
1	1	5

The 1 in the subject slot represents *chief*. The verb is *rules*, a covert verb. The 5 requires an object. *Fitonoun* fits *Stockholm* in as object:

1	2	3
S	V	O
1	1	2

A chief that rules Stockholm.

Then *tr* and *impo* become 'false' and we return to CANTWICE, as we can go through the subsequent set of rules twice. A row of Slots is anticipated by *Lower* and set up by *Setrow*:

1	2	3
S	V	O
1	1	0

The 0 in Slot 3 blocks the object. *Fitonoun* fits *Stockholm* in as a locative of place:

1	2	3	4	5	6	7
S	V	O	Instr.	Loc.pl.	Loc.tm.	Manner
1	1	0	0	2	0	0

nbool is false for all the other functions, so we conclude Setvnoun with

A chief that rules Stockholm
A chief that rules in Stockholm

in the Slots.

(3b) Let us now pursue the path of a verb which can imply its own object, but where (unlike Stockholm chief) the verb is in the modifier: fighting line, in the first sense of line (as in a straight line, as opposed to airline). nbool is true only for the verb function: f becomes 2 for that function. tr becomes 'true'; impo becomes 'true'. Since the verb is in the modifier, tr and impo are inspected, and tr becomes 'false'. After CANTWICE, a row of Slots is anticipated by Lower and set up by Setrow:

1	2	3
S	V	O
4	2	0

The 2 in the verb slot represents fighting. The 0 in the object slot blocks the slot. Fitonoun allows line to fill the subject slot as it has not the features to fill any of the other slots:

1	2	3
S	V	O
1	2	0

Setvnoun, cont'd.

A line[1] that fights.

At the label TEST, impo is found to be 'true', so impo becomes 'false' and tr becomes 'true'. We return to CANTWICE. A row of Slots is anticipated by Lower and set up by Setrow:

1	2	3
S	V	O
4	2	5

The 5 requires an object. Fitonoun fits line[1] in as an object:

1	2	3
S	V	O
4	2	1

nbool is false for all the other functions, so we conclude Setvnoun with

A line[1] that fights;
A line[1] that someone fights.

It will have been observed that Setvnoun yields a transitive sentence before an intransitive one where the verb is supplied by the head, but yields an intransitive before a transitive one where the verb is supplied by the modifier.

There are only two exceptions to this:

(i) where the verb is supplied by the head, and the modifier is a locative of time, e.g. evening breeze:

A breeze that blows in an evening or evenings;

(ii) where there are verbs in the modifier and head, both denoting the activity (e.g. speech), so that parting speech yields:

<u>Setvnoun, cont'd</u>.

The speech when someone parts.

(4) Let us now pursue the path of a causative (or ergative) verb, e.g. <u>salary increase</u>, where one can say

The salary increases

as well as

Someone increases the salary.

On its first round, testing for a subject in <u>increase</u>, <u>nbool</u> becomes 'false', but on its second round, testing for an 'activity' (i.e. a verb meaning) for <u>increase</u>, it becomes 'true'. Thus <u>f</u> becomes 2. As for other transitive verbs, <u>tr</u> becomes 'true'. <u>caus</u> (for causative) is set 'true', and as a result <u>tr</u> becomes 'false' but <u>impo</u> becomes 'true'. The verb is in the head. <u>tr</u> takes the value of the verb features 'agent' or 'gerund', both yielding 'false'. After CANTWICE, a row of Slots is anticipated by <u>Lower</u> and set up by <u>Setrow:</u>

1	2	3
S	V	0
4	1	0

The 1 in the verb slot represents <u>increase</u>. The 0 in slot 3 blocks the object function. The subject slot is given 5 instead of 4.

<u>Fitonoun</u> places <u>salary</u> in the subject slot:

1	2	3
S	V	0
2	1	0

The increase of a salary,

Setvnoun, cont'd.

derived from

A salary increases.

At the label TEST, impo is found to be 'true', so impo becomes 'false', and tr (which is 'false') becomes 'true'. We return to CANTWICE. A row of Slots is anticipated by Lower and set up by Setrow:

1	2	3
S	V	O
4	1	5

The 5 in Slot 3 requires an object. Fitonoun places salary in the object slot:

1	2	3
S	V	O
4	1	2

nbool is 'false' for all the other functions, so we conclude Setvnoun with

The increase of a salary.

This is derived from

(i) A salary increases;
(ii) Someone increases a salary.

(5) Let us now pursue the path of a transmissive verb, e.g. food poisoning. nbool is true only for the verb function: f becomes 2 for that function. As the verb is transmissive, impo and tr become 'true'. After CANTWICE, a row of Slots is anticipated by Lower and set up by Setrow:

Setvnoun, cont'd.

1	2	3
S	V	O
4	1	5

The 1 in the verb slot represents poisoning. Fitonoun fits the modifier, food, into the object slot:

1	2	3
S	V	O
4	1	2

Someone poisons food.

At the label TEST, impo is found to be 'true', so impo and tr become 'false'. We return to CANTWICE. A row of Slots is anticipated by Lower and set up by Setrow:

1	2	3
S	V	O
4	1	0

The trsmiss feature causes the 4 in the subject slot to be altered to 5, i.e. it can take a non-human subject. Because of this alteration, Fitonoun fits food into the subject slot:

1	2	3
S	V	O
2	1	0

Food poisons.

The feature trsmiss causes Slots [3, g,1] to become 5. This will cause something or someone to be output:

Food poisons something or someone.

Setvnoun, cont'd.

When this job is done we move back to the beginning of Setvnoun. nbool is 'false' for all the other functions, so we conclude Setvnoun.

Shiftup (x, y, z)

Called from Tidy.

When a type number has been removed from the 'left-hand side' of the Nest (i.e. where x is negative), this procedure shifts to the right any numbers other than 0 that are on its left, and puts 0 into the leftmost location, Nest [-7, y, z].

Skipch

Called from Cardin and the Mainprogram.

Skipch skips over the character about to be read. E.g. in Cardin, an undesired end-of-line symbol may be present, depending on the local representation of a card. If such a symbol is present, it is skipped.

Slotout (g) boolean

Called from Fledge. Calls An, Ergive, Fledge, Nounp, Sentout and Writetext.

Slotout outputs a paraphrase from the array Slots containing one or more sentences, e.g.

A knife that someone cuts bread with

for bread-knife.

Slotout yields 'false' if a serious error is encountered. g denotes a position on the g-axis (the second dimension) of Slots.

Slotout, cont'd.

Bread-knife[9] is represented as follows:

1	2	3	4
S	V	O	Instr.
4	1	2	1

g is -1 for this example, denoting the first row of Slots.

vhead becomes 'true'.

The number 3 is placed in Slots [f, g, 1], i.e. the instrumental slot. Then the variable headslot takes the value of f, i.e. 4. y is recovered from Slots [f, g, 2]. n is recovered from Nest [1, y, z]. If n is not a negative number, the procedures An and Nounp are used to print

A knife.

vhead becomes 'false'. Slots [2, g, 1] does not contain 4, so we move down to the label THAT, and print that:

A knife that

f becomes 0. Slotout calls Sentout, with the parameters f, g and vhead having the values 0, -1, 'false'. As described under Sentout, the rest of the sentence is printed, to give

A knife that someone cuts bread with.

In riding-breeches, both nouns have verbs activated (breeches has wears). Two rows of Slots have been set up:

	0	1	2	3	4	5	6	7
		S	V	O	Instr.	Loc.Pl.	Loc.Tm.	Manner
-1	3	4	1	1	0	0	-2	0
-2	2	4	2	0	0	0	0	0

Slotout, cont'd.

If Slots [2, g, 1] is 1, i.e. if the verb is provided by the head noun, vhead becomes 'true'. It does so in this case. Then the variable f takes the value of the head slot, the value being stored in Slots [0, g, 1]. In this row it is 3, for breeches.

The number 3 is placed in Slots [f, g, 1], i.e. the object slot, to block an output of this word. Then the variable headslot takes the value of f, i.e. 3. y is recovered from Slots [f, g, 2]. n is recovered from Nest [1, y, z]. It here denotes breeches. As the verb (wears) is a covert verb, Slotout prints the noun breeches. Passing the label TWOLOCS, we move down towards the end of Slotout. The procedure prints that. f is altered to 0. Then the procedure calls Sentout.

During the remainder of the analysis, Sentout (called recursively for riding) yields

Breeches that someone wears when someone rides.

Slotout allows for a negative n (showing that the noun is nested) by searching the 'left-hand side' of the Nest and fitting into its phrase any interpretation that is found there. In this case it calls Fledge recursively.

Slotout deals with sequences of time and place. If the verb slot contains a 4, it has been placed there by the procedure Timeplace, for examples such as Autumn land, where Slotout prints as it, later to yield

The land as it is in the Autumn.

If the locative denotes a building or furniture, Slotout prints that, later to yield

A house that someone is in in the summer.

Is is yielded by Sentout in these cases.

Slotout, cont'd.

At the end of each of its operations, Slotout calls Sentout and the remainder of the paraphrase is output.

Tail (c) boolean

Called from Nestfill.

This procedure becomes 'true' if the card has any characters after the nouns are paired off. It moves c along the card.

The (n)

Called from Nounout. Calls Writetext.

Unless the noun n has the 10th primary feature (i.e. does not take an article), this procedure prints the.

Tidy (hx, hy, z)

Called from Anafledge. Calls Shiftup.

This procedure is designed to remove from the Nest any interpretation of a nested sequence that is not incorporated at a higher level. This is done by removing, from any level below -1, any reference to a row of Slots where the head is an 'activity': i.e. where Slots [0, g, 1] = 2. For instance, for farthing (rush + light), the program makes the correct interpretation:

> Light of rushes that costs or is worth a
> farthing or farthings.

(The of is the material of: a light made of rushes.) There is a possible interpretation based on the sentence

> A rush or rushes shines.

Tidy, cont'd.

However, the number referring to this is removed from the Nest, as the head word is shines, an 'activity' noun only. (This is unlike the rake in coal-rake, which provides the verb but is also an instrument.)

There is an exception made in Tidy. If it is the modifier that is nested, and the interpretation gives the Equative type 5014, the nested sequence is not removed: e.g. (where the nested 'activity' word is underlined):

(computer design) work
(fire-fighting) work.

However, Tidy sometimes acts undesirably: it would remove shines from a sentence where it would be an acceptable subject:

50 pence shoeshine:
The shine of a shoe costs or is worth 50 pence.

Timeplace (lfg, lx, mod, y, z, OLAB)

Called from Locfind. Calls Lower and Record.

This procedure sets up a sentence (in a row of Slots) for a sequence such as Autumn land, to be output as

The land as it is in the Autumn.

Lower produces a fresh row of Slots. The fact that the verb slot contains a 4 signifies the Timeplace meaning to the output procedure. A reference to the row of Slots is placed by Record in the Nest.

Toosmall (string)

Called from Nestfill and Polyin. Calls Writetext.

Toosmall, cont'd.

This procedure is used when the arrays Level, Nest and Nouns overflow. If the string is 'Nest', for example, Toosmall writes:

Array Nest too small. Card skipped.

Tryitem (f, g, on) boolean

Called from Fitonoun.

We have a row of Slots whose verb is provided by one of the nouns in a sequence. This procedure tries the other noun (on) in functions in the row of Slots. The noun being tried (on) may be a head or a modifier, e.g. eating apple, apple eating. It may be nested, e.g. (crab - apple) eating. It may have verbness, e.g. school entrance, but if so it should not denote the action, although this procedure does not exclude it from doing so.

g denotes the row of Slots. f yields the function of on. The procedure yields 'true' and sets f if a slot is found. f becomes one of:

1 subject
3 object
4 instrument
5 locative of place
6 locative of time
7 manner.

vn denotes the noun with the verb, that has set up the current row of Slots.

The following rules operate in order, and as soon as f takes a value, the rest of the rules are skipped.

If vn is transmissive (e.g. slide, shut) and the Subject slot requires a non-human noun, f becomes 1. If the Subject slot requires a human noun, and the Object slot is free, f becomes 3.

Tryitem, cont'd.

If the Object slot is open to a non-human noun, vn may require a non-material noun. In that case, if on is non-material, f becomes 3. If vn has no such requirement, f becomes 3.

If the Object slot requires a human noun, and on is human or denotes a human organisation, f becomes 3.

Where on is locative, (house, day), or is the locative of an overt verb (stand) or a covert verb (school), if on is temporal (day), f becomes 6; if a place (house), f becomes 5 (provided that Slot 6 or 5 is empty).

Where on is the Instrument of a verb (overt or covert), provided Slot 4 is free, f becomes 4.

Where on has a verb but is not its Instrument, if it has a locative function (halt) and Slot 5 is free, f becomes 5.

Where on is an Instrument (e.g. gear) or belongs to the Mechanical semantic field, provided Slot 4 is free, f becomes 4.

Where on is a Manner word (way), if Slot 7 is free, f becomes 7.

When all the above have failed, if the Subject slot can take either a human or a non-human noun, f becomes 1.

If the above fails, then when the verb in the row has been provided by a head-noun (eating in apple-eating), and Slot 4 is free, we inspect vn. If vn denotes a part of the body (hand) or denotes a material (glass), f becomes 4.

If f has found a value above 0, Tryitem yields 'true'. The value of f is passed up to Fitonoun.

Trysent (f, g, on) boolean

Called from Fitonoun.

We have a row of Slots, row g, whose verb is provided by one of the nouns in a sequence. Another row is provided by on, the other noun in the sequence. This procedure tries the sentence provided by the other noun in the available functions of the former row, e.g. riding-breeches:

Breeches that someone wears when someone rides.

g denotes the row of Slots. f yields the function of the sentence set up by on. The procedure yields 'true' and sets f if a slot is found. f becomes one of:

1 subject
3 object
4 instrument
6 locative of time (while)
7 manner (as)

hed takes the value of the noun whose verb has provided row g of Slots, e.g. 1 for the breeches of riding-breeches.

The following rules operate in order, and as soon as f takes a value, the rest of the rules are skipped.

Where the Object slot in row g holds 4 or 5 and hed can take a sentence as object, f is set to 3, e.g. dancing lesson:

Someone teaches something
Someone dances
Someone teaches that someone dances,
(i.e. someone teaches dancing).

flow obstruction:

Someone obstructs something
Someone (or something) flows
Someone obstructs that someone (or something) flows.

Where hed is causative and the Subject slot is available, f becomes 1, e.g. attraction increase:

Trysent, cont'd.

Someone (or something) increases

Someone (or something) attracts something (or someone)

That someone attracts someone increases (i.e. the attraction of someone for someone else increases).

When the verb of on is causative, e.g. work song, or can imply its object, e.g. riding-breeches, or is intransitive, e.g. birth pangs, and the time slot is available, f becomes 6, e.g.

A coat that someone wears when someone rides.

When the verb of on is transitive, and the instrument slot is available, f becomes 4, e.g. dog-handler competition:

Someone competes by that someone handles a dog or dogs.

Finally, by default, if the manner slot is free, f becomes 7, e.g. security guard:

Someone that guards like or in security.

If f has found a value above 0, Trysent yields 'true'.

The value of f is passed up to Fitonoun.

Twoloc (head, mod, lx, y, z, OVER)

Called from Locfind. Calls Fields and Relate.

This procedure deals with sequences where both nouns are locatives of the same kind (i.e. both place or both time). Findfields will already have operated before Twoloc is called, and will have dealt with e.g. castle dungeon.

The following rules operate in order, and as soon as one set of conditions is found applicable, the rest of the rules are skipped.

Twoloc, cont'd.

Where the head and modifier are time words, if the modifier has an adjective, 3030 (C3) is yielded; if it has no adjective, 3011 (C1 subtype 1) is yielded:

Ten-hour day (i.e. the number of hours worked):

A day for or containing ten hours.

Monday afternoon:

An afternoon in or on Monday.

Where the head takes to, provided that the sequence has not already been dealt with by Findfields, 3016 (C1 subtype 6) is yielded:

London road:

A road to London.

Even if the sequence has already been dealt with by Findfields, 3011 (C1 subtype 1) is yielded:

A road in or on London.

When the head belongs to the field of buildings and the modifier to the field of furniture, 3030 is yielded:

bedroom:

A room for or containing a bed or beds.

Where the modifier belongs to the field of buildings and the head to the field of furniture, 3011 and 3014 are yielded:

kitchen table:

Twoloc, cont'd.

A table in or on a kitchen

The kind of table found in or on a kitchen.

Where the modifier is a proper noun, 3011 and 3030 are yielded:

Innisfree lake:

A lake in or on Innisfree

A lake for or containing Innisfree

(Innisfree is in fact an island.)

Where the modifier has an adjective, 3030 is yielded:

<*ten-*>*acre field*:

A field for or containing ten acres [or: ten-acre]

Finally, if none of the preceding conditions is met, types 3030 and 3011 are yielded:

jungle wall:

A wall for or containing the jungle;

A wall in or on a jungle.

Twoloc yields 'true' if one or more of the types has been yielded.

Typout (y, z)

Called from *Typout* and the Mainprogram. Calls *Print*, *Printch*, *Typout*, *Typwd* and *Writetext*.

This procedure prints one or more type numbers from the 'left-hand side' of the Nest, after the example has been printed

Typout, cont'd.

and before the underlying sentence and the paraphrases are printed. The name of the type is printed, e.g. Annex. Then its number is printed. If the noun sequence has more than one interpretation, a stroke is printed between each of the type designators. Where there is a sentence type, the word sentence is printed, followed by the number of the row of Slots in which the sentence is stored.

If called with y = -1, this procedure gives all the type numbers for the sequence. Where there are nested sequences, it acts recursively, bracketing its results.

Thus for factory chimney we get

Annex 4020 / Locative 3011 / Sentence 1

and for bed + room corridor:

(Locative 3030 / Sentence 1) Locative 3016 /
Equative 5011 / Locative 3011.

Typwd (t)

Called from Typout. Calls Writetext.

This procedure prints a word denoting the type of a noun sequence, e.g. Locative for 3011 to 3030 inclusive, Equative for 5010 to 5020 inclusive. When a phrase or sentence has been included in a higher sentence and left behind only a low type number, Typwd prints Included or unspecified.

For example, the underlying sentences for (towel disposal) bin are:

Someone disposes of a towel or towels;
Someone disposes of a towel or towels in a bin or bins.

The former sentence is included in the latter, with no

Typwd, cont'd.

independent interpretation. So the type designators read: (Included or unspecified) Sentence 2.

Underout

Called from the Mainprogram. Calls Newline, Sentout and Writetext.

This procedure prints, after the type numbers, any underlying sentences that have been formed for an example during the analysis. It takes them from the array Slots, using Sentout. E.g. towel disposal bin:

Someone disposes of a towel or towels;

Someone disposes of a towel or towels in a bin or bins;

(squawk box) switch:

Someone squawks in a box or boxes;

Someone switches on a box that someone squawks in with a switch or switches.

Verbalfind boolean

Called from Analyze. Calls Relate and Verbinterp.

This procedure seeks a verb. If Verbinterp yields 'true', Verbalfind becomes 'true'. Besides the complex procedure Verbinterp, several other conditions yield a Verb interpretation.

Where the modifier is a proper noun denoting a human being or a human organisation, two interpretations are pursued. Firstly, where the head is locative or denotes a mechanism or furniture, an Ownership type, 1040, is yielded: Council house:

A house made by or belonging to a Council;

Lincoln car:

A car made by or belonging to Lincoln;

Knoll desk:

A desk made by or belonging to Knoll.

Secondly, where none of the three latter conditions applies, if the head exists physically, an Ownership type, 1050, is yielded:

Police truncheon:

A truncheon belonging to the Police.

When the head denotes a disease, the Disease type, 1030, is yielded: hay fever:

A disease causing or caused by hay.

When the head denotes a mechanism and the modifier a material, the Fuel type, 1020, is yielded: steam boat:

A boat powered by steam.

Verbalfind is one of the eight procedures in Analyze which have been permuted during the development of the program.

Verbinterp (lfg, lx, head, mod, y, z, headeepest, modeepest, OLAB) boolean

Called from Verbalfind. Calls Code, Fitonoun, Function, Hasverb, Horse, Man, Record and Setvnoun.

lfg and lx denote the last filled row of Slots and the last filled location in the negative part of the Nest. y and z are the current values along the second and third axes of the Nest.

Verbinterp, cont'd.

headeepest and modeepest are 'true' when the head and the modifier are at their deepest possible level: e.g. for disposal in (towel disposal) bin, modeepest is 'false', so a reference to the sentence set up by disposal is recovered from the lower level of the Nest. OLAB is the label to go to if the type number fails to be recorded, i.e. if the Nest or Slots overflow.

This procedure seeks a verb in the head and the modifier. It becomes 'true' if it finds one, and if it satisfactorily fills one or more rows of Slots. It sets up rows, or finds them if the word with the verb is in a nested sequence. It moves lfg when it sets up a row of Slots. It puts references to rows of Slots into the Nest at lx, moving lx to the left before putting a relationship number into Nest [lx, y, z]. lx should be 0 when Verbinterp is called.

The overall structure of the procedure is:

If the head has a verb,
if the head is at its deepest, e.g. coal-rake, do (a); if not, e.g. Sunday (horse-riding) do (b).

If the head has no verb,
if the modifier is at its deepest, e.g. fly-leaf, do (c); if the modifier is nested, e.g. (horse-riding) afternoon, do (d); where (a), (b), (c) and (d) stand for complex activities which will now be described.

Where (a) the head has a verb and is at its deepest level, the first attempt at an interpretation is made for the words man, woman and horse. Each of these nouns has the 11th primary feature, which shows that there is a procedure, named according to a noun, by which one verb is chosen from the several verbs available, according to the features of the other noun. If the modifier has a verb, we jump to SEEMOD. Otherwise we inspect the noun. Horse has pulls and carries. Man has five verbs; when the other noun is a food, for instance in barm-man, the verb sells is activated, yielding ultimately

Verbinterp, cont'd.

A man that sells barm.

The noun woman picks up the procedure Man, to yield, for the food feature,

A woman that sells an apple or apples.

We then jump to SEEMOD.

To continue with the description of Verbinterp: if the head denotes clothing and the modifier denotes a part of the body, the locative feature is added to the modifier, to be picked up later for e.g. thigh-boots; also under these conditions, if the modifier has to added to its verb, then the head is made to take to. The function of the head is obtained: e.g. subject for Stockholm chief, instrument for coal-rake.

Where the modifier, as well as the head, has a verb, the modifier is tested for the 11th primary feature, e.g. horse-tram, where tram has travels but pulls is activated, to give ultimately

A tram that a horse or horses pulls.

We then jump to SEEMOD. If the noun with the 11th primary feature is not horse, we jump to KEEPON.

To continue with the first part of Verbinterp: the functions of the modifier are obtained, e.g. riding in riding-coat has the verb function, leading to

A coat that someone wears when someone rides.

If both the head and the modifier have the verb function, e.g. jog-trot, an equative type, 5014, is yielded:

A trot that is a jog.

Verbinterp, cont'd.

Where the modifier is a subject and its verb is overt, or where the head is the subject, its verb is overt and the modifier is a subject, an equative type, 5012, is yielded:

boarder pupil,[10] fighter-bomber.

We now proceed from the label KEEPON. The procedure Setvnoun is called, to set up a sentence, with the verb in the head providing the verb of the sentence. If it succeeds, e.g. coal-rake:

Someone rakes coal with a rake,

we jump to FOUND; otherwise we jump to SEEMOD.

(b) Where the head is not at its deepest level, e.g. Sunday (horse-riding), the 'left-hand side' of the Nest is inspected. If a sentence is found, e.g.

Someone rides a horse,

the procedure Fitonoun is called to fit the other noun into the sentence.

Someone rides a horse in or on Sunday.

(c) At the label SEEMOD, where the modifier has a verb and is at its deepest level, the first attempt at an interpretation is made for the word horse: e.g. tram-horse. Then the functions of the modifier are obtained: e.g. the verb function for riding in riding afternoon, the subject function for fly in fly-leaf.

Where the modifier can be the subject, if its verb is overt, an Equative type, 5013, is yielded:

A leaf that is a fly. (NED supports this.)

Verbinterp, cont'd.

Next, Setvnoun is called, to set up a sentence, with the verb in the modifier providing the verb of the sentence:

riding afternoon:

Someone rides in or on the afternoon.

If it succeeds, we jump to FOUND, otherwise we jump to OUT and thus end Verbinterp.

(d) Where the modifier is not at its deepest level, e.g.

(horse-riding) afternoon,

the 'left-hand side' of the Nest is inspected. If a sentence is found, e.g.

Someone rides a horse,

the procedure Fitonoun is called to fit the other noun into the sentence:

Someone rides a horse in or on the afternoon.

We then proceed to the label FOUND, where Verbinterp is set 'true'. Finally we pass the label OUT, and Verbinterp is concluded.

Verbp (x, y, z) boolean

Called from Sentout. Calls Code, Horse, Man, Printch and Writetext.

This procedure prints one or more verbs from vector n of the array Verbs, e.g. speaks from Mongo language. n is the

Verbp, cont'd.

contents of Nest [x, y, z]. The array Verbs has the vectors [m, n, v], where m contains the verb (in graphic form, e.g. SPEAKS), n contains a reference to the noun connected with the verb (e.g. language), and v holds the total of verbs connected with this noun, up to a maximum of 5.

If the 11th primary feature is found on the noun n, and if the verb to be printed is provided by the head, j takes the value of the modifier. j pursues it through any nesting, using a loop at LP, until it has the value of the modifier at its lowest position.

Where x denotes the head and the head-noun is not horse, Verbp calls Man; otherwise, if x denotes the modifier and the modifying noun is horse, Verbp calls Horse. These will cause the appropriate verb to be printed, e.g. sells for man in barm man, and pulls for horse in horse-tram.

The work connected with the 11th primary feature has now been described. It now merges with the normal course of Verbp.

To continue with the normal course, the verb connected with x, where x implies the head noun or the modifier, e.g. language, is printed from the array Verbs. If there is more than one verb connected with x, all the verbs are printed, using the loop at the label LOOP, and linked by or.

Writetext (string)

Called from An, Anafledge, C1S4, C1S5, Carderror, Codig, Ergive, F2AND3, G1, Infledge, Notin2, Nounout, Nounp, Phrase, Polytest, Sentout, Slotout, The, Toosmall, Typout, Typwd, Underout, Verbp, and the Mainprogram and the Outerprogram.

This procedure causes a given string of characters to be printed, e.g. made by or belonging to for Lincoln car:

A car made by or belonging to Lincoln.

<u>End of Index to Procedures</u>

The Outerprogram exists to find the size of the dictionary so that the Mainprogram can set up an array of the right size for it.

<u>Procedures called from the Outerprogram</u>

<u>Read</u>

<u>Writetext</u>.

<u>Procedures called from the Mainprogram in order of first occurrence</u>

<u>Read</u>

<u>Writetext</u>

<u>Nextch</u>

<u>Skipch</u>

<u>Newline</u>

<u>Cardin</u>

<u>Printch</u>

<u>Nestfill</u>

<u>Initslots</u>

<u>Anafledge</u>

<u>Addpref</u>

<u>Order</u>

<u>Typout</u>

<u>Print</u>

<u>Underout</u>

<u>Fledge</u>.

Footnotes to Appendix III

1 The only major one is E2: *divorce case*, *weather theme*. There are a few minor cases, e.g. *bread-knife* (contrast coal-*rake*, where the verb is the same as the noun).

2 I.e. a two-dimensional array which is part of a three-dimensional array.

3 A 'human' feature on the modifier would yield

A fellow that is a passenger.

The program still yields some erroneous interpretations, e.g. for *fellow-servant*.

4 E.g. *a building designed on a computer*. (The more usual meaning is *a building for or containing a computer*.)

5 The data do not include a clear example of this, so an example outside the data is used for the illustration. An example in the data is (*rail + way*) *station*.

6 *F5* is output using the phrase from *F4*.

7 E.g. if *colour* were a homograph, and colour<ed> were in the array Nouns, part of the <ed> would be overwritten, to give colour[1] .

8 *Slotout* would yield for *bread-knife*: *A knife that* ..., but *rake* is represented by *something* to avoid the repetition in *a rake that someone rakes coal with*.

9 Bread-knife is chosen to illustrate Slotout at this point because it illustrates the use of an explicit subject (contrast coal-rake: something that someone rakes coal with). Bread-knife also has an explicit object (contrast breakfast apparatus: apparatus that someone breakfasts with). Bread-knife is not in the data, but the latter sequences are.

10 There is a counter-example being used in Britain, heard in a conversation in June 1984; probably from the U.S.A.:

designer jeans

i.e. jeans designed by a prestigious designer (and costing more than ordinary jeans).

APPENDIX IV

SAMPLES OF INTERPRETATIONS

APPENDIX IV

SAMPLES OF INTERPRETATIONS

The format of this output has been altered slightly

(a) to conform to the format of this book;

(b) to insert the scoring shown in the evaluations of the interpretations.

Bracketed scores indicate sequences represented elsewhere in the interpretations.

If the program meets an unforeseen element in the data, it will print an error warning.

```
ANALYSIS OF NOUN SEQUENCES.
THE DICTIONARY HAS BEEN READ IN.
IT CONTAINS     1911   NOUNS AND      511   VERBS.


          .........................................

MARSH        0300        <">*CONVERSATION<"> CHAIR


HOMOGRAPHIC VARIANT NO.  1   , PREFERENCE NO.  1
SENTENCE     1

HOMOGRAPHIC VARIANT NO.  2   , PREFERENCE NO.  2
SENTENCE     4

UNDERLYING SENTENCE(S):

 SOMEONE SITS IN A CHAIR[1] OR CHAIR[1]S WHEN SOMEONE
 CONVERSES

 SOMEONE CONVERSES

 SOMEONE SITS IN A CHAIR[1] OR CHAIR[1]S

 SOMEONE TRAVELS IN OR CARRIES A CHAIR[2] OR CHAIR[2]S WHEN
 SOMEONE CONVERSES

 SOMEONE CONVERSES

 SOMEONE TRAVELS IN OR CARRIES A CHAIR[2] OR CHAIR[2]S


INTERPRETATION(S) IN ORDER OF HOMOGRAPHIC PREFERENCE:

 A CHAIR[1] THAT SOMEONE SITS IN WHEN SOMEONE CONVERSES. ✓✓

 A CHAIR[2] THAT SOMEONE TRAVELS IN OR CARRIES WHEN SOMEONE
 CONVERSES.

          .........................................

DEIGHTON    0340         <*AMALGAMATED> *MINERALS CHEQUE

MATERIAL  6010  /SENTENCE     1  /OWNERSHIP  1050
```

UNDERLYING SENTENCE(S):

SOMEONE PAYS FOR *AMALGAMATED *MINERALS WITH A CHEQUE OR CHEQUES

INTERPRETATION(S):

A CHEQUE OF *AMALGAMATED *MINERALS.

A CHEQUE THAT SOMEONE PAYS FOR *AMALGAMATED *MINERALS WITH.

A CHEQUE BELONGING TO *AMALGAMATED *MINERALS. √

....

DEIGHTON 0290 <*BAY> *STREET FRIEND

LOCATIVE 3012 /LOCATIVE 3011

INTERPRETATION(S):

A FRIEND THAT LIVES IN OR COMES FROM THE *BAY *STREET. √√

A FRIEND IN OR ON A *BAY *STREET.

....

BRAINE 0400 <*BULLDOG >*DRUMMOND TYPE

HOMOGRAPHIC VARIANT NO. 1 , PREFERENCE NO. 1
ANNEX 4010 /OWNERSHIP 1050

HOMOGRAPHIC VARIANT NO. 2 , PREFERENCE NO. 2
OWNERSHIP 1040

INTERPRETATION(S) IN ORDER OF HOMOGRAPHIC PREFERENCE:

THE TYPE[1] OF *BULLDOG *DRUMMOND. √√

A TYPE[1] BELONGING TO *BULLDOG *DRUMMOND.

TYPE[2] MADE BY OR BELONGING TO *BULLDOG *DRUMMOND.

....

FIELDING 0790 <*COVENT->*GARDEN CHURCH

LOCATIVE 3011 /LOCATIVE 3030

INTERPRETATION(S):

A CHURCH IN OR ON A *COVENT- *GARDEN. √√

A CHURCH FOR OR CONTAINING A *COVENT- *GARDEN OR *COVENT- *GARDENS.

....

THACKERAY 0360 <*EAST >*INDIA *REGISTER

LOCATIVE 3011 /LOCATIVE 3030

INTERPRETATION(S):

THE *REGISTER IN OR ON *EAST *INDIA.

THE *REGISTER FOR OR CONTAINING *EAST *INDIA. √

....

BRAINE 0200 <*FAIR >*ISLE CARDIGAN

LOCATIVE 3011

INTERPRETATION(S):

A CARDIGAN IN OR ON *FAIR *ISLE. **X?**

....

RICHARDSON 0240 <ANOTHER->GUISE SORT <OF HEART>

ERROR ON CARD, IN LOC 46
MATERIAL 6040 /ANNEX 4040

INTERPRETATION(S):

A SORT OF ANOTHER- GUISES.

A SORT WITH A ANOTHER- GUISE OR ANOTHER- GUISES. ✓

....

DEIGHTON 0130 <ARMOURED> CAR COMPANY

SENTENCE 1 /LOCATIVE 3013

UNDERLYING SENTENCE(S):

A COMPANY OR COMPANYS MAKES OR USES A ARMOURED CAR OR ARMOURED CARS

INTERPRETATION(S):

A COMPANY THAT MAKES OR USES A ARMOURED CAR OR ARMOURED CARS. ✓✓

A COMPANY THAT LIVES IN OR WORKS IN A ARMOURED CAR.

....

DEIGHTON 0510 <ARTIFICIAL> SILK SCARF

MATERIAL 6010 /SENTENCE 1

UNDERLYING SENTENCE(S):

ARTIFICIAL SILK WEARS A SCARF OR SCARFS

INTERPRETATION(S):

A SCARF OF ARTIFICIAL SILK. ✓✓

A SCARF THAT ARTIFICIAL SILK WEARS.

....

BRAINE 0340 <BARBED >WIRE FENCE

MATERIAL 6010 /ANNEX 4040 /SENTENCE 1

UNDERLYING SENTENCE(S):

A FENCE OR FENCES SURROUNDS BARBED WIRE

INTERPRETATION(S):

A FENCE OF BARBED WIRE. √√

A FENCE WITH BARBED WIRE.

A FENCE THAT SURROUNDS BARBED WIRE.

....

SCOTT 0510 <BEND->LEATHER-GUN

MATERIAL 6010 /SENTENCE 1 /SENTENCE 2 /FUEL 102
0

UNDERLYING SENTENCE(S):

SOMEONE SHOOTS BEND- LEATHER WITH A GUN OR GUNS

BEND- LEATHER SHOOTS WITH A GUN OR GUNS

INTERPRETATION(S):

A GUN OF BEND- LEATHER. √√

A GUN THAT SOMEONE SHOOTS BEND- LEATHER WITH.

A GUN THAT BEND- LEATHER SHOOTS WITH.

A GUN POWERED BY BEND- LEATHER.

....

BENNETT 0220 <BLACK->CURRANT JAM

ANNEX 4040 /SENTENCE 1 /SENTENCE 2

UNDERLYING SENTENCE(S):

SOMEONE SQUEEZES A BLACK- CURRANT OR BLACK- CURRANTS

A BLACK- CURRANT OR BLACK- CURRANTS SQUEEZES JAM

INTERPRETATION(S):

JAM WITH A BLACK- CURRANT OR BLACK- CURRANTS. √√?

THE JAM OF A BLACK- CURRANT OR BLACK- CURRANTS.

JAM THAT A BLACK- CURRANT OR BLACK- CURRANTS SQUEEZES.

....

DEIGHTON 0500 <BROWN> PAPER BUNDLE

MATERIAL 6040 /LOCATIVE 3011

INTERPRETATION(S):

A BUNDLE OF BROWN PAPER. √√

A BUNDLE IN OR ON BROWN PAPER.

....

BRAINE 0070 <CARBONATED->WATER SENSATION

SENTENCE 1 /SENTENCE 2 /LOCATIVE 3011

UNDERLYING SENTENCE(S):

SOMEONE FEELS CARBONATED- WATER

SOMEONE FEELS A SENSATION OR SENSATIONS IN CARBONATED- WATER

INTERPRETATION(S):

THE SENSATION OF CARBONATED- WATER. √√

A SENSATION THAT SOMEONE FEELS IN CARBONATED- WATER.

A SENSATION IN OR ON CARBONATED- WATER.

....

RADCLIFFE 0200 <COMMON->PLACE REMARK

SENTENCE 1 /SENTENCE 2

UNDERLYING SENTENCE(S):

A COMMON- PLACE OR COMMON- PLACES REMARKS

SOMEONE REMARKS IN A COMMON- PLACE OR COMMON- PLACES

INTERPRETATION(S):

THE REMARK OF A COMMON- PLACE OR COMMON- PLACES.

THE REMARK IN A COMMON- PLACE OR COMMON- PLACES. ✓

....

THACKERAY 0250 <COW'S->SKIN TRUNK

MATERIAL 6010 /LOCATIVE 3030

INTERPRETATION(S):

A TRUNK OF COW'S- SKINS. ✓✓

A TRUNK FOR OR CONTAINING A COW'S- SKIN OR COW'S- SKINS.

....

BENNETT 0050 <EVERY>DAY CROCKERY

SENTENCE 1 /SENTENCE 2 /LOCATIVE 3011

UNDERLYING SENTENCE(S):

SOMEONE EATS WITH CROCKERY IN A EVERY DAY OR EVERY DAYS

SOMEONE EATS A EVERY DAY OR EVERY DAYS WITH CROCKERY

INTERPRETATION(S):

CROCKERY THAT SOMEONE EATS WITH IN A EVERY DAY OR EVERY DAYS. ✓✓

CROCKERY THAT SOMEONE EATS A EVERY DAY OR EVERY DAYS WITH.

CROCKERY IN OR ON A EVERY DAY.

....

BRONTE 0540 <EVERY >DAY COUNTENANCE

LOCATIVE 3013

INTERPRETATION(S):

A COUNTENANCE THAT LIVES IN OR WORKS IN A EVERY DAY. X

....

THACKERAY 0540 <EVERY->DAY LIFE

SENTENCE 1 /LOCATIVE 3011

UNDERLYING SENTENCE(S):

SOMEONE LIVES IN A EVERY- DAY OR EVERY- DAYS

INTERPRETATION(S):

THE LIFE IN A EVERY- DAY OR EVERY- DAYS. ✓✓

LIFE IN OR ON A EVERY- DAY.

....

BENNETT 0260 <FIRST->FLOOR CORRIDOR

LOCATIVE 3016 /ANNEX 4040 /LOCATIVE 3011

INTERPRETATION(S):

A CORRIDOR TO A FIRST- FLOOR.

A CORRIDOR WITH A FIRST- FLOOR OR FIRST- FLOORS.

A CORRIDOR IN OR ON A FIRST- FLOOR. ✓

....

SCOTT 0560 <FIRST->RATE MAN/OF/WAR

HOMOGRAPHIC VARIANT NO. 1 , PREFERENCE NO. 1
ANNEX 4040 /SENTENCE 1 /SENTENCE 2

HOMOGRAPHIC VARIANT NO. 2 , PREFERENCE NO. 2
SENTENCE 4

UNDERLYING SENTENCE(S):

A MAN/OF/WAR OR MAN/OF/WARS SAILS OR FIGHTS LIKE OR IN A FIRST- RATE[1] OR FIRST- RATE[1]S

A MAN/OF/WAR OR MAN/OF/WARS SAILS OR FIGHTS A FIRST-RATE[1] OR FIRST- RATE[1]S

A MAN/OF/WAR OR MAN/OF/WARS SAILS OR FIGHTS

A MAN/OF/WAR OR MAN/OF/WARS SAILS OR FIGHTS A FIRST-RATE[2] OR FIRST- RATE[2]S

INTERPRETATION(S) IN ORDER OF HOMOGRAPHIC PREFERENCE:

A MAN/OF/WAR WITH A FIRST- RATE[1] OR FIRST- RATE[1]S.

A MAN/OF/WAR THAT SAILS OR FIGHTS LIKE OR IN A FIRST-RATE[1] OR FIRST- RATE[1]S. √?

A MAN/OF/WAR THAT SAILS OR FIGHTS A FIRST- RATE[1] OR FIRST- RATE[1]S.

A MAN/OF/WAR THAT SAILS OR FIGHTS A FIRST- RATE[2] OR FIRST- RATE[2]S.

....

LAWRENCE 0160 <FIRST->RATE PREACHER

HOMOGRAPHIC VARIANT NO. 1 , PREFERENCE NO. 1
ANNEX 4040 /SENTENCE 1

HOMOGRAPHIC VARIANT NO. 2 , PREFERENCE NO. 2
SENTENCE 3 /SENTENCE 4

UNDERLYING SENTENCE(S):

A PREACHER OR PREACHERS PREACHES LIKE OR IN A FIRST- RATE[1] OR FIRST- RATE[1]S

A PREACHER OR PREACHERS PREACHES

SOMEONE PAYS A PREACHER OR PREACHERS

A PREACHER OR PREACHERS PAYS A FIRST- RATE[2] OR FIRST- RATE[2]S

INTERPRETATION(S) IN ORDER OF HOMOGRAPHIC PREFERENCE:

A PREACHER WITH A FIRST- RATE[1] OR FIRST- RATE[1]S.

SOMEONE THAT PREACHES LIKE OR IN A FIRST- RATE[1] OR FIRST- RATE[1]S. **√?**

A PREACHER THAT SOMEONE PAYS.

A PREACHER THAT PAYS A FIRST- RATE[2] OR FIRST- RATE[2]S.

....

BRAINE 0200 <FIRST->RATE TAILORING

HOMOGRAPHIC VARIANT NO. 1 , PREFERENCE NO. 1
ANNEX 4040 /SENTENCE 1 /SENTENCE 2

HOMOGRAPHIC VARIANT NO. 2 , PREFERENCE NO. 2
EQUATIVE 5014 /SENTENCE 3 /SENTENCE 4

UNDERLYING SENTENCE(S):

SOMEONE TAILORS A FIRST- RATE[1] OR FIRST- RATE[1]S

SOMEONE TAILORS LIKE OR IN A FIRST- RATE[1] OR FIRST- RATE[1]S

SOMEONE TAILORS A FIRST- RATE[2] OR FIRST- RATE[2]S

A FIRST- RATE[2] OR FIRST- RATE[2]S TAILORS

```
INTERPRETATION(S) IN ORDER OF HOMOGRAPHIC PREFERENCE:

 A TAILORING WITH A FIRST- RATE[1] OR FIRST- RATE[1]S.

 THE TAILORING OF A FIRST- RATE[1] OR FIRST- RATE[1]S.

 THE TAILORING LIKE OR IN A FIRST- RATE[1] OR FIRST-
 RATE[1]S. ✓

 A TAILORING THAT IS A FIRST- RATE[2].

 THE TAILORING OF A FIRST- RATE[2] OR FIRST- RATE[2]S.

 THE TAILORING OF A FIRST- RATE[2] OR FIRST- RATE[2]S.

          ......................................

BRONTE      1000        <FIRST->RATE TREAT


HOMOGRAPHIC VARIANT NO.  1  , PREFERENCE NO.  1
ANNEX  4040  /SENTENCE    1  /SENTENCE    2

HOMOGRAPHIC VARIANT NO.  2  , PREFERENCE NO.  2
EQUATIVE  5014  /SENTENCE    3  /SENTENCE    4

UNDERLYING SENTENCE(S):

 SOMEONE TREATS A FIRST- RATE[1] OR FIRST- RATE[1]S

 SOMEONE TREATS LIKE OR IN A FIRST- RATE[1] OR FIRST-
 RATE[1]S

 SOMEONE TREATS A FIRST- RATE[2] OR FIRST- RATE[2]S

 A FIRST- RATE[2] OR FIRST- RATE[2]S TREATS


INTERPRETATION(S) IN ORDER OF HOMOGRAPHIC PREFERENCE:

 A TREAT WITH A FIRST- RATE[1] OR FIRST- RATE[1]S.

 THE TREAT OF A FIRST- RATE[1] OR FIRST- RATE[1]S.

 THE TREAT LIKE OR IN A FIRST- RATE[1] OR FIRST- RATE[1]S. ✓

 A TREAT THAT IS A FIRST- RATE[2].
```

THE TREAT OF A FIRST- RATE[2] OR FIRST- RATE[2]S.

THE TREAT OF A FIRST- RATE[2] OR FIRST- RATE[2]S.

....

DEIGHTON 0400 <FIVE> DOLLAR BILL

HOMOGRAPHIC VARIANT NO. 2 , PREFERENCE NO. 1
SENTENCE 2

HOMOGRAPHIC VARIANT NO. 1 , PREFERENCE NO. 2
SENTENCE 1

UNDERLYING SENTENCE(S):

A BILL[1] OR BILL[1]S COSTS OR IS WORTH A FIVE DOLLAR OR FIVE DOLLARS

SOMEONE PAYS OR PAYS FOR OR ADVERTIZES A FIVE DOLLAR OR FIVE DOLLARS WITH A BILL[2] OR BILL[2]S

INTERPRETATION(S) IN ORDER OF HOMOGRAPHIC PREFERENCE:

A BILL[2] THAT SOMEONE PAYS OR PAYS FOR OR ADVERTIZES A FIVE DOLLAR OR FIVE DOLLARS WITH.

A BILL[1] THAT COSTS OR IS WORTH A FIVE DOLLAR OR FIVE DOLLARS. ✓

....

BRAINE 0360 (*LAMPTON-*LUFFORD) *REPORT

(EQUATIVE 5010 /OWNERSHIP 1050 /ADDITIVE 7010)SENTENC
E 1 /OWNERSHIP 1050 /LOCATIVE 3030

UNDERLYING SENTENCE(S):

SOMEONE REPORTS *LUFFORD THAT IS *LAMPTON OR *LUFFORD BELONGING TO *LAMPTON OR *LUFFORD AND *LAMPTON IN THE *REPORT

INTERPRETATION(S):

SOMETHING THAT SOMEONE REPORTS *LUFFORD THAT IS *LAMPTON OR *LUFFORD BELONGING TO *LAMPTON OR *LUFFORD AND *LAMPTON IN.

THE *REPORT BELONGING TO X *LUFFORD THAT IS *LAMPTON OR *LUFFORD BELONGING TO *LAMPTON OR *LUFFORD AND *LAMPTON. ✓

THE *REPORT FOR OR CONTAINING *LUFFORD THAT IS *LAMPTON OR *LUFFORD BELONGING TO *LAMPTON OR *LUFFORD AND *LAMPTON.

....

LAWRENCE 0100 (*LION *WALLACE) BOOTH

(EQUATIVE 5010)LOCATIVE 3030 /OWNERSHIP 1040

INTERPRETATION(S):

A BOOTH FOR OR CONTAINING ✓✓ *WALLACE THAT IS A *LION. ✓✓

A BOOTH MADE BY OR BELONGING TO *WALLACE THAT IS A *LION.

....

DEIGHTON 0350 (*SECURITY *GUARD) CAP <AND> (GUN BE
LT)

ERROR ON CARD, IN LOC 48
(SENTENCE 1 /SENTENCE 2)EQUATIVE 5012 /SENTENCE
3 /OWNERSHIP 1050

UNDERLYING SENTENCE(S):

A *GUARD OR *GUARDS GUARDS *SECURITY

A *GUARD OR *GUARDS GUARDS LIKE OR IN *SECURITY

SOMEONE THAT GUARDS *SECURITY OR SOMEONE THAT GUARDS LIKE OR IN *SECURITY WEARS A CAP OR CAPS

INTERPRETATION(S):

A CAP THAT IS SOMEONE THAT GUARDS *SECURITY OR SOMEONE THAT

GUARDS LIKE OR IN *SECURITY.

A CAP THAT SOMEONE THAT GUARDS *SECURITY OR SOMEONE THAT GUARDS LIKE OR IN *SECURITY WEARS.

A CAP BELONGING TO SOMEONE THAT GUARDS *SECURITY OR SOMEONE THAT GUARDS LIKE OR IN *SECURITY.

....

DEIGHTON 0350 (*SECURITY *GUARD) COAT

(SENTENCE 1 /SENTENCE 2)EQUATIVE 5012 /SENTENCE 3 /OWNERSHIP 1050

UNDERLYING SENTENCE(S):

A *GUARD OR *GUARDS GUARDS *SECURITY

A *GUARD OR *GUARDS GUARDS LIKE OR IN *SECURITY

SOMEONE THAT GUARDS *SECURITY OR SOMEONE THAT GUARDS LIKE OR IN *SECURITY WEARS A COAT OR COATS

INTERPRETATION(S):

A COAT THAT IS SOMEONE THAT GUARDS *SECURITY OR SOMEONE THAT GUARDS LIKE OR IN *SECURITY.

A COAT THAT SOMEONE THAT GUARDS *SECURITY OR SOMEONE THAT GUARDS LIKE OR IN *SECURITY (√) WEARS. √

A COAT BELONGING TO SOMEONE THAT GUARDS *SECURITY OR SOMEONE THAT GUARDS LIKE OR IN *SECURITY.

....

BRAINE 0190 (*SHERATON-TYPE) FURNITURE

HOMOGRAPHIC VARIANT NO. 1 , PREFERENCE NO. 1
(ANNEX 4010 /OWNERSHIP 1050)ANNEX 4040 /SENTENCE
1

HOMOGRAPHIC VARIANT NO. 2 , PREFERENCE NO. 2
(OWNERSHIP 1040)SENTENCE 2

UNDERLYING SENTENCE(S):

SOMEONE FURNISHES THE TYPE[1] OF *SHERATON OR A TYPE[1] BELONGING TO *SHERATON WITH FURNITURE

SOMEONE FURNISHES TYPE[2] MADE BY OR BELONGING TO *SHERATON WITH FURNITURE

INTERPRETATION(S) IN ORDER OF HOMOGRAPHIC PREFERENCE:

FURNITURE WITH √√ THE TYPE[1] OF √√ *SHERATON OR A TYPE[1] BELONGING TO *SHERATON.

SOMETHING THAT SOMEONE FURNISHES THE TYPE[1] OF *SHERATON OR A TYPE[1] BELONGING TO *SHERATON WITH.

SOMETHING THAT SOMEONE FURNISHES TYPE[2] MADE BY OR BELONGING TO *SHERATON WITH.

....

MARSH 0370 (SCHOOL-GIRL) *FRENCH

(ANNEX 4030 /LOCATIVE 3013 /SENTENCE 1 /SENTENCE 2 /OWNERSHIP 1050)MATERIAL 6050 /ANNEX 4010 /SENTENCE 3 /SENTENCE 4

UNDERLYING SENTENCE(S):

A GIRL OR GIRLS STUDIES IN A SCHOOL OR SCHOOLS

SOMEONE STUDIES A GIRL OR GIRLS IN A SCHOOL OR SCHOOLS

SOMEONE SPEAKS A GIRL IN THE SCHOOL OR A GIRL THAT LIVES IN OR WORKS IN A SCHOOL OR A GIRL THAT STUDIES IN A SCHOOL OR SCHOOLS OR A GIRL THAT SOMEONE STUDIES IN A SCHOOL OR SCHOOLS OR A GIRL BELONGING TO A SCHOOL LIKE OR IN *FRENCH

A GIRL IN THE SCHOOL OR A GIRL THAT LIVES IN OR WORKS IN A SCHOOL OR A GIRL THAT STUDIES IN A SCHOOL OR SCHOOLS OR A GIRL THAT SOMEONE STUDIES IN A SCHOOL OR SCHOOLS OR A GIRL BELONGING TO A SCHOOL SPEAKS LIKE OR IN *FRENCH

INTERPRETATION(S):

*FRENCH OF A GIRL IN THE SCHOOL OR A GIRL THAT LIVES IN OR WORKS IN A SCHOOL OR A GIRL THAT STUDIES IN A SCHOOL OR SCHOOLS OR A GIRL THAT SOMEONE STUDIES IN A SCHOOL OR SCHOOLS OR A GIRL BELONGING TO A SCHOOL.

*FRENCH OF A GIRL IN THE SCHOOL OR A GIRL THAT LIVES IN OR WORKS IN A SCHOOL OR A GIRL THAT STUDIES IN A SCHOOL OR SCHOOLS OR A GIRL THAT SOMEONE STUDIES IN A SCHOOL OR SCHOOLS OR A GIRL BELONGING TO A SCHOOL.

*FRENCH THAT SOMEONE SPEAKS A GIRL IN THE SCHOOL OR A GIRL THAT LIVES IN OR WORKS IN A SCHOOL OR A GIRL THAT STUDIES IN A SCHOOL OR SCHOOLS OR A GIRL THAT SOMEONE STUDIES IN A SCHOOL OR SCHOOLS OR A GIRL BELONGING TO A SCHOOL IN.

*FRENCH THAT A GIRL IN THE SCHOOL (√√) OR A GIRL THAT LIVES IN OR WORKS IN A SCHOOL OR A GIRL THAT STUDIES IN A SCHOOL OR SCHOOLS OR A GIRL THAT SOMEONE STUDIES IN A SCHOOL OR SCHOOLS OR A GIRL BELONGING TO A SCHOOL SPEAKS IN. √

....

BRAINE 0350 (SCHOOL+ROOM) SMELL

(ANNEX 4020 /LOCATIVE 3030 /LOCATIVE 3011 /SENTENCE
1 /SENTENCE 2 /OWNERSHIP 1040)SENTENCE 3 /SE
NTENCE 4 /SENTENCE 5

UNDERLYING SENTENCE(S):

A ROOM OR ROOMS STUDIES IN A SCHOOL OR SCHOOLS

SOMEONE STUDIES A ROOM OR ROOMS IN A SCHOOL OR SCHOOLS

THE ROOM OF A SCHOOL OR A ROOM FOR OR CONTAINING A SCHOOL OR SCHOOLS OR A ROOM IN OR ON A SCHOOL OR A ROOM THAT STUDIES IN A SCHOOL OR SCHOOLS OR A ROOM THAT SOMEONE STUDIES IN A SCHOOL OR SCHOOLS OR A ROOM MADE BY OR BELONGING TO A SCHOOL SMELLS

SOMETHING OR SOMEONE SMELLS IN THE ROOM OF A SCHOOL OR A ROOM FOR OR CONTAINING A SCHOOL OR SCHOOLS OR A ROOM IN OR ON A SCHOOL OR A ROOM THAT STUDIES IN A SCHOOL OR SCHOOLS OR A ROOM THAT SOMEONE STUDIES IN A SCHOOL OR SCHOOLS OR A ROOM MADE BY OR BELONGING TO A SCHOOL

SOMEONE SMELLS THE ROOM OF A SCHOOL OR A ROOM FOR OR CONTAINING A SCHOOL OR SCHOOLS OR A ROOM IN OR ON A SCHOOL

OR A ROOM THAT STUDIES IN A SCHOOL OR SCHOOLS OR A ROOM THAT SOMEONE STUDIES IN A SCHOOL OR SCHOOLS OR A ROOM MADE BY OR BELONGING TO A SCHOOL

INTERPRETATION(S):

THE SMELL OF √√ THE ROOM OF A SCHOOL (√√) OR A ROOM FOR OR CONTAINING A SCHOOL OR SCHOOLS OR A ROOM IN OR ON A SCHOOL OR A ROOM THAT STUDIES IN A SCHOOL OR SCHOOLS OR A ROOM THAT SOMEONE STUDIES IN A SCHOOL OR SCHOOLS OR A ROOM MADE BY OR BELONGING TO A SCHOOL.

THE SMELL IN THE ROOM OF A SCHOOL OR A ROOM FOR OR CONTAINING A SCHOOL OR SCHOOLS OR A ROOM IN OR ON A SCHOOL OR A ROOM THAT STUDIES IN A SCHOOL OR SCHOOLS OR A ROOM THAT SOMEONE STUDIES IN A SCHOOL OR SCHOOLS OR A ROOM MADE BY OR BELONGING TO A SCHOOL.

THE SMELL OF THE ROOM OF A SCHOOL OR A ROOM FOR OR CONTAINING A SCHOOL OR SCHOOLS OR A ROOM IN OR ON A SCHOOL OR A ROOM THAT STUDIES IN A SCHOOL OR SCHOOLS OR A ROOM THAT SOMEONE STUDIES IN A SCHOOL OR SCHOOLS OR A ROOM MADE BY OR BELONGING TO A SCHOOL.

....

DEIGHTON 0180 (SECURITY GUARD) <PEAKED> CAP

(SENTENCE 1 /SENTENCE 2)EQUATIVE 5012 /SENTENCE 3 /OWNERSHIP 1050

UNDERLYING SENTENCE(S):

A GUARD OR GUARDS GUARDS SECURITY

A GUARD OR GUARDS GUARDS LIKE OR IN SECURITY

SOMEONE THAT GUARDS SECURITY OR SOMEONE THAT GUARDS LIKE OR IN SECURITY WEARS A PEAKED CAP OR PEAKED CAPS

INTERPRETATION(S):

A PEAKED CAP THAT IS SOMEONE THAT GUARDS SECURITY OR SOMEONE THAT GUARDS LIKE OR IN SECURITY.

A PEAKED CAP THAT √ SOMEONE THAT GUARDS SECURITY OR SOMEONE

THAT GUARDS LIKE OR IN SECURITY (V) WEARS.

A PEAKED CAP BELONGING TO SOMEONE THAT GUARDS SECURITY OR SOMEONE THAT GUARDS LIKE OR IN SECURITY.

....

DEIGHTON 0170 (SECURITY GUARD) CAP

(SENTENCE 1 /SENTENCE 2)EQUATIVE 5012 /SENTENCE 3 /OWNERSHIP 1050

UNDERLYING SENTENCE(S):

A GUARD OR GUARDS GUARDS SECURITY

A GUARD OR GUARDS GUARDS LIKE OR IN SECURITY

SOMEONE THAT GUARDS SECURITY OR SOMEONE THAT GUARDS LIKE OR IN SECURITY WEARS A CAP OR CAPS

INTERPRETATION(S):

A CAP THAT IS SOMEONE THAT GUARDS SECURITY OR SOMEONE THAT GUARDS LIKE OR IN SECURITY.

A CAP THAT SOMEONE THAT GUARDS SECURITY OR SOMEONE THAT GUARDS LIKE OR IN SECURITY WEARS.

A CAP BELONGING TO SOMEONE THAT GUARDS SECURITY OR SOMEONE THAT GUARDS LIKE OR IN SECURITY.

....

DEIGHTON 0130 (SECURITY GUARD) UNIFORM

(SENTENCE 1 /SENTENCE 2)EQUATIVE 5012 /SENTENCE 3 /OWNERSHIP 1050

UNDERLYING SENTENCE(S):

A GUARD OR GUARDS GUARDS SECURITY

A GUARD OR GUARDS GUARDS LIKE OR IN SECURITY

SOMEONE THAT GUARDS SECURITY OR SOMEONE THAT GUARDS LIKE OR IN SECURITY WEARS AN UNIFORM OR UNIFORMS

INTERPRETATION(S):

AN UNIFORM THAT IS SOMEONE THAT GUARDS SECURITY OR SOMEONE THAT GUARDS LIKE OR IN SECURITY.

AN UNIFORM THAT ✓ SOMEONE THAT GUARDS SECURITY OR SOMEONE THAT GUARDS LIKE OR IN SECURITY (✓) WEARS.

AN UNIFORM BELONGING TO SOMEONE THAT GUARDS SECURITY OR SOMEONE THAT GUARDS LIKE OR IN SECURITY.

....

MARSH 0390 (SHARK+SKIN) TROUSERS

(ANNEX 4020 /MATERIAL 6020)MATERIAL 6010 /SENTENCE 1 /LOCATIVE 3011

UNDERLYING SENTENCE(S):

SOMEONE WEARS TROUSERS IN THE SKIN OF A SHARK OR A SKIN FOR SHARKS OR A SKIN IN THE FORM OF A SHARK

INTERPRETATION(S):

TROUSERS MADE OF ✓✓ THE SKIN OF A SHARK (✓✓) OR A SKIN FOR SHARKS OR A SKIN IN THE FORM OF A SHARK.

TROUSERS THAT SOMEONE WEARS IN THE SKIN OF A SHARK OR A SKIN FOR SHARKS OR A SKIN IN THE FORM OF A SHARK.

TROUSERS IN OR ON THE SKIN OF A SHARK OR A SKIN FOR SHARKS OR A SKIN IN THE FORM OF A SHARK.

....

BRAINE 0360 (SHOULDER-LENGTH) HAIR

(ANNEX 4010)ANNEX 4040

INTERPRETATION(S):

HAIR WITH ✓✓ THE LENGTH OF A SHOULDER. X

....

BENNETT 0150 (SHOW+ROOM) DOOR

(SENTENCE 1 /SENTENCE 2)LOCATIVE 3016 /ANNEX 4
020 /LOCATIVE 3016 /LOCATIVE 3014 /LOCATIVE 3015

UNDERLYING SENTENCE(S):

SOMETHING OR SOMEONE SHOWS IN A ROOM OR ROOMS

SOMEONE SHOWS A ROOM OR ROOMS

INTERPRETATION(S):

A DOOR TO √√ A ROOM THAT SOMETHING OR SOMEONE SHOWS IN (√√) OR A ROOM THAT SOMEONE SHOWS.

THE DOOR OF A ROOM THAT SOMETHING OR SOMEONE SHOWS IN OR A ROOM THAT SOMEONE SHOWS.

A DOOR TO A ROOM THAT SOMETHING OR SOMEONE SHOWS IN OR A ROOM THAT SOMEONE SHOWS.

THE KIND OF DOOR USED IN OR ON A ROOM THAT SOMETHING OR SOMEONE SHOWS IN OR A ROOM THAT SOMEONE SHOWS.

THE KIND OF DOOR FOUND IN OR ON A ROOM THAT SOMETHING OR SOMEONE SHOWS IN OR A ROOM THAT SOMEONE SHOWS.

....

BENNETT 0210 (SHOW+ROOM) STAIR

(SENTENCE 1 /SENTENCE 2)LOCATIVE 3016 /ANNEX 4
020 /LOCATIVE 3011

UNDERLYING SENTENCE(S):

SOMETHING OR SOMEONE SHOWS IN A ROOM OR ROOMS

SOMEONE SHOWS A ROOM OR ROOMS

INTERPRETATION(S):

A STAIR TO √√ A ROOM THAT SOMETHING OR SOMEONE SHOWS IN (√√) OR A

ROOM THAT SOMEONE SHOWS.

THE STAIR OF A ROOM THAT SOMETHING OR SOMEONE SHOWS IN OR A ROOM THAT SOMEONE SHOWS.

A STAIR IN OR ON A ROOM THAT SOMETHING OR SOMEONE SHOWS IN OR A ROOM THAT SOMEONE SHOWS.

....

DEIGHTON 0490 (SILK SCARF) MAP

(MATERIAL 6010 /SENTENCE 1)LOCATIVE 3030 /SENTENCE 2

UNDERLYING SENTENCE(S):

SILK WEARS A SCARF OR SCARFS

SILK WEARS A SCARF OR SCARFS IN A MAP OR MAPS

INTERPRETATION(S):

A MAP FOR OR CONTAINING X A SCARF OF SILK √√ OR A SCARF THAT SILK WEARS.

A MAP THAT SILK WEARS A SCARF OR SCARFS IN.

....

MARSH 0260 (SLEEPING-CAR) ATTENDANT

(SENTENCE 1 /SENTENCE 4 /SENTENCE 7 /SENTENCE 10)EQUATIVE 5012 /SENTENCE 13 /LOCATIVE 3013

UNDERLYING SENTENCE(S):

A CAR OR CARS TRAVELS SOMETHING OR SOMEONE WHEN SOMEONE SLEEPS

SOMEONE SLEEPS

A CAR OR CARS TRAVELS SOMETHING OR SOMEONE

A CAR OR CARS TRAVELS WHEN SOMEONE SLEEPS

SOMEONE SLEEPS

A CAR OR CARS TRAVELS

SOMEONE TRAVELS SOMETHING OR SOMEONE IN A CAR OR CARS WHEN SOMEONE SLEEPS

SOMEONE SLEEPS

SOMEONE TRAVELS SOMETHING OR SOMEONE IN A CAR OR CARS

SOMEONE TRAVELS IN A CAR OR CARS WHEN SOMEONE SLEEPS

SOMEONE SLEEPS

SOMEONE TRAVELS IN A CAR OR CARS

AN ATTENDANT OR ATTENDANTS ATTENDS ON OR TO A CAR THAT TRAVELS SOMETHING OR SOMEONE WHEN SOMEONE SLEEPS OR A CAR THAT TRAVELS WHEN SOMEONE SLEEPS OR A CAR THAT SOMEONE TRAVELS SOMETHING OR SOMEONE IN WHEN SOMEONE SLEEPS OR A CAR THAT SOMEONE TRAVELS IN WHEN SOMEONE SLEEPS

INTERPRETATION(S):

AN ATTENDANT THAT IS A CAR THAT TRAVELS SOMETHING OR SOMEONE WHEN SOMEONE SLEEPS OR A CAR THAT TRAVELS WHEN SOMEONE SLEEPS OR A CAR THAT SOMEONE TRAVELS SOMETHING OR SOMEONE IN WHEN SOMEONE SLEEPS OR A CAR THAT SOMEONE TRAVELS IN WHEN SOME ONE SLEEPS.

SOMEONE THAT ATTENDS ON OR TO ✓ A CAR THAT TRAVELS SOMETHING OR SOMEONE WHEN SOMEONE SLEEPS OR A CAR THAT TRAVELS WHEN SOMEONE SLEEPS OR A CAR THAT SOMEONE TRAVELS SOMETHING OR SOMEONE IN WHEN SOMEONE SLEEPS OR A CAR THAT SOMEONE TRAVELS IN WHEN SOMEONE SLEEPS. **(✓)**

AN ATTENDANT THAT LIVES IN OR WORKS IN A CAR THAT TRAVELS SOMETHING OR SOMEONE WHEN SOMEONE SLEEPS OR A CAR THAT TRAVELS WHEN SOMEONE SLEEPS OR A CAR THAT SOMEONE TRAVELS SOMETHING OR SOMEONE IN WHEN SOMEONE SLEEPS OR A CAR THAT SOMEONE TRAVELS IN WHEN SOMEONE SLEEPS.

....

GREENE 0120 (SODA-WATER) SIPHON

(ANNEX 4040 /LOCATIVE 3030)SENTENCE 1 /LOCATIVE 3

011

UNDERLYING SENTENCE(S):

SOMEONE SIPHONS WATER WITH SODA OR WATER FOR OR CONTAINING SODA WITH A SIPHON OR SIPHONS

INTERPRETATION(S):

SOMETHING THAT SOMEONE SIPHONS √√ WATER WITH SODA (√√) OR WATER FOR OR CONTAINING SODA WITH.

A SIPHON IN OR ON WATER WITH SODA OR WATER FOR OR CONTAINING SODA.

....

DEIGHTON 0410 (SQUAWK BOX) SWITCH

(SENTENCE 1)ANNEX 4020 /SENTENCE 2 /LOCATIVE 3
011

UNDERLYING SENTENCE(S):

SOMEONE SQUAWKS IN A BOX OR BOXS

SOMEONE SWITCHES ON A BOX THAT SOMEONE SQUAWKS IN WITH A SWITCH OR SWITCHS

INTERPRETATION(S):

THE SWITCH OF √√ A BOX THAT SOMEONE SQUAWKS IN. (√√)

SOMETHING THAT SOMEONE SWITCHES ON A BOX THAT SOMEONE SQUAWKS IN WITH.

A SWITCH IN OR ON A BOX THAT SOMEONE SQUAWKS IN.

....

BENNETT 0400 (STAIR+CASE)-DOOR

(LOCATIVE 3030 /LOCATIVE 3011)LOCATIVE 3016 /LOCATIVE 3014 /LOCATIVE 3015

INTERPRETATION(S):

A DOOR TO √√ A CASE FOR OR CONTAINING A STAIR OR STAIRS (√√) OR A CASE IN OR ON A STAIR.

THE KIND OF DOOR USED IN OR ON A CASE FOR OR CONTAINING A STAIR OR STAIRS OR A CASE IN OR ON A STAIR.

THE KIND OF DOOR FOUND IN OR ON A CASE FOR OR CONTAINING A STAIR OR STAIRS OR A CASE IN OR ON A STAIR.

....

DEIGHTON 0480 (STEWARDESS CALL)-BUTTON

(INCLUDED OR UNSPECIFIED)SENTENCE 3 /SENTENCE 4

UNDERLYING SENTENCE(S):

SOMEONE CALLS A STEWARDESS OR STEWARDESSS

A STEWARDESS OR STEWARDESSS CALLS

SOMEONE CALLS A STEWARDESS OR STEWARDESSS WITH A BUTTON OR BUTTONS

A STEWARDESS OR STEWARDESSS CALLS WITH A BUTTON OR BUTTONS

INTERPRETATION(S):

A BUTTON THAT √√ SOMEONE CALLS A STEWARDESS OR STEWARDESSS √√ WITH.

A BUTTON THAT A STEWARDESS OR STEWARDESSS CALLS WITH.

....

MARSH 0110 (STRAW+BERRY) JAM

(EQUATIVE 5011)ANNEX 4040 /SENTENCE 1 /SENTENCE 2

UNDERLYING SENTENCE(S):

SOMEONE SQUEEZES A BERRY THAT IS STRAW

A BERRY THAT IS STRAW SQUEEZES JAM

INTERPRETATION(S):

JAM WITH √√ A BERRY THAT IS STRAW. **(X)**

THE JAM OF A BERRY THAT IS STRAW.

JAM THAT A BERRY THAT IS STRAW SQUEEZES.

....

THACKERAY 0600 (TIGER-HUNTING) STORY

(INCLUDED OR UNSPECIFIED)SENTENCE 3 /SENTENCE 4

UNDERLYING SENTENCE(S):

SOMEONE HUNTS A TIGER OR TIGERS

A TIGER OR TIGERS HUNTS

SOMEONE NARRATES A STORY OR STORYS WHEN SOMEONE HUNTS A TIGER OR TIGERS

SOMEONE NARRATES A STORY OR STORYS WHEN A TIGER OR TIGERS HUNTS

SOMEONE NARRATES A STORY OR STORYS

INTERPRETATION(S):

A STORY THAT SOMEONE NARRATES √√ WHEN SOMEONE HUNTS A TIGER OR TIGERS. **X?**

A STORY THAT SOMEONE NARRATES WHEN A TIGER OR TIGERS HUNTS.

....

PEACOCK 0920 (TOLL-GATE) KEEPER

(SENTENCE 1)SENTENCE 2

UNDERLYING SENTENCE(S):

A GATE OR GATES PAYS A TOLL OR TOLLS

A KEEPER OR KEEPERS KEEPS A GATE THAT PAYS A TOLL OR TOLLS

INTERPRETATION(S):

SOMEONE THAT KEEPS √√ A GATE THAT PAYS A TOLL OR TOLLS. X

....

BRAINE 0440 (TOOTH+BRUSH) MOUSTACHE

(SENTENCE 1)ANNEX 4020 /SENTENCE 2

UNDERLYING SENTENCE(S):

SOMEONE BRUSHES A TOOTH OR TOOTHS WITH A BRUSH OR BRUSHS

A MOUSTACHE OR MOUSTACHES BRUSHES A TOOTH OR TOOTHS WITH A BRUSH OR BRUSHS

INTERPRETATION(S):

THE MOUSTACHE OF X SOMETHING THAT SOMEONE BRUSHES A TOOTH OR (√√) TOOTHS WITH.

A MOUSTACHE THAT BRUSHES A TOOTH OR TOOTHS WITH A BRUSH OR BRUSHS.

....

DEIGHTON 0440 (TOP-SPEED) WAY

(LOCATIVE 3020)ANNEX 4010 /LOCATIVE 3030

INTERPRETATION(S):

THE WAY OF X SPEED AT THE TOP. X

A WAY FOR OR CONTAINING SPEED AT THE TOP.

....

DEIGHTON 0500 (TOWEL DISPOSAL) BIN

(INCLUDED OR UNSPECIFIED)SENTENCE 2

UNDERLYING SENTENCE(S):

SOMEONE DISPOSES OF A TOWEL OR TOWELS

SOMEONE DISPOSES OF A TOWEL OR TOWELS IN A BIN OR BINS

INTERPRETATION(S):

A BIN THAT √√ SOMEONE DISPOSES OF A TOWEL OR TOWELS √√ IN.

....

BENNETT 0140 (WOOL+WORK) BUNCH

(MATERIAL 6010 /FUEL 1020)MATERIAL 6040 /SENTENCE
3

UNDERLYING SENTENCE(S):

WOOL WORKS

SOMEONE WORKS WOOL

A BUNCH OR BUNCHS WORKS WOOL

INTERPRETATION(S):

A BUNCH OF √√ A WORK OF WOOL (√√) OR A WORK POWERED BY WOOL.

A BUNCH THAT WORKS WOOL.

....

BECKFORD 2290 (WORMWOOD-COLOUR) FLY

(ANNEX 4010)ANNEX 4040 /SENTENCE 2

UNDERLYING SENTENCE(S):

A FLY OR FLYS FLIES

THE COLOUR OF WORMWOOD FLIES

INTERPRETATION(S):

A FLY WITH √√ THE COLOUR OF WORMWOOD. √√

THE FLY OF THE COLOUR OF WORMWOOD.

....

BRAINE 0370 *GRADE/*THREE WIFE

LOCATIVE 3012 /LOCATIVE 3011

INTERPRETATION(S):

A WIFE THAT LIVES IN OR COMES FROM *GRADE/*THREE.

A WIFE IN OR ON *GRADE/*THREE. √

....

BRONTE 0880 *GRANGE LIGHT

SENTENCE 1 /LOCATIVE 3011

UNDERLYING SENTENCE(S):

SOMEONE SHINES IN THE *GRANGE

INTERPRETATION(S):

THE LIGHT IN THE *GRANGE. √√

LIGHT IN OR ON THE *GRANGE.

....

FIELDING 0880 *GUILD-HALL

LOCATIVE 3030 /OWNERSHIP 1040

INTERPRETATION(S):

A HALL FOR OR CONTAINING THE *GUILD. √√

A HALL MADE BY OR BELONGING TO THE *GUILD.

....

DEFOE 0590 *GUINEA GRAIN

LOCATIVE 3015

INTERPRETATION(S):

THE KIND OF GRAIN FOUND IN OR ON *GUINEA. √√

....

DEFOE 0400 *GUINEY TRADER

SENTENCE 2 /LOCATIVE 3016 /LOCATIVE 3012 /LOCATIVE 3011

UNDERLYING SENTENCE(S):

A TRADER OR TRADERS TRADES

A TRADER OR TRADERS TRADES TO *GUINEY

INTERPRETATION(S):

SOMEONE THAT TRADES TO *GUINEY. √√

A TRADER TO *GUINEY.

A TRADER THAT LIVES IN OR COMES FROM *GUINEY.

A TRADER IN OR ON *GUINEY.

....

BRAINE 0070 *GUISELEY (SAND+STONE)

HOMOGRAPHIC VARIANT NO. 1 , PREFERENCE NO. 1
LOCATIVE 3011 /LOCATIVE 3030 (MATERIAL 6010 /LOCATIVE 3030 /LOCATIVE 3011)

HOMOGRAPHIC VARIANT NO. 2 , PREFERENCE NO. 2
LOCATIVE 3015 (MATERIAL 6010 /LOCATIVE 3015)

INTERPRETATION(S) IN ORDER OF HOMOGRAPHIC PREFERENCE:

STONE[1] OF SAND **(√√)** OR STONE[1] FOR OR CONTAINING SAND OR STONE[1] IN OR ON SAND IN OR ON *GUISELEY. **√√**

STONE[1] OF SAND OR STONE[1] FOR OR CONTAINING SAND OR STONE[1] IN OR ON SAND FOR OR CONTAINING *GUISELEY.

THE KIND OF A STONE[2] OF SAND OR THE KIND OF STONE[2] FOUND IN OR ON SAND FOUND IN OR ON *GUISELEY.

....

DEIGHTON   0450   *H*Q *SQUADRON

LOCATIVE 3012 /LOCATIVE 3011

INTERPRETATION(S):

A *SQUADRON THAT LIVES IN OR COMES FROM THE *H*Q. **√√**

A *SQUADRON IN OR ON A *H*Q.

....

BRAINE   0360   *HAMILTON WATCH

HOMOGRAPHIC VARIANT NO. 1 , PREFERENCE NO. 1
EQUATIVE 5010 /MATERIAL 6050 /SENTENCE   1 /OWNERSHIP 1050

HOMOGRAPHIC VARIANT NO. 2 , PREFERENCE NO. 2
SENTENCE   3 /OWNERSHIP 1040

UNDERLYING SENTENCE(S):

A WATCH[1] OR WATCH[1]S WATCHES *HAMILTON

A WATCH[1] OR WATCH[1]S WATCHES

*HAMILTON WEARS A WATCH[2] OR WATCH[2]S

INTERPRETATION(S) IN ORDER OF HOMOGRAPHIC PREFERENCE:

A WATCH[1] THAT IS *HAMILTON.

A WATCH[1] OF *HAMILTON.

SOMEONE THAT WATCHES *HAMILTON.

A WATCH[1] BELONGING TO *HAMILTON.

A WATCH[2] THAT *HAMILTON WEARS.

A WATCH[2] MADE BY OR BELONGING TO *HAMILTON. ✓

....

THACKERAY 0250 *HAMMERSMITH *SEMIRAMIS

LOCATIVE 3012 /LOCATIVE 3011

INTERPRETATION(S):

*SEMIRAMIS THAT LIVES IN OR COMES FROM *HAMMERSMITH. ✓✓

*SEMIRAMIS IN OR ON *HAMMERSMITH.

....

GREENE 0150 *HEINZ BEAN<S>

OWNERSHIP 1050

INTERPRETATION(S):

A BEAN BELONGING TO *HEINZ. X

....

DEIGHTON 0110 *HEPPLEWHITE (BOOK+CASE)

LOCATIVE 3030 /OWNERSHIP 1040 (LOCATIVE 3030 /LOCATIVE 30
11 /SENTENCE 1)

UNDERLYING SENTENCE(S):

SOMEONE READS A BOOK OR BOOKS IN A CASE OR CASES

INTERPRETATION(S):

A CASE FOR OR CONTAINING A BOOK OR BOOKS OR A CASE IN OR ON A BOOK OR A CASE THAT SOMEONE READS A BOOK OR BOOKS IN FOR OR CONTAINING *HEPPLEWHITE.

A CASE FOR OR CONTAINING A BOOK OR BOOKS (√√) OR A CASE IN OR ON A BOOK OR A CASE THAT SOMEONE READS A BOOK OR BOOKS IN MADE BY OR BELONGING TO *HEPPLEWHITE. √

....

BRAINE 0170 *HEYWOOD FLAVOUR

ANNEX 4010

INTERPRETATION(S):

THE FLAVOUR OF *HEYWOOD. √√

....

SCOTT 0260 *HIGHLAND GLEN

LOCATIVE 3011 /LOCATIVE 3030

INTERPRETATION(S):

A GLEN IN OR ON THE *HIGHLAND. √√

A GLEN FOR OR CONTAINING THE *HIGHLAND.

....

RICHARDSON 0320 *HOLLAND LINEN

LOCATIVE 3011

INTERPRETATION(S):

LINEN IN OR ON *HOLLAND. X?

....

PEACOCK 0070 *HOLYHEAD MAIL

```
HOMOGRAPHIC VARIANT NO.  1  , PREFERENCE NO.  1
SENTENCE     1  /LOCATIVE  3016  /LOCATIVE  3011

HOMOGRAPHIC VARIANT NO.  2  , PREFERENCE NO.  2
SENTENCE     2  /LOCATIVE  3011

HOMOGRAPHIC VARIANT NO.  3  , PREFERENCE NO.  3
SENTENCE     3  /SENTENCE    4  /SENTENCE    5  /SENTENCE
   6  /LOCATIVE  3016  /LOCATIVE  3011

UNDERLYING SENTENCE(S):

 SOMEONE DELIVERS MAIL[1] TO *HOLYHEAD

 SOMEONE WEARS MAIL[2] IN *HOLYHEAD

 A MAIL[3] OR MAIL[3]S TRAVELS *HOLYHEAD

 A MAIL[3] OR MAIL[3]S TRAVELS TO *HOLYHEAD

 SOMEONE TRAVELS *HOLYHEAD IN A MAIL[3] OR MAIL[3]S

 *HOLYHEAD TRAVELS IN A MAIL[3] OR MAIL[3]S


INTERPRETATION(S) IN ORDER OF HOMOGRAPHIC PREFERENCE:

 MAIL[1] THAT SOMEONE DELIVERS TO *HOLYHEAD.

 MAIL[1] TO *HOLYHEAD.

 MAIL[1] IN OR ON *HOLYHEAD.

 MAIL[2] THAT SOMEONE WEARS IN *HOLYHEAD.

 MAIL[2] IN OR ON *HOLYHEAD.

 A MAIL[3] THAT TRAVELS *HOLYHEAD.

 A MAIL[3] THAT TRAVELS TO *HOLYHEAD. √

 A MAIL[3] THAT SOMEONE TRAVELS *HOLYHEAD IN.

 A MAIL[3] THAT *HOLYHEAD TRAVELS IN.
```

A MAIL[3] TO *HOLYHEAD.

A MAIL[3] IN OR ON *HOLYHEAD.

....

PEACOCK 0200 *HOLYHEAD ROAD

LOCATIVE 3016 /LOCATIVE 3011

INTERPRETATION(S):

A ROAD TO *HOLYHEAD. √√

A ROAD IN OR ON *HOLYHEAD.

....

BRAINE 0090 *HOME *COUNTY

LOCATIVE 3011 /LOCATIVE 3030

INTERPRETATION(S):

THE *COUNTY IN OR ON *HOME. √√

THE *COUNTY FOR OR CONTAINING *HOME.

....

BENNETT 0190 *HOWE (SEWING-MACHINE)

SENTENCE 4 /OWNERSHIP 1040 (SENTENCE 1)

UNDERLYING SENTENCE(S):

SOMEONE MAKES THAT SOMEONE SEWS WITH A MACHINE OR MACHINES

SOMEONE SEWS

SOMEONE MAKES SOMETHING OR SOMEONE WITH A MACHINE OR MACHINES

*HOWE MAKES THAT SOMEONE SEWS WITH A MACHINE OR MACHINES

INTERPRETATION(S):

A MACHINE THAT *HOWE MAKES THAT SOMEONE SEWS WITH.

A MACHINE THAT SOMEONE MAKES THAT SOMEONE SEWS WITH (√√?) MADE BY OR BELONGING TO *HOWE. √

....

THACKERAY 0430 *INDIA PATTERN

ANNEX 4010 /LOCATIVE 3011

INTERPRETATION(S):

THE PATTERN OF *INDIA.

A PATTERN IN OR ON *INDIA. √

....

SCOTT 0500 *KELSO RACE

SENTENCE 1 /SENTENCE 2 /SENTENCE 3

UNDERLYING SENTENCE(S):

*KELSO RACES

SOMETHING OR SOMEONE RACES IN *KELSO

SOMEONE RACES *KELSO

INTERPRETATION(S):

THE RACE OF *KELSO.

THE RACE IN *KELSO. √

THE RACE OF *KELSO.

....

THACKERAY 0320 *KENSINGTON TURNPIKE

LOCATIVE 3011

INTERPRETATION(S):

A TURNPIKE IN OR ON *KENSINGTON. √√

....

DEIGHTON 0390 *KLEENEX TISSUE

ANNEX 4020 /OWNERSHIP 1050

INTERPRETATION(S):

THE TISSUE OF *KLEENEX. X

A TISSUE BELONGING TO *KLEENEX.

....

SCOTT 0410 *KNIGHT *TEMPLAR

EQUATIVE 5010 /OWNERSHIP 1050

INTERPRETATION(S):

A *TEMPLAR THAT IS A *KNIGHT. √√

A *TEMPLAR BELONGING TO A *KNIGHT.

....

DEIGHTON 0110 *KNOLL DESK

LOCATIVE 3030 /OWNERSHIP 1040

INTERPRETATION(S):

A DESK FOR OR CONTAINING *KNOLL.

A DESK MADE BY OR BELONGING TO *KNOLL. √

....

BRAINE 0340 *LABOUR *M.*P.

ANNEX 4020 /OWNERSHIP 1050

INTERPRETATION(S):

THE *M.*P. OF *LABOUR. √√?

A *M.*P. BELONGING TO *LABOUR.

....

GREENE 0560 *LAKE POET

HOMOGRAPHIC VARIANT NO. 1 , PREFERENCE NO. 1
SENTENCE 1 /SENTENCE 2 /LOCATIVE 3012 /LOCATIVE 3011

HOMOGRAPHIC VARIANT NO. 2 , PREFERENCE NO. 2
EQUATIVE 5010 /OWNERSHIP 1050

UNDERLYING SENTENCE(S):

A POET OR POETS WRITES SOMETHING OR SOMEONE IN THE *LAKE[1]

A POET OR POETS WRITES IN THE *LAKE[1]

A POET OR POETS WRITES SOMETHING OR SOMEONE

A POET OR POETS WRITES

INTERPRETATION(S) IN ORDER OF HOMOGRAPHIC PREFERENCE:

A POET THAT WRITES SOMETHING OR SOMEONE IN THE *LAKE[1]. √√

A POET THAT WRITES IN THE *LAKE[1].

A POET THAT LIVES IN OR COMES FROM THE *LAKE[1].

A POET IN OR ON THE *LAKE[1].

A POET THAT IS *LAKE[2].

A POET BELONGING TO *LAKE[2].

....

THACKERAY 0520 *LATIN *GRAMMAR

ANNEX 4010 /SENTENCE 1 /SENTENCE 2

UNDERLYING SENTENCE(S):

*GRAMMAR SPEAKS LIKE OR IN *LATIN

SOMEONE SPEAKS *GRAMMAR LIKE OR IN *LATIN

INTERPRETATION(S):

*GRAMMAR OF *LATIN. √√

*GRAMMAR THAT SPEAKS LIKE OR IN *LATIN.

*GRAMMAR THAT SOMEONE SPEAKS LIKE OR IN *LATIN.

....

THACKERAY 0320 *LIFE *GUARD

SENTENCE 1 /SENTENCE 4

UNDERLYING SENTENCE(S):

A *GUARD OR *GUARDS GUARDS THAT SOMEONE LIVES

SOMEONE LIVES

A *GUARD OR *GUARDS GUARDS SOMETHING OR SOMEONE

A *GUARD OR *GUARDS GUARDS WHEN SOMEONE LIVES

SOMEONE LIVES

A *GUARD OR *GUARDS GUARDS

INTERPRETATION(S):

SOMEONE THAT GUARDS THAT SOMEONE LIVES. √√?

SOMEONE THAT GUARDS WHEN SOMEONE LIVES.

....

DEIGHTON 0190 *LINCOLN (HIRE-CAR)

SENTENCE 6 /OWNERSHIP 1040 /LOCATIVE 3030 (SENTENCE 5)

UNDERLYING SENTENCE(S):

A CAR OR CARS TRAVELS SOMETHING OR SOMEONE

A CAR OR CARS TRAVELS

SOMEONE TRAVELS SOMETHING OR SOMEONE IN A CAR OR CARS

SOMEONE TRAVELS IN A CAR OR CARS

SOMEONE HIRES A CAR OR CARS

*LINCOLN HIRES A CAR OR CARS

INTERPRETATION(S):

A CAR THAT *LINCOLN HIRES.

A CAR THAT SOMEONE HIRES (√√) MADE BY OR BELONGING TO *LINCOLN. √

A CAR THAT SOMEONE HIRES FOR OR CONTAINING *LINCOLN.

....

RICHARDSON 0160 *LINCOLNSHIRE ESTATE

LOCATIVE 3011 /LOCATIVE 3030

INTERPRETATION(S):

AN ESTATE IN OR ON *LINCOLNSHIRE. √√

AN ESTATE FOR OR CONTAINING *LINCOLNSHIRE.

....

SCOTT 0370 *LOCHABER-AXE

SENTENCE 1 /LOCATIVE 3011

UNDERLYING SENTENCE(S):

SOMEONE CHOPS WITH AN AXE OR AXES IN *LOCHABER

INTERPRETATION(S):

AN AXE THAT SOMEONE CHOPS WITH IN *LOCHABER. √√

AN AXE IN OR ON *LOCHABER.

....

RADCLIFFE 0140 *LOMBARDY POPLAR

LOCATIVE 3015

INTERPRETATION(S):

THE KIND OF POPLAR FOUND IN OR ON *LOMBARDY. √√

....

DEIGHTON 0490 *LONDON (AIR+PORT)

HOMOGRAPHIC VARIANT NO. 1 , PREFERENCE NO. 1
LOCATIVE 3011 /LOCATIVE 3030 (LOCATIVE 3030 /LOCATIVE 3011)

HOMOGRAPHIC VARIANT NO. 2 , PREFERENCE NO. 2
LOCATIVE 3011 /LOCATIVE 3030 (LOCATIVE 3030 /SENTENCE 1)

HOMOGRAPHIC VARIANT NO. 3 , PREFERENCE NO. 3
LOCATIVE 3015 (LOCATIVE 3011)

HOMOGRAPHIC VARIANT NO. 5 , PREFERENCE NO. 4
LOCATIVE 3011 (LOCATIVE 3011)

HOMOGRAPHIC VARIANT NO. 4 , PREFERENCE NO. 5
LOCATIVE 3015 (SENTENCE 2)

HOMOGRAPHIC VARIANT NO. 6 , PREFERENCE NO. 6

LOCATIVE 3011 (SENTENCE 3)

UNDERLYING SENTENCE(S):

SOMEONE FLIES OR LANDS IN A PORT[1] OR PORT[1]S

PORT[2] FLIES OR LANDS

A PORT[3] OR PORT[3]S FLIES OR LANDS

INTERPRETATION(S) IN ORDER OF HOMOGRAPHIC PREFERENCE:

A PORT[1] FOR OR CONTAINING AIR[1] OR A PORT[1] IN OR ON AIR[1] IN OR ON *LONDON.

A PORT[1] FOR OR CONTAINING AIR[1] OR A PORT[1] IN OR ON AIR[1] FOR OR CONTAINING *LONDON.

A PORT[1] FOR OR CONTAINING AN AIR[2] OR AIR[2]S OR A PORT[1] THAT SOMEONE FLIES OR LANDS IN (✓) IN OR ON *LONDON. ✓

A PORT[1] FOR OR CONTAINING AN AIR[2] OR AIR[2]S OR A PORT[1] THAT SOMEONE FLIES OR LANDS IN FOR OR CONTAINING *LONDON.

THE KIND OF PORT[2] IN OR ON AIR[1] FOUND IN OR ON *LONDON.

A PORT[3] IN OR ON AIR[1] IN OR ON *LONDON.

THE KIND OF PORT[2] THAT FLIES OR LANDS FOUND IN OR ON *LONDON.

A PORT[3] THAT FLIES OR LANDS IN OR ON *LONDON.

....

DEIGHTON 0400 *LONDON FLIGHT

SENTENCE 1 /SENTENCE 2

UNDERLYING SENTENCE(S):

*LONDON FLIES

SOMEONE FLIES TO *LONDON

INTERPRETATION(S):

THE FLIGHT OF *LONDON.

THE FLIGHT TO *LONDON. √

....

SCOTT 0290 *MADEIRA NEGUS

LOCATIVE 3015

INTERPRETATION(S):

THE KIND OF NEGUS FOUND IN OR ON *MADEIRA. √√

....

BRAINE 0260 *MARKET *SQUARE

LOCATIVE 3011 /LOCATIVE 3030 /SENTENCE 1 /SENTENCE 2 /OWNERSHIP 1040

UNDERLYING SENTENCE(S):

THE *SQUARE SELLS IN THE *MARKET

SOMEONE SELLS THE *SQUARE IN THE *MARKET

INTERPRETATION(S):

THE *SQUARE IN OR ON THE *MARKET.

THE *SQUARE FOR OR CONTAINING THE *MARKET. √

THE *SQUARE THAT SELLS IN THE *MARKET.

THE *SQUARE THAT SOMEONE SELLS IN THE *MARKET.

THE *SQUARE MADE BY OR BELONGING TO THE *MARKET.

....

BRAINE 0280 *MARTIN TOURER

SENTENCE 1 /SENTENCE 3 /SENTENCE 4 /OWNERSHIP 1040 /LOCATIVE 3030

UNDERLYING SENTENCE(S):

A TOURER OR TOURERS TOURS *MARTIN

A TOURER OR TOURERS TOURS

SOMEONE TOURS *MARTIN IN A TOURER OR TOURERS

*MARTIN TOURS IN A TOURER OR TOURERS

INTERPRETATION(S):

SOMEONE OR SOMETHING THAT TOURS *MARTIN.

SOMETHING THAT SOMEONE TOURS *MARTIN IN.

SOMETHING THAT *MARTIN TOURS IN.

A TOURER MADE BY OR BELONGING TO *MARTIN. ✓

A TOURER FOR OR CONTAINING *MARTIN.

....

BENNETT 0380 *MAY MORNING

LOCATIVE 3011

INTERPRETATION(S):

A MORNING IN OR ON *MAY. ✓✓

....

BRAINE 0120 *MEDICI REPRODUCTION

SENTENCE 1 /SENTENCE 3 /SENTENCE 4 /SENTENCE 5 /OWNERSHIP 1050

UNDERLYING SENTENCE(S):

A REPRODUCTION OR REPRODUCTIONS REPRODUCES THE *MEDICI

A REPRODUCTION OR REPRODUCTIONS REPRODUCES

SOMEONE REPRODUCES THE *MEDICI

THE *MEDICI REPRODUCES

THE *MEDICI REPRODUCES A REPRODUCTION OR REPRODUCTIONS

INTERPRETATION(S):

SOMEONE OR SOMETHING THAT REPRODUCES THE *MEDICI.

THE REPRODUCTION OF THE *MEDICI.

THE REPRODUCTION OF THE *MEDICI.

SOMETHING THAT THE *MEDICI REPRODUCES. ✓

A REPRODUCTION BELONGING TO THE *MEDICI.

....

THACKERAY 0570 *MIDSUMMER EXAMINATION

SENTENCE 1 /SENTENCE 2

UNDERLYING SENTENCE(S):

SOMEONE EXAMINES IN *MIDSUMMER

SOMEONE EXAMINES *MIDSUMMER

INTERPRETATION(S):

THE EXAMINATION IN *MIDSUMMER. ✓✓

THE EXAMINATION OF *MIDSUMMER.

....

MARSH 0450 *MING VASE

LOCATIVE 3030 /OWNERSHIP 1040

INTERPRETATION(S):

A VASE FOR OR CONTAINING *MING. X

A VASE MADE BY OR BELONGING TO *MING.

....

GREENE 0090 *MISSISSIPPI (PADDLE-STEAMER)

SENTENCE 2 /LOCATIVE 3011 (ANNEX 4040 /SENTENCE 1)

UNDERLYING SENTENCE(S):

A STEAMER OR STEAMERS STEAMS WITH A PADDLE OR PADDLES

A STEAMER OR STEAMERS STEAMS WITH A PADDLE OR PADDLES IN THE *MISSISSIPPI

INTERPRETATION(S):

SOMEONE OR SOMETHING THAT STEAMS WITH A PADDLE OR PADDLES IN THE *MISSISSIPPI.

A STEAMER WITH A PADDLE OR PADDLES (✓) OR SOMEONE OR SOMETHING THAT STEAMS WITH A PADDLE OR PADDLES IN OR ON THE *MISSISSIPPI. ✓

....

BRAINE 0230 *MODLEY BUS

SENTENCE 1 /SENTENCE 2 /SENTENCE 3 /SENTENCE 4 /LOCATIVE 3016 /LOCATIVE 3011

UNDERLYING SENTENCE(S):

A BUS OR BUSS TRAVELS *MODLEY

A BUS OR BUSS TRAVELS TO *MODLEY

SOMEONE TRAVELS *MODLEY IN A BUS OR BUSS

*MODLEY TRAVELS IN A BUS OR BUSS

INTERPRETATION(S):

A BUS THAT TRAVELS *MODLEY.

A BUS THAT TRAVELS TO *MODLEY. ✓

A BUS THAT SOMEONE TRAVELS *MODLEY IN.

A BUS THAT *MODLEY TRAVELS IN.

A BUS TO *MODLEY.

A BUS IN OR ON *MODLEY.

....

BRAINE 0410 *MONDAY DRABNESS

ANNEX 4010 /LOCATIVE 3011

INTERPRETATION(S):

DRABNESS OF *MONDAY. ✓✓

DRABNESS IN OR ON *MONDAY.

....

DEIGHTON 0420 *MONDAY MORNING

LOCATIVE 3011

INTERPRETATION(S):

A MORNING IN OR ON *MONDAY. ✓✓

....

LAWRENCE 0680 *MONDAY NIGHT

LOCATIVE 3011

INTERPRETATION(S):

A NIGHT IN OR ON *MONDAY. ✓✓

....

GREENE 0110 *MONGO LANGUAGE

SENTENCE 1

UNDERLYING SENTENCE(S):

THE *MONGO SPEAKS A LANGUAGE OR LANGUAGES

INTERPRETATION(S):

A LANGUAGE THAT THE *MONGO SPEAKS. √√

....

MARSH 0610 *MONTE/*CARLO RALLY

SENTENCE 1 /SENTENCE 2 /SENTENCE 3

UNDERLYING SENTENCE(S):

*MONTE/*CARLO RALLIES

SOMETHING OR SOMEONE RALLIES IN *MONTE/*CARLO

SOMEONE RALLIES *MONTE/*CARLO

INTERPRETATION(S):

THE RALLY OF *MONTE/*CARLO.

THE RALLY IN *MONTE/*CARLO. √?

THE RALLY OF *MONTE/*CARLO.

....

BRAINE 0370 *N*A*L*G*O <*NATIONAL >*CHARTER

SENTENCE 1 /OWNERSHIP 1050

UNDERLYING SENTENCE(S):

SOMEONE GRANTS *N*A*L*G*O WITH A *NATIONAL *CHARTER OR
*NATIONAL *CHARTERS

INTERPRETATION(S):

A *NATIONAL *CHARTER THAT SOMEONE GRANTS *N*A*L*G*O WITH.

A *NATIONAL *CHARTER BELONGING TO *N*A*L*G*O. ✓

....

MARSH 0120 *NARCOTICS *BUREAU

SENTENCE 1 /LOCATIVE 3030

UNDERLYING SENTENCE(S):

A *BUREAU OR *BUREAUS DEALS WITH *NARCOTICS

INTERPRETATION(S):

A *BUREAU THAT DEALS WITH *NARCOTICS. ✓✓

A *BUREAU FOR OR CONTAINING *NARCOTICS.

....

BRAINE 0360 *NASH *AIRFLYTE <*EIGHT>

ERROR ON CARD, IN LOC 41
SENTENCE 1 /SENTENCE 3 /SENTENCE 4 /OWNERSHIP 1040 /LOCATIVE 3030

UNDERLYING SENTENCE(S):

A *AIRFLYTE OR *AIRFLYTES TRAVELS *NASH

A *AIRFLYTE OR *AIRFLYTES TRAVELS

SOMEONE TRAVELS *NASH IN A *AIRFLYTE OR *AIRFLYTES

*NASH TRAVELS IN A *AIRFLYTE OR *AIRFLYTES

INTERPRETATION(S):

A *AIRFLYTE THAT TRAVELS *NASH.

A *AIRFLYTE THAT SOMEONE TRAVELS *NASH IN.

A *AIRFLYTE THAT *NASH TRAVELS IN.

A *AIRFLYTE MADE BY OR BELONGING TO *NASH. ✓

A *AIRFLYTE FOR OR CONTAINING *NASH.

....

LAWRENCE 0110 MOSS=ROSE

ANNEX 4040

INTERPRETATION(S):

A ROSE WITH A MOSS OR MOSSS. X

....

THACKERAY 0270 MOTHER-TONGUE

ANNEX 4020 /SENTENCE 1 /SENTENCE 2

UNDERLYING SENTENCE(S):

SOMEONE SPEAKS A MOTHER OR MOTHERS WITH A TONGUE OR TONGUES

A MOTHER OR MOTHERS SPEAKS WITH A TONGUE OR TONGUES

INTERPRETATION(S):

THE TONGUE OF A MOTHER. ✓✓

A TONGUE THAT SOMEONE SPEAKS A MOTHER OR MOTHERS WITH.

A TONGUE THAT A MOTHER OR MOTHERS SPEAKS WITH.

....

PEACOCK 0590 MOUNTAIN-(MOON+LIGHT)

SENTENCE 2 /LOCATIVE 3011 (INCLUDED OR UNSPECIFIED)

UNDERLYING SENTENCE(S):

THE MOON SHINES

THE MOON SHINES IN A MOUNTAIN OR MOUNTAINS

INTERPRETATION(S):

THE LIGHT IN A MOUNTAIN OR MOUNTAINS (√√) OF THE MOON. √√

....

PEACOCK 0570 MOUNTAIN-ASH

HOMOGRAPHIC VARIANT NO. 2 , PREFERENCE NO. 1
ANNEX 4010 /LOCATIVE 3011

HOMOGRAPHIC VARIANT NO. 1 , PREFERENCE NO. 2
LOCATIVE 3015

INTERPRETATION(S) IN ORDER OF HOMOGRAPHIC PREFERENCE:

ASH[2] OF A MOUNTAIN.

ASH[2] IN OR ON A MOUNTAIN.

THE KIND OF ASH[1] FOUND IN OR ON A MOUNTAIN. √

....

PEACOCK 0720 MOUNTAIN-CATARACT

SENTENCE 1 /LOCATIVE 3011

UNDERLYING SENTENCE(S):

A CATARACT OR CATARACTS FALLS IN A MOUNTAIN OR MOUNTAINS

INTERPRETATION(S):

A CATARACT THAT FALLS IN A MOUNTAIN OR MOUNTAINS. √√

A CATARACT IN OR ON A MOUNTAIN.

....

PEACOCK 0800 MOUNTAIN CHAPEL

LOCATIVE 3030 /LOCATIVE 3011

INTERPRETATION(S):

A CHAPEL FOR OR CONTAINING A MOUNTAIN OR MOUNTAINS.

A CHAPEL IN OR ON A MOUNTAIN. ✓

....

PEACOCK 0650 MOUNTAIN-FRAME

SENTENCE 1 /LOCATIVE 3011

UNDERLYING SENTENCE(S):

SOMEONE FRAMES A MOUNTAIN OR MOUNTAINS WITH A FRAME OR FRAMES

INTERPRETATION(S):

A FRAME THAT SOMEONE FRAMES A MOUNTAIN OR MOUNTAINS WITH. ✓✓

A FRAME IN OR ON A MOUNTAIN.

....

PEACOCK 0920 MOUNTAIN RECESS

ANNEX 4010 /LOCATIVE 3030 /LOCATIVE 3011

INTERPRETATION(S):

THE RECESS OF A MOUNTAIN. ✓✓

A RECESS FOR OR CONTAINING A MOUNTAIN OR MOUNTAINS.

A RECESS IN OR ON A MOUNTAIN.

....

PEACOCK 0930 MOUNTAIN ROAD

LOCATIVE 3016 /LOCATIVE 3011

INTERPRETATION(S):

A ROAD TO A MOUNTAIN.

A ROAD IN OR ON A MOUNTAIN. √

....

DEIGHTON 0350 MOUNTAIN TOP

ANNEX 4010 /LOCATIVE 3011

INTERPRETATION(S):

THE TOP OF A MOUNTAIN. √√

A TOP IN OR ON A MOUNTAIN.

....

RADCLIFFE 0420 MOUNTAIN VISTA

SENTENCE 1 /SENTENCE 2 /SENTENCE 3 /LOCATIVE
3011

UNDERLYING SENTENCE(S):

SOMEONE SEES A MOUNTAIN OR MOUNTAINS

SOMEONE SEES IN A MOUNTAIN OR MOUNTAINS

SOMEONE SEES A VISTA OR VISTAS IN A MOUNTAIN OR MOUNTAINS

INTERPRETATION(S):

THE VISTA OF A MOUNTAIN OR MOUNTAINS. √√

THE VISTA IN A MOUNTAIN OR MOUNTAINS.

A VISTA THAT SOMEONE SEES IN A MOUNTAIN OR MOUNTAINS.

A VISTA IN OR ON A MOUNTAIN.

....

RADCLIFFE 0280 MOUNTAINEER CHILD

EQUATIVE 5010

INTERPRETATION(S):

A CHILD THAT IS A MOUNTAINEER. √√

....

LAWRENCE 0150 MOUSE-COLOUR

ANNEX 4010

INTERPRETATION(S):

THE COLOUR OF A MOUSE. √√

....

RADCLIFFE 0330 MUD FLOOR

MATERIAL 6010 /LOCATIVE 3030

INTERPRETATION(S):

A FLOOR OF MUD. √√

A FLOOR FOR OR CONTAINING MUD.

....

BRAINE 0280 MUD+GUARD

MATERIAL 6010 /SENTENCE 1 /SENTENCE 2

UNDERLYING SENTENCE(S):

A GUARD OR GUARDS GUARDS MUD

A GUARD OR GUARDS GUARDS WITH MUD

INTERPRETATION(S):

A GUARD OF MUD. X

SOMEONE THAT GUARDS MUD.

SOMEONE THAT GUARDS WITH MUD.

....

GREENE 0200 MUD HUT

MATERIAL 6010 /LOCATIVE 3030

INTERPRETATION(S):

A HUT OF MUD. √√

A HUT FOR OR CONTAINING MUD.

....

GREENE 0480 MUD KITCHEN

MATERIAL 6010 /LOCATIVE 3030

INTERPRETATION(S):

A KITCHEN OF MUD. √√

A KITCHEN FOR OR CONTAINING MUD.

....

BENNETT 0040 MULE-TRACK

SENTENCE 1 /SENTENCE 2 /LOCATIVE 3030

UNDERLYING SENTENCE(S):

SOMEONE TRAVELS A MULE OR MULES IN A TRACK OR TRACKS

A MULE OR MULES TRAVELS IN A TRACK OR TRACKS

INTERPRETATION(S):

A TRACK THAT SOMEONE TRAVELS A MULE OR MULES IN.

A TRACK THAT A MULE OR MULES TRAVELS IN. √

A TRACK FOR OR CONTAINING A MULE OR MULES.

....

PEACOCK 0270 MUSIC-ROOM

LOCATIVE 3030 /LOCATIVE 3011 /SENTENCE 1

UNDERLYING SENTENCE(S):

SOMEONE PLAYS MUSIC IN A ROOM OR ROOMS

INTERPRETATION(S):

A ROOM FOR OR CONTAINING MUSIC. √√

A ROOM IN OR ON MUSIC.

A ROOM THAT SOMEONE PLAYS MUSIC IN.

....

THACKERAY 0590 MUSLIN FROCK

HOMOGRAPHIC VARIANT NO. 1 , PREFERENCE NO. 1
MATERIAL 6010

HOMOGRAPHIC VARIANT NO. 2 , PREFERENCE NO. 2
MATERIAL 6010

INTERPRETATION(S) IN ORDER OF HOMOGRAPHIC PREFERENCE:

A FROCK[1] OF MUSLIN. √√

A FROCK[2] OF MUSLIN.

....

RICHARDSON 0420 MUSLIN TUCKER

MATERIAL 6010

INTERPRETATION(S):

A TUCKER OF MUSLIN. √√

....

DEFOE 0490 MUSQUET-BORE

HOMOGRAPHIC VARIANT NO. 1 , PREFERENCE NO. 1
ANNEX 4010 /SENTENCE 1

HOMOGRAPHIC VARIANT NO. 2 , PREFERENCE NO. 2
SENTENCE 2

UNDERLYING SENTENCE(S):

SOMEONE BORES A MUSQUET OR MUSQUETS

A BORE[2] OR BORE[2]S BORES A MUSQUET OR MUSQUETS

INTERPRETATION(S) IN ORDER OF HOMOGRAPHIC PREFERENCE:

THE BORE[1] OF A MUSQUET. √√

THE BORE[1] OF A MUSQUET OR MUSQUETS.

SOMEONE THAT BORES A MUSQUET OR MUSQUETS.

....

BENNETT 0090 MUSTARD-TINT<ED>

ANNEX 4010

INTERPRETATION(S):

THE TINT OF MUSTARD. √√

....

THACKERAY 0520 MUTTON-CANDLE

MATERIAL 6010

INTERPRETATION(S):

A CANDLE OF MUTTON. √√?

....

FIELDING 0760 NAME+SAKE

ANNEX 4010

INTERPRETATION(S):

THE SAKE OF A NAME. √√

....

LAWRENCE 0500 NAVEL STRING

ANNEX 4010 /MATERIAL 6020

INTERPRETATION(S):

STRING OF A NAVEL. √√

STRING FOR NAVELS OR STRING IN THE FORM OF A NAVEL.

....

THACKERAY 0340 NECK+CLOTH

SENTENCE 1 /MATERIAL 6020

UNDERLYING SENTENCE(S):

SOMEONE WIPES OR COVERS OR LINES A NECK OR NECKS WITH CLOTH

INTERPRETATION(S):

CLOTH THAT SOMEONE WIPES OR COVERS OR LINES A NECK OR NECKS WITH. √√

CLOTH FOR NECKS OR CLOTH IN THE FORM OF A NECK.

....

RICHARDSON 0330 NECK+LACE

SENTENCE 1 /MATERIAL 6020

UNDERLYING SENTENCE(S):

A NECK OR NECKS WEARS LACE

INTERPRETATION(S):

LACE THAT A NECK OR NECKS WEARS. X

LACE FOR NECKS OR LACE IN THE FORM OF A NECK.

....

DEIGHTON 0190 NECK STRING

ANNEX 4010 /MATERIAL 6020

INTERPRETATION(S):

STRING OF A NECK. X

STRING FOR NECKS OR STRING IN THE FORM OF A NECK.

....

DEIGHTON 0420 NECK+TIE

HOMOGRAPHIC VARIANT NO. 2 , PREFERENCE NO. 1
EQUATIVE 5011

HOMOGRAPHIC VARIANT NO. 1 , PREFERENCE NO. 2
SENTENCE 1 /SENTENCE 2 /SENTENCE 3

UNDERLYING SENTENCE(S):

A TIE[1] OR TIE[1]S TIES A NECK OR NECKS

SOMEONE TIES A NECK OR NECKS

A NECK OR NECKS TIES A TIE[1] OR TIE[1]S

INTERPRETATION(S) IN ORDER OF HOMOGRAPHIC PREFERENCE:

A TIE[2] THAT IS A NECK. X

SOMEONE OR SOMETHING THAT TIES A NECK OR NECKS.

THE TIE[1] OF A NECK OR NECKS.

SOMETHING THAT A NECK OR NECKS TIES.

....

THACKERAY 0220 NEEDLE+WORK

SENTENCE 1 /SENTENCE 2

UNDERLYING SENTENCE(S):

SOMETHING OR SOMEONE WORKS WITH A NEEDLE OR NEEDLES

SOMEONE WORKS A NEEDLE OR NEEDLES

INTERPRETATION(S):

THE WORK WITH A NEEDLE OR NEEDLES. √√

THE WORK OF A NEEDLE OR NEEDLES.

....

DEFOE 0580 NEGRO SLAVE

EQUATIVE 5010 /SENTENCE 1

UNDERLYING SENTENCE(S):

A SLAVE OR SLAVES SERVES A NEGRO OR NEGROS

A SLAVE OR SLAVES SERVES

INTERPRETATION(S):

A SLAVE THAT IS A NEGRO. √√

A SLAVE THAT SERVES A NEGRO OR NEGROS.

....

SCOTT 0480 NEIGHBOUR *PLUMDAMAS

EQUATIVE 5010

INTERPRETATION(S):

*PLUMDAMAS THAT IS A NEIGHBOUR. √√

....

MARSH 0250 NET BAG

MATERIAL 6010 /LOCATIVE 3030 /SENTENCE 1

UNDERLYING SENTENCE(S):

SOMEONE CATCHES OR CONFINES A BAG OR BAGS WITH NET

INTERPRETATION(S):

A BAG OF NET. √√

A BAG FOR OR CONTAINING NET.

A BAG THAT SOMEONE CATCHES OR CONFINES WITH NET.

....

DEIGHTON 0110 NEWS+PAPER

LOCATIVE 3030 /SENTENCE 1

UNDERLYING SENTENCE(S):

SOMEONE PUBLISHES NEWS IN PAPER

INTERPRETATION(S):

PAPER FOR OR CONTAINING NEWS.

PAPER THAT SOMEONE PUBLISHES NEWS IN. √

....

THACKERAY 0430 1ST, L NIGHT ATTACK

SENTENCE 1 /SENTENCE 2

UNDERLYING SENTENCE(S):

SOMEONE ATTACKS IN A NIGHT OR NIGHTS

SOMEONE ATTACKS A NIGHT OR NIGHTS

INTERPRETATION(S):

THE ATTACK IN A NIGHT OR NIGHTS. √√

THE ATTACK OF A NIGHT OR NIGHTS.

....

THACKERAY 0430 NIGHT-CAP

SENTENCE 1 /LOCATIVE 3011

UNDERLYING SENTENCE(S):

SOMEONE WEARS A CAP OR CAPS IN A NIGHT OR NIGHTS

INTERPRETATION(S):

A CAP THAT SOMEONE WEARS IN A NIGHT OR NIGHTS. √√

A CAP IN OR ON A NIGHT.

....

BRAINE 0350 NIGHT CLUB

SENTENCE 1 /SENTENCE 2

UNDERLYING SENTENCE(S):

A CLUB OR CLUBS BELONGS TO OR JOINS IN A NIGHT OR NIGHTS

IS IN A CLUB OR CLUBS IN A NIGHT OR NIGHTS

INTERPRETATION(S):

A CLUB THAT BELONGS TO OR JOINS IN A NIGHT OR NIGHTS. X

A CLUB AS IT IS IN A NIGHT OR NIGHTS.

....

MARSH 0380 NIGHT+DRESS

SENTENCE 1 /LOCATIVE 3011

UNDERLYING SENTENCE(S):

SOMEONE WEARS A DRESS OR DRESSS IN A NIGHT OR NIGHTS

INTERPRETATION(S):

A DRESS THAT SOMEONE WEARS IN A NIGHT OR NIGHTS. √√

A DRESS IN OR ON A NIGHT.

....

RADCLIFFE 0490 NIGHT-FALL

SENTENCE 1 /SENTENCE 2

UNDERLYING SENTENCE(S):

A NIGHT OR NIGHTS FALLS

SOMEONE FALLS IN A NIGHT OR NIGHTS

INTERPRETATION(S):

THE FALL OF A NIGHT OR NIGHTS. √√

THE FALL IN A NIGHT OR NIGHTS.

....

MARSH 0480 NIGHT+GOWN

SENTENCE 1 /LOCATIVE 3011

UNDERLYING SENTENCE(S):

SOMEONE WEARS A GOWN OR GOWNS IN A NIGHT OR NIGHTS

INTERPRETATION(S):

A GOWN THAT SOMEONE WEARS IN A NIGHT OR NIGHTS. √√

A GOWN IN OR ON A NIGHT.

....

DEIGHTON 0330 NIGHT SKY

SENTENCE 1

UNDERLYING SENTENCE(S):

IS IN THE SKY IN A NIGHT OR NIGHTS

INTERPRETATION(S):

THE SKY AS IT IS IN A NIGHT OR NIGHTS. √√

....

DEIGHTON 0290 NOMINEE BID

SENTENCE 1 /SENTENCE 2

UNDERLYING SENTENCE(S):

SOMEONE BIDS A NOMINEE OR NOMINEES

A NOMINEE OR NOMINEES BIDS

INTERPRETATION(S):

THE BID OF A NOMINEE OR NOMINEES.

THE BID OF A NOMINEE OR NOMINEES. ✓

....

DEIGHTON 0320 NOMINEE COMPANY

EQUATIVE 5010 /MATERIAL 6050 /SENTENCE 1

UNDERLYING SENTENCE(S):

A COMPANY OR COMPANYS MAKES OR USES A NOMINEE OR NOMINEES

INTERPRETATION(S):

A COMPANY THAT IS A NOMINEE. ✓✓

A COMPANY OF NOMINEES.

A COMPANY THAT MAKES OR USES A NOMINEE OR NOMINEES.

....

DEIGHTON 0190 NOTE+BOOK

SENTENCE 1 /LOCATIVE 3030

UNDERLYING SENTENCE(S):

A NOTE OR NOTES READS A BOOK OR BOOKS

INTERPRETATION(S):

A BOOK THAT A NOTE OR NOTES READS.

A BOOK FOR OR CONTAINING A NOTE OR NOTES. ✓

....

DEIGHTON 0130 NOVELTY COMPANY

SENTENCE 1

UNDERLYING SENTENCE(S):

A COMPANY OR COMPANYS MAKES OR USES A NOVELTY OR NOVELTYS

INTERPRETATION(S):

A COMPANY THAT MAKES OR USES A NOVELTY OR NOVELTYS. √√

....

GREENE 0400 NOVICE MASTER

EQUATIVE 5010 /SENTENCE 1

UNDERLYING SENTENCE(S):

A MASTER OR MASTERS CONTROLS OR TEACHES A NOVICE OR NOVICES

A MASTER OR MASTERS CONTROLS OR TEACHES

INTERPRETATION(S):

A MASTER THAT IS A NOVICE.

A MASTER THAT CONTROLS OR TEACHES A NOVICE OR NOVICES. √

....

BRONTE 0610 OAK CASE

MATERIAL 6010 /LOCATIVE 3030

INTERPRETATION(S):

A CASE OF OAK. √√

A CASE FOR OR CONTAINING OAK.

....

BRONTE 0660 OAK CLOSET

MATERIAL 6010 /LOCATIVE 3030

INTERPRETATION(S):

A CLOSET OF OAK. √√

A CLOSET FOR OR CONTAINING OAK.

....

BRONTE 0470 OAK DRESSER

HOMOGRAPHIC VARIANT NO. 1 , PREFERENCE NO. 1
MATERIAL 6010

HOMOGRAPHIC VARIANT NO. 2 , PREFERENCE NO. 2
MATERIAL 6010 /SENTENCE 1 /SENTENCE 2

UNDERLYING SENTENCE(S):

A DRESSER[2] OR DRESSER[2]S DRESSES SOMEONE WITH OAK

A DRESSER[2] OR DRESSER[2]S DRESSES WITH OAK

INTERPRETATION(S) IN ORDER OF HOMOGRAPHIC PREFERENCE:

A DRESSER[1] OF OAK. √√

A DRESSER[2] OF OAK.

SOMEONE THAT DRESSES SOMEONE WITH OAK.

SOMEONE THAT DRESSES WITH OAK.

....

END OF DATA.

END OF RUN.

BIBLIOGRAPHY

Linguistic and Computer Works

Dictionaries are listed at the end.

Adams, Valerie, An Introduction to Modern English Word-Formation (Longman, London, 1973).

ALGOL ICL student edition (1970). 'This publication is a Student Edition of the ICL 1900 Series manual Algol: Language (Technical Publication 3340), first published in 1965 and last revised in March 1970', International Computers Limited, Reading, Berkshire.

Bierwisch, M. and Heidolph, K.E., eds., Progress in Linguistics (Mouton, The Hague, 1970).

Brekle, H.E., Generative Satzsemantik und Transformationelle Syntax im System der Englischen Nominalkomposition (Wilhelm Fink Verlag, München, 1970).

Chomsky, Noam, 'Remarks on Nominalization', in: Jacobs, R. and Rosenbaum, P. (eds.), Readings in English Transformational Grammar (Blaisdell, Waltham, Mass., 1970), 184-221.

Cook, Walter A., Introduction to Tagmemic Analysis (Holt, Rinehart and Winston, Inc., New York, 1969). (Undated on title page, but copyright 1969.)

Downing, Pamela, 'On the creation and use of English compound nouns', Language, Vol. 53, No. 4 (1977), 810-842.

Fillmore, Charles J., 'The Case for Case' in: Bach, Emmon and Harms, Robert T. (eds.), Universals in Linguistic Theory (Holt, Rinehart and Winston, London, 1968; first published in Great Britain, 1970).

Firbas, Jan, 'Thoughts on the communicative function of the verb in English, German and Czech', Brno Studies in English, Vol. 1 (Praha, 1959), 39-63.

Firbas, Jan, 'On defining the Theme in Functional Sentence Analysis', Travaux Linguistiques de Prague, 1 (1964), 267-280.

Firbas, Jan, 'Non-Thematic Subjects in Contemporary English', Travaux Linguistiques de Prague, 2 (1966), 239-256.

Friedman, Joyce, with Bredt, Thomas H., Doran, Robert W., Pollack, Bary W. and Martner, Theodore S., A Computer Model of _Transformational Grammar_ (American Elsevier Publishing Company, Inc., New York, 1971).

Gruber, Jeffrey S., 'Topicalization in Child Language' (first published 1967), in: Reibel, D.A. and Schane, S.A. (eds.), _Modern Studies in English_ (Prentice-Hall, Inc., Englewood Cliffs, New Jersey, 1969).

Halliday, M.A.K., 'Categories of the Theory of Grammar', _Word_ 17.3 (1961), 241-92.

Halliday, M.A.K., 'Notes on Transitivity and Theme in English', _Journal of Linguistics_, Vol. 3 (1967), 37-81, 199-244, and Vol. 4 (1968), 179-215.

Halliday, M.A.K., _Grammar, Society and the Noun_ (Inaugural Lecture), (H.K. Lewis & Co., Ltd., London, 1967 b).

Halliday, M.A.K., 'Functional diversity in language as seen from a consideration of modality and mood in English', _Foundations of Language_, 6 (1970), 322-361.

Jacobs, R. and Rosenbaum, P., (eds.), _Readings in English Transformational Grammar_ (Blaisdell, Waltham, Mass., 1970).

Jespersen, Otto, _A Modern English Grammar on Historical Principles_ (George Allen & Unwin Ltd., London, 1909-49; reprinted 1961).

Katz, Jerrold J. and Fodor, Jerry A., 'The Structure of a Semantic Theory', _Language_ 39 (1963), 170-210. (Reprinted in Fodor and Katz, _The Structure of Language: Readings in the Philosophy of Language_ (Prentice-Hall, Englewood Cliffs, N.J., 1964.)

Katz, Jerrold J., _Semantic Theory_ (Harper and Row, New York, 1972).

Kaufmann, A., _Introduction to the Theory of Fuzzy Subsets_: Vol. I: Fundamental Theoretical Elements (Academic Press, London, 1975).

Kelly, E.F. and Stone, P.J., _Computer Recognition of English Word Senses_ (North-Holland Publishing Company, Amsterdam and Oxford, 1975).

Kučera, Henry and Francis, Nelson W., _Computational Analysis of Present-Day American English_ (Brown University, Providence, Rhode Island, U.S.A., 1967).

Laffal, Julius, A Concept Dictionary of English (Gallery Press, Essex, Connecticut, and Halstead Press, a division of John Wiley and Sons, New York and London, 1973).

Leech, Geoffrey N., Towards a Semantic Description of English, (Longmans, Green and Co. Ltd., London, 1969).

Leech, Geoffrey N., Semantics (Penguin Books Ltd., Harmondsworth, Middlesex, 1974).

Lees, R.B., The Grammar of English Nominalizations (First pub. Bloomington, Indiana, 1960; Mouton & Co., The Hague, 1964).

Lees, R.B., 'On a transformational analysis of compounds: A reply to Hans Marchand', Indogermanische Forschungen, 71 (1966), 1-13.

Lees, R.B., 'Problems in the grammatical analysis of English nominal compounds' in: Bierwisch and Heidolph (1970).

Leonard, Rosemary, The Types and Currency of Noun + Noun Sequences in Prose Usage 1750-1950, unpublished thesis for the degree of M.Phil. in the University of London (1968).

Levi, Judith N., 'Where do all those other adjectives come from?' in: Corum, Claudia, Smith-Stark, T. Cedric, and Weiser, Ann (eds.), Papers from the ninth regional meeting: Chicago Linguistic Society (Chicago Linguistic Society, Chicago, 1973), 332-345.

Levi, Judith N., 'On the alleged idiosyncrasy of nonpredicate NPs', in: LaGaly, Michael W., Fox, Robert A. and Bruck, Anthony (eds.), Papers from the tenth regional meeting: Chicago Linguistic Society (Chicago Linguistic Society, Chicago, 1974), 402-415.

Levi, Judith N., The syntax and semantics of nonpredicating adjectives in English, unpublished doctoral dissertation, The University of Chicago (1975). Distributed by the Indiana University Linguistics Club.

Levi, Judith N., The Syntax and Semantics of Complex Nominals (Academic Press, New York and London, 1978).

Lyons, John, Semantics (Cambridge University Press, Cambridge, 1977).

Marchand, Hans, The Categories and Types of Present-day English Word-formation (Otto Harrassowitz, Wiesbaden, 1960).

Marchand, Hans, The Categories and Types of Present-day English Word-formation (C.H. Beck'sche Verlagsbuchhandlung, München, 1969).

Quirk, R., Greenbaum, S., Leech, G. and Svartvik, J., A Grammar of Contemporary English (Longman Group Ltd., London; Seminar Press Inc., New York, 1972).

Saussure, F. de, Cours de Linguistique Générale (Payot, Paris, 1916). English translation by Wade Baskin, A Course in General Linguistics (Philosophical Library, New York, 1959).

Schwartz, A., 'On Interpreting Nominalizations', in: Bierwisch, M. and Heidolph, K.E. (1970), 295-305.

Sweet, H., A New English Grammar, Part I (Oxford University Press, Oxford, 1891).

Ullmann, Stephen, The Principles of Semantics (Basil Blackwell, Oxford, 1957; first edition 1951, with additional bibliographical material, 1959 and 1963).

Vachek, J., The Linguistic School of Prague (Indiana University Press, Bloomington and London, 1966).

Van Overbeke, Maurice, 'La Décomposition Automatique des Composes Néerlandais', Revue (L.A.S.L.A., 110 Boulevard de la Sauvenière, Liège, 1971), 151-174.

Walker, Donald E., 'Speech Understanding Through Syntactic and Semantic Analysis' in: Proceedings International Joint Conference on Artificial Intelligence (1973), Artificial Intelligence Center, Technical Note 80, SRI Project 1526, Stanford Research Institute, Menlo Park, California 94025.

Warren, Beatrice, Semantic Patterns of Noun-Noun Compounds (Gothenburg Studies in English 41, Acta Universitatis Gothoburgensis, Göteborg, Sweden, 1978).

Wilks, Yorick, 'Preference Semantics', Stanford Artificial Intelligence Laboratory, Memo No. AIM-206; Computer Science Department, Report No. CS-377 (July 1973). 'This paper was presented at the Colloquium on the Formal Semantics of Natural Language, Cambridge, April 1973 and will appear in the Proceedings, (ed. E. Keenan), Cambridge University Press, 1974.'

Wilks, Yorick, 'Natural Language Inference', Stanford Artificial Intelligence Laboratory, Memo. No. AIM-211; Computer Science Department, Report No. CS-383 (August 1973).

Winograd, Terry, Understanding Natural Language (Edinburgh University Press, 1972).

Woods, William A., Kaplan, R.M., and Nash-Webber, B., The Lunar Sciences Natural Language Information System, Final Report. B.B.N. Report No. 2378, Job No. 11501 (Bolt Beranek and Newman Inc., 50 Moulton Street, Cambridge, Massachusetts, 1972; prepared for The Language Research Foundation, 131 Mt. Auburn Street, Cambridge, Massachusetts.)

Chambers Twentieth Century Dictionary, ed. A.M. Macdonald, W. and R. Chambers (Edinburgh and London, 1972). (Referred to as Chambers (1972).)

The Concise Oxford Dictionary of Current English, ed. Fowler, H.W. and Fowler, F.G., fifth edition (Oxford University Press, Oxford, 1966; reprinted with corrections 1966). (Referred to as COD (1966).)

The Concise Oxford Dictionary of Current English, ed. J.B. Sykes, 6th edition (Oxford University Press, Oxford, 1976). (Referred to as COD (1976).)

A New English Dictionary on Historical Principles, ed. Sir James A.H. Murray, Henry Bradley, W.A. Craigie and C.T. Onions (Clarendon Press, Oxford, 1888-1933). (Referred to as the NED (1888-1933).)

Nuttall's Standard Dictionary of the English Language, ed. and revised by W.J. Gordon (Frederick Warne & Co. Ltd., London, 1929). (Referred to as Nuttall's (1929).)

The Penguin English Dictionary, compiled by G.N. Garmonsway with Jacqueline Simpson (Penguin Books Ltd., Harmondsworth, Middlesex, 1965). (Referred to as Penguin (1965).)

The Shorter Oxford English Dictionary on Historical Principles, ed. C.T. Onions (Clarendon Press, Oxford, third edition 1944; reprinted with corrections 1964). (Referred to as the Shorter Oxford (1964).)

Webster's Third New International Dictionary of the English Language, ed. Philip B. Gove, copyright 1971 by G. & C. Merriam Co. (Encyclopaedia Britannica, Inc., Chicago, London, etc., 1971). (Referred to as Webster (1971).)

Texts used for selection of noun sequences

First editions are listed immediately after the modern editions. The details of their title-pages are preserved, unless they are merely texts cited from Leonard (1968).

Austen, Jane, Pride and Prejudice, printed for T. Egerton (London, 1813).

Beckford, William, Vathek, translated from the original French by Samuel Henley, in: Shorter Novels: Eighteenth Century (Dent, London, 1967).

[Beckford] 'AN ARABIAN TALE, FROM AN UNPUBLISHED MANUSCRIPT ... LONDON: Printed for J. JOHNSON, in ST. PAUL'S CHURCH-YARD ... MDCCLXXXVI.' [i.e. Vathek]

Bennett, Arnold, The Old Wives' Tale, Everyman's Library (Dent, London, 1966).

'THE OLD WIVES' TALE A NOVEL BY ARNOLD BENNETT LONDON CHAPMAN & HALL, LTD. 1908'

Braine, John, Room at the Top (Penguin Books, Harmondsworth, Middlesex, 1959).

'Room at the top John Braine EYRE & SPOTTISWOODE LONDON 1957'

Brontë, Emily, Wuthering Heights (Penguin Books, Harmondsworth, Middlesex, 1965).

[Brontë] 'WUTHERING HEIGHTS A NOVEL, By ELLIS BELL ... LONDON: THOMAS CAUTLEY NEWBY, PUBLISHER, 72, MORTIMER ST., CAVENDISH Sq., 1847'

Defoe, Daniel, The Life and Adventures of Robinson Crusoe (Penguin Books, Harmondsworth, Middlesex, 1965).

[Defoe] 'THE LIFE AND STRANGE SURPRIZING ADVENTURES OF ROBINSON CRUSOE, OF YORK, MARINER ... LONDON: Printed for W. TAYLOR at the Ship in Pater-Noster-Row. MDCCXIX'

Deighton, Len, Only When I Larf (Sphere Books Limited, London, 1968). [This is the first edition.]

Dickens, Charles, Master Humphrey's Clock (Chapman and Hall, London) in weekly parts beginning April 4th, 1840.

Dickens, Charles, The Old Curiosity Shop (Blackie and Son Ltd., London, 1894; reprinted 1904). First published 1840-41.

[Dickens] The Old Curiosity Shop (Chapman and Hall, London, 1841).

Fielding Henry, The History of Tom Jones (Penguin Books, Harmondsworth, Middlesex, 1966).

[Fielding] 'THE HISTORY OF TOM JONES, A FOUNDLING.' 'LONDON: Printed for A. MILLAR, over-against Catherine-street in the Strand. MDCCXLIX.'

Greene, Graham, A Burnt-Out Case (Penguin Books, Harmondsworth, Middlesex, 1963).

'GRAHAM GREENE A Burnt-Out Case HEINEMANN LONDON' ' © GRAHAM GREENE 1960 This English language edition first published 1961'

Isherwood, Christopher, Down There on a Visit (Methuen and Co. Ltd., London, 1962).

Isherwood, Christopher, 'Mr. Lancaster', London Magazine (October 1959), pp. 17 ff.

Johnson, Samuel, The Prince of Abissinia, printed for R. and J. Dodsley and W. Johnston (London, 1759). i.e.[Rasselas]

Lawrence, D.H., Sons and Lovers (Penguin Books, Harmondsworth, Middlesex, 1948).

'SONS AND LOVERS BY D.H. LAWRENCE ... LONDON: DUCKWORTH & CO. HENRIETTA STREET, COVENT GARDEN 1913'

Mair, Alistair, Turning Point (Heinemann, London, 1973).

Marsh, Ngaio, Spinsters in Jeopardy (Collins, Fontana Books, London, 1960).

'"Spinsters in Jeopardy", Ngaio Marsh (Published for the Crime Club by Collins St James's Place London). 1954'

Meredith, George, The Ordeal of Richard Feverel (Chapman and Hall, London, 1859).

Peacock, Thomas Love, Headlong Hall, in Headlong Hall Nightmare Abbey (Dent, London, 1965).

[Peacock] 'HEADLONG HALL ... LONDON: PRINTED FOR T. HOOKHAM, JUN. AND CO. OLD BOND ST ... 1816.'

Radcliffe, Ann, The Mysteries of Udolpho (Everyman's Library, Dent, London, 1965).

[Radcliffe] 'THE MYSTERIES OF UDOLPHO ... By ANN RADCLIFFE ... LONDON: PRINTED FOR G.G. AND J. ROBINSON, PATERNOSTER ROW 1794' [I trust this is the first edition: there were 2 issues in 1794.]

Richardson, Samuel, Pamela (Everyman's Library, Dent, London, 1966).

[Richardson] 'PAMELA: OR, VIRTUE Rewarded.' 'LONDON: Printed for C. RIVINGTON, in St. Paul's Church-Yard; and J. OSBORN, in Pater-noster Row. MDCCXLI.' [This is the second edition. The first edition was published in 1740. I worked from the second.]

Scott, Sir Walter, The Heart of Midlothian (Collins, London, 1952).

[Scott] 'TALES OF MY LANDLORD, Second Series, COLLECTED AND ARRANGED BY JEDEDIAH CLEISHBOTHAM ... EDINBURGH: PRINTED FOR ARCHIBALD CONSTABLE AND COMPANY. 1818.' [i.e. The Heart of Midlothian]

Shakespeare, William, Macbeth, ed. Muir, Kenneth (Methuen and Co. Ltd., London, 1957).

Shaw, G.B., Plays: Pleasant and Unpleasant, ed. Grant Richards (London, 1898).

Thackeray, W.M., Vanity Fair (Collins, London, 1954).

[Thackeray] 'VANITY FAIR ... LONDON: BRADBURY AND EVANS, 11, BOUVERIE STREET, 1848.'

Thompson, Charles, Bing The authorised biography (W.H. Allen, London, 1975).

Walpole, Horace, The Castle of Otranto, in Shorter Novels: Eighteenth Century (Dent, London, 1967).

[Walpole] 'THE CASTLE OF OTRANTO ... Translated by WILLIAM MARSHAL, Gent. From the original ITALIAN of ONUPHRIO MURALTO ... LONDON: Printed for THO. LOWNDS in Fleet-Street. MDCCLXV.'

INDEX OF AUTHORS